# LIVING BEYOND LOSS

Listening to the bereaved—really listening—brings into sharp focus two things: their pain and their questions. In *Living Beyond Loss: Questions and Answers About Grief and Bereavement,* noted psychologist Robert Neimeyer compassionately engages the heartfelt inquiries of real bereaved people who have lost parents and partners, siblings and children, to illness, tragic accident, suicide and violence and offers practical counsel on how to move forward toward a life that can again have meaning. Drawing on more than 50 years of experience in grief therapy and grounded in contemporary research on loss and resilience, this book is an indispensable guide to understanding the nuances of grief and adaptation, which is equally relevant to the bereaved themselves and to the therapists and professionals who strive to support them.

**Robert A. Neimeyer, PhD,** directs the Portland Institute for Loss and Transition; actively practices as a trainer, consultant and coach; and has published extensively on grieving as a meaning-making process.

# THE SERIES IN DEATH, DYING, AND BEREAVEMENT

Series Editors: Robert A. Neimeyer, PhD
*Portland Institute for Loss and Transition, Oregon, USA*
and
Darcy L. Harris, PhD
*Western University Canada, Ontario, Canada*

Volumes published in the Series in Death, Dying and Bereavement are representative of the multidisciplinary nature of the intersecting fields of death studies, suicidology, end-of-life care, and grief counseling. The series meets the needs of clinicians, researchers, paraprofessionals, pastoral counselors, and educators by providing cutting edge research, theory, and best practices on the most important topics in these fields—for today and for tomorrow.

**NEW TECHNIQUES OF GRIEF THERAPY**
Bereavement and Beyond
*Edited by Robert A. Neimeyer*

**PEDIATRIC PALLIATIVE CARE**
A Model for Exemplary Practice
*Betty Davies, Rose Steele, and Jennifer Baird*

**THE RESTORATIVE NATURE OF ONGOING CONNECTIONS WITH THE DECEASED**
Exploring Presence Within Absence
*Laurie A. Burke and Edward (Ted) Rynearson*

**COMPASSION-BASED APPROACHES IN LOSS AND GRIEF**
*Darcy L. Harris and Andy H. Y. Ho*

**GRIEVING BEYOND GENDER**
Understanding Diverse Grieving Styles, 3rd ed
*Kenneth J. Doka and Terry L. Martin*

**LIVING BEYOND LOSS**
Questions and Answers About Grief and Bereavement
*Robert A. Neimeyer*

For more information about this series, please visit www.routledge.com/Series-in-Death-Dying-and-Bereavement/book-series/SE0620

"Robert Neimeyer is a global authority on bereavement and grief. *Living Beyond Loss* is a treasure trove of stories told by people trying to navigate the painful labyrinth of bereavement. It offers guidance for those who are bereft, while modeling compassion and wisdom for those who try to help them find their way."
**Harvey Max Chochinov, OC, OM, MD, PhD, FRCPC, FRSC,** *Distinguished Professor of Psychiatry at the University of Manitoba and author of* Dignity in Care: The Human Side of Medicine

"*Living Beyond Loss* is a wonderful resource written by an internationally recognized authority in the field. Readers will find sensitive suggestions, gentle guidance, and practical ideas to help grieving individuals navigate the most difficult aspects of grief and loss. This is truly a must-read book that explores important topics related to grief for clinicians, family, friends, and bereaved individuals themselves."
**Darcy Harris, PhD,** *author of* Principles and Practice of Grief Counseling

"Robert Neimeyer's *Living Beyond Loss: Questions and Answers About Grief and Bereavement* is a wonderful contribution to the field and a great gift to those struggling with loss and grief. Here we have a well-recognized grief therapist and researcher answering poignant questions by both those who grieve and the professionals who support them. Bob offers wise answers in clear, simple, but always compassionate ways, lighting a path for living beyond loss."
**Kenneth J. Doka, PhD,** *senior vice president at The Hospice Foundation of America and professor emeritus at The College of New Rochelle*

"For years, every Monday morning I've rushed to see Bob Neimeyer's latest response to a challenging question about loss posed by a bereaved individual or a concerned caregiver in AfterTalk's "Ask Dr. Neimeyer" column. Nowhere else have I ever seen such clinically and empirically informed information used to compassionately support and validate each questioner, succinctly frame each issue, and then provide not just perspective but specific guidance for how to therapeutically address it and cope most effectively. Inevitably, I would save each column for future reference, as his distillation of so much complex material into a brief answer would amaze me. Now, the combined wealth of Dr. Neimeyer's wisdom, experience, and sensitivity is offered in one volume that focuses on challenging questions stemming from losses of all types of loved ones and all types of death, while also providing further guidance for professionals. As it elucidates complex notions about grief and makes specific self-help recommendations, this book will be an incomparable asset that personally speaks to the bereaved and informs those who care for them. It is a must have!"
**Therese A. Rando, PhD, BCETS, BCBT**, *The Institute for the Study and Treatment of Loss, Warwick, Rhode Island*

# LIVING BEYOND LOSS

## Questions and Answers About Grief and Bereavement

### Robert A. Neimeyer, PhD

NEW YORK AND LONDON

Designed cover image: Rickie Simpson, *Promise*,
pencil and pastel on paper

First published 2025
by Routledge
605 Third Avenue, New York, NY 10158

and by Routledge
4 Park Square, Milton Park, Abingdon, Oxon, OX14 4RN

*Routledge is an imprint of the Taylor & Francis Group, an informa business*

© 2025 Robert A. Neimeyer

The right of Robert A. Neimeyer to be identified as author of this work has been asserted in accordance with sections 77 and 78 of the Copyright, Designs and Patents Act 1988.

All rights reserved. No part of this book may be reprinted or reproduced or utilised in any form or by any electronic, mechanical, or other means, now known or hereafter invented, including photocopying and recording, or in any information storage or retrieval system, without permission in writing from the publishers.

*Trademark notice*: Product or corporate names may be trademarks or registered trademarks, and are used only for identification and explanation without intent to infringe.

ISBN: 978-0-367-14347-3 (hbk)
ISBN: 978-0-367-14348-0 (pbk)
ISBN: 978-0-429-05907-0 (ebk)

DOI: 10.4324/9780429059070

Typeset in Bembo
by Apex CoVantage, LLC

# CONTENTS

| | |
|---|---|
| *Preface* | ix |
| *Series Editor's Foreword By Darcy L. Harris* | xi |
| *About the Author* | xiii |

**PART 1**
## Introduction     1

1  Listening to the Bereaved     3

2  How to Use This Book     6

**PART 2**
## Who We Lose     9

3  Loss of a Husband     11

4  Loss of a Wife     33

5  Loss of a Partner or Close Relation     50

6  Loss of a Parent     60

7  Loss of a Child     80

8  Loss of a Sibling     91

9  Complicated Relationships     100

**PART 3**
## How We Lose     111

10  Fatal Illness     113

11  Fatal Accident     122

| | | |
|---|---|---|
| 12 | Suicide and Overdose | 136 |
| 13 | Homicide and Mass Tragedies | 161 |

## PART 4
## Further Questions — 173

| | | |
|---|---|---|
| 14 | Practical and Philosophic Questions | 175 |
| 15 | Questions From Professionals | 188 |
| 16 | Training Resources for Professionals | 232 |

*Index* — 234

# PREFACE

**Who Are We? AfterTalk and Dr. Robert A. Neimeyer**

This book is a collaboration between world authority in loss and bereavement, Dr. Robert A. Neimeyer, and AfterTalk, an online nonprofit, non-denominational organization created by Lisa Bogatin and Larry Lynn. As readers soon will see, AfterTalk offers a place for comfort and sharing for those who have experienced loss, as well as a resource for addressing the often-anguishing questions that rise up from the well of grief. As AfterTalk's mission statement describes it:

> AfterTalk's *Private Conversations* space is a sanctuary where you can write to your loved one and save your writing, photos or videos for as long as you wish. Our *Hospice Memory Archiving* is your private space to document, share and preserve what you want your loved ones to know today and for the future. Our *AfterTalk Blog* is home to a plethora of articles and inspirational quotes and a safe place to share your feedback as well.
>
> Our *Ask Dr. Neimeyer* column is where renowned grief expert Dr. Robert Neimeyer answers readers' questions about grieving as well as anticipatory grief. And in our *Resource Center* you'll find books and grief counseling resources for guidance and healing along with information related to financial, insurance and estate planning.

AfterTalk's partner in this project is Robert A. Neimeyer, PhD, Professor Emeritus of the Department of Psychology, University of Memphis, who also maintains an active consulting and coaching practice. He directs the Portland Institute for Loss and Transition (www.portlandinstitute.org), which provides online and onsite training internationally in grief therapy. Neimeyer has published 35 books, including *New Techniques of Grief Therapy: Bereavement and Beyond* and *The Handbook of Grief Therapies*, and serves as editor of the journal *Death Studies*. The author of over 600 articles and

## PREFACE

book chapters and a frequent workshop presenter, he is currently working to advance a more adequate theory of grieving as a meaning-making process. Neimeyer served as president of the Association for Death Education and Counseling (ADEC) and chair of the International Work Group for Death, Dying, & Bereavement. In recognition of his scholarly contributions, he has been granted the Eminent Faculty Award by the University of Memphis, made a fellow of the Clinical Psychology Division of the American Psychological Association, and given Lifetime Achievement Awards by both ADEC and the International Network on Personal Meaning.

We are proud to partner in this book-length engagement with the questions and concerns of real people suffering real losses, who reached out to AfterTalk through the "Ask Dr. Neimeyer" column for guidance and support. In a fundamental sense, the meaningful dialogue captured in these pages owes at least as much to the candor and openness of our readers and contributors as it does to our own efforts.

# SERIES EDITOR'S FOREWORD

Many of us wish there were answers to the questions that swirl around us when we encounter life-changing losses and the grief that accompanies them. How do we care for ourselves in such a painful place? How should we approach someone in our family or in our care who is hurting deeply? What about the "tricky" scenarios that often accompany complicated losses and ambivalent relationships? The ripples extend widely in a lake of grief, and it is easy to feel like we are drowning—or barely keeping our head above water. If only we could find a lifeline that would help us as we desperately try to tread water! And now we can, in the form of this book.

*Living Beyond Loss: Questions and Answers About Grief and Bereavement* is a profoundly rich resource, where grieving individuals and those who care about them have written their earnest and urgent queries about a vast range of grief-related concerns to Dr. Robert Neimeyer, one of the most internationally respected scholars and therapists in the field of bereavement. This volume contains his thoughtful and sensitive replies to these queries. The responses are based on current research and theory, but, more importantly, they arise from his spending more than five decades working alongside the bereaved in grief therapy. As a result, the answers he provides are informed by the head and by the heart and proffer wise, practical, and compassionate guidance for both laypersons and professionals alike.

The topics covered are extensive. The book is grouped into sections that focus on specific types of relationships—the losses of parents, spouses, children and significant others; the circumstances of the death, both natural and violent; and consultation requested by professionals striving to better accompany clients and patients contending with heart-rending anguish. The bereaved raise concerns about how to manage overwhelming emotions, what to tell children, where to find meaning in their reduced lives and how to deal with traumatic images or resolve conflicts in their families or with the dead themselves. Many of the questions bear on the impact of social norms and expectations upon grieving individuals, identifying when grief becomes so intense, complicated or entrenched that it requires more than well-intended support, as well as about specialized approaches to therapy that can address the residual effects of exhausting caregiving, the pangs of profound loneliness or the intrusive images that accompany suicide, homicide or a fatal accident. Most of the questions are highly personal, citing feelings of shame, guilt, regret, anger and disenfranchisement—the sense that one's grief "doesn't count" or remains invisible to others. Often such questions are of a kind that might be very hard to ask someone in person—if one could even find someone with the patience, empathy and wisdom to engage them. However, in this unique book, all questions are welcomed and treated with the same thoughtful sensitivity. In fact, readers will often have the sense that they are finding answers to their own silent questions—the ones in their hearts that they couldn't find the words to ask.

Reading this book is like sitting down to have a meaningful conversation with a dear friend—who also happens to know an awful lot about navigating life after all semblance of meaning has been obliterated by a profound loss. This is a book to give to a grieving friend, to share with individuals who support those who are in the throes of grief and to serve as a resource for therapists and caregivers who will appreciate the sensitive way that Neimeyer responds to individuals in their most vulnerable moments, as well as to tough clinical questions voiced by his fellow professionals in several disciplines.

In the book, Neimeyer underscores the importance of having someone bear witness to our experiences, stepping toward us rather than pulling away during the darkest and most painful times in our lives. Reading *Living Beyond Loss*, grieving individuals will readily identify with the various dialogues, ultimately realizing that they are not alone in their painfully private questions about what they have experienced and the unknown future they now face. Indeed, the "lessons" of loss found in these pages are the reminders of our interconnectivity with each other and the inevitable pain we experience when those connections are irrevocably altered by a loved one's irreversible physical absence. And in the end, it is a resource that offers hope for living beyond the pain and perplexity of early grief, as we build a continuing bond with the deceased, find meaning in our mourning and engage a changed life and relationships that are no less precious for having been touched by loss.

*Darcy Harris, PhD, FT*

# ABOUT THE AUTHOR

**Robert A. Neimeyer, PhD**, is Professor Emeritus of the Department of Psychology, University of Memphis, and maintains an active consulting and coaching practice. He also directs the Portland Institute for Loss and Transition, which provides online and onsite training internationally in grief therapy. Since completing his doctoral training at the University of Nebraska in 1982, he has conducted extensive research on the topics of death, grief, loss, and suicide intervention.

Neimeyer has published 35 books, including *New Techniques of Grief Therapy: Bereavement and Beyond* and *The Handbook of Grief Therapies*, the latter with Edith Steffen and Jane Milman. The author of over 600 articles and book chapters, he is currently working to advance a more adequate theory of grieving as a meaning-making process, both in his published work and through his frequent professional workshops for national and international audiences.

Neimeyer is the editor of the respected international journal, *Death Studies*, and served as president of the Association for Death Education and Counseling. In recognition of his scholarly contributions, he has been granted the Distinguished Research Award, the Distinguished Teaching Award and the Eminent Faculty Award by the University of Memphis; elected chair of the International Work Group on Death, Dying, and Bereavement; and given the Research Recognition, Clinical Practice and Lifetime Achievement Awards by the Association for Death Education and Counseling (ADEC). Most recently, he has been granted Lifetime Achievement Awards from both ADEC and the International Network for Personal Meaning.

# Part 1

# INTRODUCTION

What can the reader hope to find in the pages to follow? These brief opening chapters provide orientation to the question–answer exchanges that constitute the book, explain where the questions arose and offer suggestions for safely "dosing" the readers' exposure to the pithy and painful stories they will encounter as they peruse the various sections. I also offer some practical suggestions for how bereaved readers might use the book to promote compassionate clarity about their own losses as well as necessary self-change, and for professional readers to draw on the dialogue between the contributors of questions and myself in their own clinical practice.

# 1
# LISTENING TO THE BEREAVED

Listening to the bereaved—really listening—brings into sharp focus two things: their pain and their questions. In ordinary conversation or correspondence, both are often muffled under social convention, the need to present a brave front and to spare the listener the discomfort of feeling a measure of their suffering and uncertainty. But when a safe space is opened to hear the truth of tragic loss, what emerges is often the deep devastation that attends the death of someone dear, coupled with the fear of stepping into a future that is devoid of their friendship and companionship. At other times, it is the anger or guilt stemming from the complexity or ambivalence of the relationship that finds expression and that needs to be heard and addressed. This book took shape in an attempt to engage such raw and sometimes lingering grief and the existential questions to which it gives rise, offering a compassionate perspective and practical advice for people attempting to rebuild a world of meaning that has been challenged, and sometimes shattered, by loss.

What can readers—themselves likely to be struggling with bereavement in their own lives or in those of others for whom they care—expect to find in the pages that follow? First and foremost, they will encounter the authentic voices of other bereaved people, as they address the hard but unvarnished questions that are uniquely their own, that arise from the death of just this special partner or parent, this unique child or confidante or this complicated but close person in their lives. As the writers find words for their distress and disorientation, readers will be invited into the intimate particulars of lives made strange by loss. But in this same movement into the circumstances of a specific death, readers also will hear echoes of feelings and frustrations that resonate with their own. Inevitably, when people speak most honestly for themselves, they speak for all humanity.

By the same token, I have tried to speak with similar honesty and directness, offering what understanding I can, based on what contemporary bereavement studies have to tell us or teach us about the dynamics of grieving. But more directly, I have drawn inspiration from the many hundreds, perhaps thousands, of bereaved parents, partners, family and friends I have encountered in 50 years of experience as a practicing grief therapist, who have shared with me not only their pain but also their progress toward lives of renewed meaning and, yes, even joy and satisfaction. Both of these ways of knowing—through the twin lenses of carefully documented research and the practical wisdom of shared experience—ultimately converge on the hopeful conclusion that people can transcend tragedy and even grow through grief, though the path forward is rarely easy. By meeting the bereaved where they are, sometimes in the immediate aftermath of a life-altering loss, sometimes many years later, I have tried to address the "stuck" points, the impasses or roadblocks that seem to impose impossible obstacles to beginning or resuming that journey.

The great variety of losses addressed in the pages that follow understandably give rise to a huge range of emotions. The death of a child to cancer, of a partner to suicide, of a parent in a house fire, of a loved one to murder, of multiple family members in a vehicular accident or even of anonymous strangers to war or terrorism can all trigger unique feelings of helplessness, guilt, horror, anger and disconsolate depression. Like a Pandora's box of human struggles, the grieving heart pours out a vast and varied torrent of troubles, and the bereaved are left having to address them all, too often without the full support of others. The purpose of this book is to stand with mourners as they do so, to grasp what is uniquely hard in their particular loss, to hear in it the strains of universal human predicaments and to offer useful counsel that will speak to a specific mourner but in a way that has more general applicability to those readers who have not yet found the words or settings in which to express their own questions.

Where did the questions that structure this book come from? The great majority were sent to a unique website named AfterTalk (www.aftertalk.com), designed by two friends, Larry Lynn and Lisa Bogatin, to provide a special kind of bereavement support by encouraging users to have healing conversations with those they have loved and lost. This remarkable resource is based on the conviction—which I share—that grieving commonly involves not a process of "letting go" of the deceased, but instead of finding new and sustainable ways to "hold on," to maintain a psychologically meaningful bond rather than relinquish it. Accordingly, AfterTalk provides a free, web-based format for encouraging people to speak not only *about* the deceased and memorialize them but also to speak *to* the deceased in the form of earnest letters, sometimes prompted by available "conversation starters," to express their love and their longing, their hurt and their hope. The result can be a sense of reopening the relationship between the living and dead, an opportunity to "say hello again," as my colleague Michael White once put it, rather than to say a final "goodbye" or alternatively to address lingering issues that were left unresolved at the point of the death. With a restoration of relationship and a conservation of continuity between the past and present, people then have greater resources for moving toward a changed future.

However, death also poses troubling questions that the deceased alone cannot answer. It is for this reason that Lisa and Larry invited me from the beginning of the site to offer a kind of advice column, addressing just such questions from users in an "Ask Dr. Neimeyer" column that is a regular service of the site and, according to our user satisfaction survey, is one of its most helpful features. Listening between the lines of the stories the bereaved tell themselves and others, I have tried to offer both a philosophic perspective on what makes a particular loss particularly hard, and concrete counsel—often of a counterintuitive and detailed kind—intended to be "news you can use" for any bereaved person struggling with similar questions. By compiling these questions and answers in this book and organizing them by the nature of the relationship to the deceased and the circumstances of the death itself, we have tried to give readers clear guidance leavened with compassionate understanding, ultimately addressing their anguish, while respecting their resilience. We hope that many more bereaved find consolation and counsel in the pages that follow and, of course, invite any further comments and questions that result from the reading.

—*Robert A. Neimeyer, PhD, Portland, Oregon*

# 2

# HOW TO USE THIS BOOK

It is appropriate to begin this book by providing some orientation to the reader, especially as most will bring more than mere curiosity about the topics of death and grief to the reading. Almost inevitably, they also will be bringing their own experiences with loss, and for most, these experiences will be achingly fresh and sometimes shattering. Indeed, even those professionals who support the bereaved—the counselors, therapists, social workers, nurses, chaplains, death doulas and others who accompany them prior to or following the death of an intimate companion or family member—will inevitably bring to the reading their own history of loss, which can sometimes be activated once more by the struggles presented by their patients or clients. So, a few words are in order to orient both audiences.

First, recognize at the outset that the grieving persons writing the questions are often describing losses in some detail that could parallel the reader's own. Although this is likely the very reason that most readers have picked up *Living Beyond Loss* in the first place, hoping to encounter situations with which they identify, this same identification can touch on understandable vulnerabilities in their own lives and losses, sometimes activating troubling feelings that deserve more of an audience than the printed pages of a book can offer. Moreover, our goal was to allow the bereaved to speak in their own authentic voices, without censorship, with only modest editing of their words for the sake of readability, resulting in descriptions of the losses and their impact that are often anguishing to read, even for those of us seasoned by working many years or decades alongside people with similar struggles. I therefore encourage readers to exercise a principle of self-compassion and step *back* from any part of the reading that feels like "too much" to take in. Instead, if this feeling arises, I encourage them to consider stepping *toward* a trusted relationship of a personal or professional sort to more fully reflect on the emotional implications of their own loss, on what they need and are ready for at a given moment, as they seek a way forward. Another way of saying this is that this book is not intended as a substitute for psychological or spiritual counsel by peers or professionals, but instead as a supplement to these social resources.

DOI: 10.4324/9780429059070-3

Beyond this caveat, I encourage readers seeking perspective or advice on their own losses to read the dialogues that follow in an active way, engaging personally with both the questions and answers. Rather than rushing through the text, take time to sit with each letter, asking, *How does this fit for me? What can I use here, by way of consolation, perspective or direction? What small action step might I take based on this passage?* Implicit in this advice is the idea that words alone do not mitigate the pain of grief, enlarge a world made smaller by loss or cultivate our resilience to move through the darkness and, in a sense, even befriend it. Instead, these valued outcomes grow naturally when we connect the words to our own emotions, yearnings, experiences and personal strengths and begin to integrate them into our behavior and ways of being with others. Reading slowly, selectively and soulfully moves us in this direction, as can journaling about personal insights, applications or lessons learned after a few pages of such reading.

Finally, for fellow professionals offering support or therapy for the bereaved, I should underscore the obvious: that the responses that follow do not constitute professional consultation on your own challenging cases, though I hope they might suggest relevant principles or practices to consider. Instead, they simply represent my own best attempt to harvest the lessons of loss arising in my own five decades as a grief therapist and researcher, as a means of offering compassionate counsel directly to the bereaved and—I hope—encouragement for the healing intentions of valued colleagues who join me in this effort.[1]

For both readerships—the bereaved themselves and the grief professionals who accompany them—I hope the earnest exchanges in the pages that follow will not only lay bare the suffering and struggles of the writers but also suggest principles and practices that promote growth through grief, despite its rigors. Indeed, it is the reality of resilience in the aftermath of tragic transitions that is the basic message of *Living Beyond Loss*, reflecting the human capacity to find meaning in mourning. I appreciate the simple courage and hard-won wisdom of all those who have opened this book, as I do those who have shared their stories.

### Note

1 For those professionals interested in a deeper dive into online or onsite training in grief therapy, consult the rich curriculum of the Portland Institute for Loss and Transition at www.portlandinstitute.org.

# Part 2

# WHO WE LOSE

Perhaps more than any other emotion except love, grief is *about* something and, most especially, about *someone*. Far from being a generic response to loss, our bereavement is configured largely by our connection to a specific person, a specific relationship, one that is precious, problematic or perhaps both simultaneously. This part of the book therefore groups questions according to the character of the bond that has been broken, or at least challenged, by death, whether to a spouse, partner, parent, child, sibling or other close relation, with the pain of this rupture in attachment commonly being at the core of the griever's anguish. Finally, we conclude with a handful of questions that bear on especially complicated relationships with the deceased or with the larger family or social system of which they are a part. In each case, of course, the questions within a chapter highlight the uniqueness of the loss and, ultimately, of the person formulating the question.

Readers interested in further web-based resources relative to the loss of particular relationships are encouraged to explore the list provided by AfterTalk at the following link: https://www.aftertalk.com/grief_organizations.

# 3
# LOSS OF A HUSBAND

### Grieving for a Husband/Father During Holiday Season

*Dear Dr. Neimeyer,*

My husband Don died 9 months ago after a rapid decline; and his lungs basically stopped working, even with oxygen treatments. His death has been hard for us as a family in many ways, as he lived only about 6 months after getting the diagnosis, and we are now facing the first Christmas without him. He was always the "social magnet" for every occasion with family and friends, the one who would take them fishing, cook the meals and tell the stories. So it is hard to imagine going through the season without him.

But my main question is, how can I talk with my four grown children about the "elephant in the room" created by their father's death when we get together for the first holiday with his family in California for a week? All but one of them live in different states, but I write them every week, and often share thoughts and hopes their father had for their lives. But I'm not much of a telephone person. And I guess I also don't call much because I hate to break down in tears and bring them down whenever I get them on the line.

So what should I do when we are together for a week? If I ask them how they are doing, they'll just say "Fine." But it really feels like we are just walking on eggshells. We can get through the gift exchanges and dinners, but I know we really need to connect more if we still are going to be a family.

**Mary**

*Dear Mary,*

I can imagine that this will be a very different holiday for you, in another state both geographically and emotionally in the wake of Don's illness and death. And your story makes clear that your grief, like most people's, is something that happens both within you as individuals and between you as members of a family trying to reorganize without his big presence in your family get-togethers. And so, in the uncomfortable silence that can arise in the presence of his family and your own, you are now thrust into the role of being the conversation manager, a role that might have naturally fallen to Don.

So how can you make opportunities for meaningful encounters, especially with your children, rather than practice a kind of vigilant mutual avoidance of the most important and obvious topic of the season, namely your shared loss? Fortunately, the holidays typically provide multiple natural opportunities for "real" moments of meeting and meaning, even if these are brief and punctuated by attention to the many activities and topics that will also naturally occupy your attention during this period. Here are a few ideas.

1. *Give the gifts that keep on giving.* Might you select a small gift, perhaps something of Don's, to give to each child on his behalf? No doubt you can think of many things that could symbolize some kind of bond with each of the kids: maybe a special fishing lure, book, article of clothing or memento of a family trip. Such things can provide both a cherished "linking object" that honors their unique bond with their father and also serve as "conversation starters" about shared memories of a heartwarming or humorous type. The fact that this gift exchange will occur in the presence of his extended family—who might also be recipients of such gifts—can increase this effect, as each invites an explanation to those less familiar with its meaning, or who might have shared relevant times with him fishing, enjoying meals and more, who could have their own stories to tell. Whatever their commercial value, the gifts labeled with a tag "From Dad" or "From Don" are likely to be treasured for both of these reasons for years to come.
2. *Make room for him on the tree.* Consider contributing an ornament to the Christmas tree that invokes Don's presence: perhaps it is a little wooden fishing boat or an ornament he himself bought on a family outing. You can be sure that its simple presence on the tree will invite his presence in the room and in the thoughts of those who walk by, conveying the feeling that he is indeed with you during this season in your hearts and minds.
3. *Invite Don to the table.* Given that Don apparently cooked for special occasions and likely had favorite foods, might you individually or you as a family cook a favorite dish of his to share? Almost certainly such dishes, like the gifts, will both honor him and prompt shared memories. And if you really want to invoke his presence, set an extra place at the table for him. The empty chair could be a strong ritual statement of both his presence and absence—perhaps too strong for some families, but perfect for others. Keeping in mind the principle behind the practice, you'll be able to find the symbolic statement that fits just right for your family.

In sum, the holidays naturally afford opportunities for remembrance and renewal, though these need not pervade every context and conversation as you find new ways to move forward together as a family. Experimenting with a few ideas like those noted earlier will let you find creative ways to beckon Don into the gatherings as an invited rather than intrusive presence. And as voices and stories begin to fill the silence, you will have lit a symbolic candle in a time that otherwise might be dark.

—Dr. Neimeyer

## Recent Loss to Cancer

*Dear Dr. Neimeyer,*

I lost my dearest husband 3 months ago after almost 8 years of battling cancer. Our attachment deepened even more when he was diagnosed since we got to be with each other 24/7. This perhaps is the reason why until now I can't seem to move on. It's as if time doesn't heal all wounds.

Visiting his grave has become a part of my daily routine. I try to get busy with other things, but he is always in my thoughts. Am I suffering from depression? I have done almost everything to ease the pain of losing him. . . . I have made a memorial table in loving memory of him. . . . I have collected photos to create a memorial album, etc.

I find solace in the chirps of the birds, the drizzling water from the fountain and the sounds from the wind chimes. But I'm really torn into pieces. I am heartbroken. . . . Life seems meaningless without my beloved.

Praying and hoping that you could help me get through this, Doc.

**Renata**

*Dear Renata,*

To experience keen heartbreak just three months after the death of your life partner is certainly a common experience with which countless bereaved spouses can identify. And it is easy to imagine, as you suggest, that the intense bonding required to negotiate his lengthy illness could have made a close relationship all that much closer. If, as your "24/7" description of togetherness implies, pulling together to contend with his cancer perhaps inevitably also entailed pulling away from others, this too would tie your heartstrings so fully to his that severing them could be especially anguishing, almost like being surgically separated from a Siamese twin. And you are right that time alone does little to heal such wounds, as studies of prolonged grief reactions tell us. Instead, it is what we do with the time that counts.

And so what might you do with the time to help you adapt to this changed world into which his death has thrown you? Some ideas are provided by contemporary understandings of grief. For a visual aid of one useful theory, adapted from the Dual Process Model of Coping with Bereavement (DPM) by my colleagues Maggie Stroebe and Henk Schut, try this:

> Draw a wide oblong oval on a sheet of paper, from side to side. Label this "Everyday Life Experience."
> 
> Then, within this oval, add two egg-like shapes standing up, one near either end, with a gap between them. Label the one on the left "Loss" and the one on the right "Life."
> 
> Finally, starting near the top of the eggs, draw a zig-zag line going back and forth between them, from top to bottom. Label this "Pendulum Swing."

Now sit back and take a look at the "Map of Mourning" that you've drawn. Imagine that the Loss sphere contains the raw pain of grief, the loneliness, the longing, the attempt to reconnect with your husband, to restore the bond. And imagine that the Life sphere contains everything else: buying groceries, relating to friends and family, pursuing projects, working, trying new things, taking on new roles. Both are important. Both are part of grief. The pendulum swing between them—even if initially much more time is spent in the Loss orientation—reminds us that we naturally are drawn to and require both. Perhaps at first we have only a few moments of "time out" from our grief when engaged in something that requires our concentration, but these moments are crucial to embrace, nurture and enlarge, to provide a natural counterbalance to the absorption in loss. At the heart of the DPM is an audacious notion: that we make progress through grief when we give ourselves permission, even encouragement, to make time to grieve . . . and time not to. We need the former to learn how to love someone in his or her physical absence, and we need the latter in order to learn to live differently but with meaning in the changed world.

Now make an honest inventory of all of the thoughts, actions and projects you undertake in an average day or week. Of those you mention, nearly all focus on the left side of the model, falling within the Loss orientation: visiting the grave daily, constructing a memorial table, compiling a memorial album, etc. No doubt each is an act of love and is deeply meaningful. But only "trying to get busy with other things" falls into the right side of the map, the Life orientation, and the way you phrase it suggests that the things you try to get busy with have much less meaning for you. To balance the pendulum, what might you add consciously to that side of the model? How about visiting a new or beloved place daily with a special friend? Rearranging a table top to feature a display of arts or crafts that you find beautiful? Making an album of new photographs you take yourself that touch or inspire you, such as the birds, fountain or natural scenes to which you are drawn? The idea would be to promote a natural back-and-forth between loss and life, grief and growth, in a way that carries you forward in both domains.

One of the subtler implications of the DPM is that adapting to loss is not a straight arrow that moves from left to right on the map; it's rarely that easy. Loss is a part of our everyday life experience as bereaved people . . . but only a part. With intention, tenacity and good company, we can also refresh and reinvent ourselves by giving the Life side of the equation equal time. Ask yourself if your husband would want that for you. If the answer is yes, you may owe it to him as much as to yourself and others who care about you to move forward by stepping first with your left foot, and then with your right, shifting your balance between Loss and Life, as naturally as walking toward a self-set goal . . . knowing that you will take your husband along with you, walking hand in hand.

—Dr. Neimeyer

## How to Live Without Him

*Dear Dr. Neimeyer,*

My husband died in November. He was in his early 40s. We were together nearly 25 years; he was my other half. We did everything together. It is so hard for me. All I do is cry. I know that's not going to bring him back, but I'm so heartbroken. It is like I'm dying inside. Each day I talk to him and I get goosebumps on my right arm and my hand gets numb. Is that a sign? Is it true that they come to you? I just wonder if he misses me as much as I miss him. How can I live without him? It's killing me.

**Netta**

*Dear Netta,*

Although we live in a culture that emphasizes individualism, the reality is that we are wired for attachment. As the feeling of yearning that you express poignantly conveys, we need others—and particularly a few "special" others—to feel whole. This is why one common feature of profound grief is the sense that a part of ourselves has died; in a psychologically real sense, it has. To lose a partner so early in life reduces us, and even our earnest attempts to retain a connection to him or her can feel like a pallid alternative to the gift of our loved one's full presence. Learning to live with this very present absence often requires a considerable effort over time.

For all of these reasons, intense grief alone is not something pathological, something to be worried about. Certainly, missing our deceased loved ones keenly and experiencing tearfulness when we think about them is common early in mourning, and probably occurs in proportion to our love. But as you move into your seventh or eighth month of bereavement, if you find that the tears are a constant companion and that pleasure is a stranger, if you seem to have lost touch with the uniquely valuable aspects of yourself, if you find yourself cutting off from others and having trouble functioning at home or at work, and especially if things seem to be getting worse rather than better, then consciously taking steps to reclaim your life may be in order.

So, what to do if this description seems to fit? One thing is to follow your instincts to talk with your husband, not only about your missing him—though that surely would be part of it—but also to share the highlights of your day, discuss your plans for the week or solicit his advice about an important decision you are facing. AfterTalk can provide a portal for just this sort of communication: messages that affirm life as well as loss. Just as a weekly phone call to a parent or child living in another state naturally would include conversations about interesting and important updates on your activities; so too can a written letter to your husband continue to include him as an audience to your life in a way he might appreciate, not only in a way that would cause him concern. Your letter even suggests that you believe he may have a spiritual presence in your life, missing you in return. If so, you might sit quietly for a moment after writing and re-reading your letter and try to sense what his response might be. Giving it voice in a letter written back to yourself can help strengthen your bond, and perhaps even offer you helpful advice and encouragement on setting aside your grief at times in order to reengage other people and projects. Though it is not a panacea for the pain of loss, reaffirming a living bond as a part—though not the entirety—of life can help ensure that the second six months after the loss is not merely a darker version of the first.

—Dr. Neimeyer

## A Husband's Sudden Death

*Hi Dr. Neimeyer,*

My husband's sudden death happened unexpectedly five years ago at the age of 54. We were together for 33 years. He dropped dead in front of me with no warning. They said that he was gone before he hit the floor. We had a very good marriage, and I am thankful for the time that we had. We ran a business together for 30 years and have two grown children. I keep very busy, and that has been the most helpful, along with the fact that I do have a lot of close family nearby. My problem is that I don't see a future for myself. I work, do errands and household chores, and that's about it. I just don't know what to do next or how to move on. I will be 59 in three months. I miss what I had, but I know I can't get it back. I also feel that I don't have closure because I wasn't able to say goodbye! My son says that I need to get out of my comfort zone, but I don't know how to go about doing this. I know that in some ways five years is a long time, but for me it's like it was yesterday.

Thanks for your time!

**Cynthia**

*Dear Cynthia,*

When we lose someone suddenly, as you have, we are denied so many things: a chance to adapt, to anticipate the looming loss and discuss it with our loved one, an opportunity to affirm love, say goodbye and, when relevant, seek and extend forgiveness for wrongs or disappointments across years of relationship. Not only do we miss this special person, but we also miss the opportunity to address what needed to be addressed and say what needed to be said. After-Talk letters can take a long step toward helping us do this even beyond death, restoring a sense of connection that lets us convey what is in our hearts and even seek the loved one's counsel on our changed lives.

And this latter point introduces a key feature of your own grief experience: in losing your husband as a physical presence in your life, you also lost all of the future roles and goals that were tied to his being there. This is partly what people mean when they say that it feels as if a part of them had died with their partner, leaving them with a sense of merely going through the motions. Keeping busy helps, no doubt—it provides a buffer against the sort of rumination that can reinforce depression and helplessness. But it is not a long-term substitute for purposeful activity organized around new goals and roles or that addresses the questions, "Who am I now?" and "What now matters to me?"

These are big questions, but not impossible ones to ask and answer. One place to start is by looking at previous sources of pleasure and meaning. Across the course of your life, when did you feel most alive? Was it when you were spending time with close friends? Learning new things? Creating something beautiful? Helping others? When did you feel most like you were growing as a person, and what direction of growth might be suitable for you now? In one sense your son is probably right: change of any kind moves us out of our comfort zone, or we risk stagnation. The secret is to find the right balance of challenge and support as you explore new options. Start small—at least twice a week, shop in a different grocery store, ask a friend to join you for lunch in a new restaurant, wear different clothes. And then try adding activities that link to the long-term interests referred to earlier—perhaps an art class, or volunteer work or an out-of-town trip. With each small step the way will become clearer, and you will discover or rediscover the person you are now meant to be.

—Dr. Neimeyer

## A Daughter's Upcoming Wedding

*Dear Dr. Neimeyer,*

My husband Burt died two years ago, and for the most part my family and I are doing fine. The first year was very hard, but it was made easier by a lovely memorial service we had for him on a beach where he used to sail, when we had a family clambake and bonfire, told stories and read passages of poetry that had meant a lot to Burt or that said a lot to us about the kind of values he had—for family and for the natural environment. Now, as my son and daughter move into their own adult lives, I admit that I feel a bit lonely in the new home that we bought before we learned Burt was ill, but I love my work as a special education teacher, stay in touch with the kids and have a circle of friends.

But recently I've been struggling with Burt's loss again, as our daughter, Carrie, in her late 20s, has gotten engaged to a man from another part of the country whose family comes from a higher social sphere than we do; they are used to fancy social gatherings in posh settings and probably have never hiked a trail, lit a campfire or pitched a tent in their lives. They're nice enough, really, and Carrie and Joel seem to be well-matched, but his parents are accustomed to arranging big events, and so are marching ahead with making big plans for the wedding.

My problem is that as Carrie prepares to take this step, I'm feeling Burt's absence more than ever . . . and I think she might be, too. It just feels so wrong to have to rely on her uncle to walk her down the aisle and to know that it is her father's arm she should be holding. I want so much for Burt to be recognized in some way, but I worry that Joel's parents would say that this is not about him—they never met him, after all—but about our children. On top of that, I'm sort of an introvert, and Joel's mother is really a force of nature, and I don't know how to talk with her about this, or if Carrie would even want me to.

I'm so confused, and even a little tearful. What advice would you give someone like me?

**Shirley**

*Dear Shirley,*

It seems to be the way of grief, just as it is the way of love, to have to keep redefining the terms of our connection to our loved ones as life moves forward. Surely you would not be the first widow, nor Carrie the first bride, to feel a husband's or father's absence keenly during a subsequent marriage or other life passage. After all, Burt is half the reason that she is even in the world to walk down that aisle, and to bar him from even symbolic presence at the event seems to compound the sense of injustice that surrounds his absence. So what might be done to address this, for the sake of all parties?

The first thing to do is to talk with Carrie. Explain how you are feeling and see if she shares some of your concerns and wishes, as very probably she will. Then brainstorm together some creative or ritual ways that you might bring Burt into the wedding weekend in appropriate places while keeping the spotlight on the couple. This needn't be hard, as some of these might be quite unobtrusive: perhaps your son might wear one of your husband's ties, a song might be included that had special meaning to Burt or a wedding gift given to the couple that reinforces your family's love of nature and invites Joel more fully into it. Or Burt might make a somewhat fuller symbolic appearance on the occasion, as you toast the couple in the rehearsal dinner on his behalf, reserve an empty seat alongside you in the pew or suggest to the wedding celebrant a reading or story that would have a special meaning to both father and daughter. Not all of this needs to be negotiated between you, of course—some things can simply be a welcome surprise—but if you learn that Carrie too would welcome a tip of the hat to her father in the service and that Joel would not object, then you could arrange a mother-to-mother talk with your counterpart and solicit her understanding and creative input as well.

In summary, in the several hours that most wedding functions last, and given the role traditionally played by proud parents in blessing their children's new lives, it seems appropriate that all four of them have some brief opportunity to participate in this meaningful ritual of family transition—even in absentia. Bringing Burt in to play a symbolic celebratory role may prove bittersweet, but the whole family is likely to feel enlarged and affirmed by your doing so.

—Dr. Neimeyer

## Loss of Her Rock

*Dr. Neimeyer,*

My wonderful husband passed away six months ago. It was very unexpected, and he was the love of my life. I'm just having a hard time adjusting without him. He was my rock.

**Sabrina**

*Dear Sabrina,*

When we lose an intimate life companion like your husband, we feel displaced, uprooted, without the grounding and connection that relationship afforded, often for many years. Like a ship without an anchor, we may feel adrift on stormy seas, with no idea how to make our way to the secure harbor that person once provided. This is true when we lose all sorts of attachment relationships, but may be especially true for those, like you, who lose loving partners, or children who lose loving parents. Grieving is the emotional acknowledgment of the severity of that loss.

And yet, as natural as it is to focus on the immensity of our loss, in doing so exclusively we can fail to recognize how much we have retained. Indeed, nearly all children will one day lose their parents, if only in adulthood, though the lessons learned at their hand and ideally the security developed in that bond will remain with them for the rest of their lives. This is no less true in widowhood, when we can review, sometimes by journaling, the many "life imprints" left by the loved one. What might we notice, for example, about what we carry forward from the relationship, at any or all of the following levels:

- our mannerisms or gestures
- our ways of speaking or relating to others
- our pastimes, hobbies or interests
- our vocations or volunteer activities
- our basic personalities
- our core values and beliefs

By writing a bit about each of these layers or levels of imprint, we often come to see more clearly the cherished legacy of our loved one, which remains very much alive in our lives. Indeed, in a certain sense, we continue their lives in our own. A meaningful extension of this reflection would be to write an AfterTalk letter of gratitude to our loved one to express the depth of our appreciation for this lasting gift and to share our ideas about how we can constructively continue to manifest it in the future.

Of course, this thoughtful and creative response does not erase the grief we feel, but it can ennoble it, and remind us that even in the physical absence of someone we have loved and lost, we need not erase his deeper presence in our ongoing lives.

—Dr. Neimeyer

### Losing the Final Piece of Him

*Dear Dr. Neimeyer,*

My husband passed away nearly a dozen years ago, and I have been receiving his Social Security benefits since that time. On my birthday next spring I will be taking my own Social Security. My question is: Why do I feel so apprehensive about taking mine and giving up my husband's? This is the last thing that I have that was his and mine . . . I feel as though if I give it up, I am losing the final piece of him. Is this normal even after 12 years?

Thank you,

**Moira**

*Dear Moira—*

Ah, Moira. Even in matters of the heart, we human beings are drawn to symbolism and significance. And just as you say, the Social Security provided posthumously by your husband had profound meaning for you that went well beyond a monthly check or electronic deposit. In an important sense, it was not simply a monthly deposit to a banking account—it was a deposit to a love account. And now, even if your financial needs are met by your own retirement benefits, your emotional needs are not, and you feel the shadow of an old grief flicker across your vision of the future.

Understandable as this disquieting feeling is, it could also hold the key to its own solution. That is, what seems required is the development of psychological security to replace the Social Security, to discern more clearly the many ways he is still very much with you. Very likely many things in your home, from the chairs and tables that support your body and meals to the lamps that disperse the darkness bear his fingerprints or sense of presence, and perhaps the home itself is one that sheltered you both. More intangibly, but ultimately more importantly, much of who you are as a person likely bears the imprint of your years of loving connection. You could find it helpful to reflect, perhaps in an AfterTalk letter or journal entry, on the "life imprint" he left on you, at levels ranging from your mannerisms and ways of speaking, through your ways of relating to others and yourself, to your choice of pastimes or interests and ultimately to your core values and purposes. Meditating on these, and perhaps expressing in that symbolic letter to him the gratitude you have for the many ways he is still very much with you, could help bridge the transition from one expression of a continuing bond in the form of your joint Social Security check to a form of psychological security expressed in a dozen more durable connections.

—Dr. Neimeyer

## Opening to New Love

*Dear Dr. Neimeyer,*

I lost my husband to a sudden death which involved a vehicle accident when he suffered a pulmonary embolism at the age of 59. This happened over a year ago just days before our 34th anniversary.

I began reading many books [and] articles on sudden death and all the emotions and phases you will most likely go through. I have a strong faith in God and truly believe he has given me the strength to make it through this past year. I have been blessed in so many ways to stay in my home, continue to work, etc. Having said all that, lately I have been longing for companionship and thinking possibly of trying to meet someone new. I enjoyed being married and we had a good marriage, with the usual ups and downs. That is when I ran into your website and AfterTalk.

At times I have so much guilt, then some strong anxiety about a new relationship, then feeling like I am getting too old and there won't be anyone for me, and I read how there seems to be a little bit of "steer clear of widows" attitude that could complicate finding the right person. How do you work through all of these emotions, and how do you go about meeting someone and dating again?

**Rachel**

*Dear Rachel,*

Surely the best practice for a successful second partnership is having enjoyed a satisfying earlier relationship. Not only does it provide a training ground for future intimacy, but it also offers a model for what a good marriage might look like, so that you can be alert to when those conditions are not met in future dating situations. This said, your mix of interest and hesitation in approaching dating as a widow is a common one, and a few principles might offer support for your new quest for companionship. Here are seven tips as you explore this brave new world:

1. *Center in your values.* The best relationships begin with shared core values, such as your strong faith. Of course, this need not imply that you limit your options to members of your specific religious denomination, but core similarities in belief and in the other values that shape choices of activities and interests are worth exploring before broaching commitment.
2. *Consider what you have to give.* Though we often look for a partner to complete our life, it balances the equation to spend some time reminding ourselves of what we have to offer, as well as what we need. Psychologist Abraham Maslow once distinguished between "D-love" and "B-love," the former focused on remediating the deficits or inadequacies in our lives, and the latter, healthier variety built on "being" rather than deficiency, being who we are. Your description of yourself and your work suggests you have much to offer to the right person, just as that person will have much to offer you.
3. *Seek someone who can be open about your individual pasts, as well as a possible shared future.* Your previous marriage sounds long and rich, and to shroud it in silence could come to feel like erasing much of who you are—and the same would likely be true for your partner. Seek a relationship that is not threatened by appreciative recollections of previous spouses, any

more than by recollections of your respective childhoods. Both have contributed to the people you have become.

4. *Avoid invidious comparisons.* The previous point notwithstanding, it is important to avoid elevating a previous partner to sainthood or using him as a paragon of virtue, in comparison to whom a second partner is found wanting. Of course, our reluctance to think ill of the dead, combined with the inevitable rough spots in negotiating any new relationship, can contribute to this common dynamic, but look for opportunities to appreciate differences as well as similarities across relationships, and you'll be off to a good start.

5. *Expect anxiety.* By definition, steering into the unknown stirs up anxiety for most of us, and dating again after a long marriage is likely to feel unfamiliar, strange and probably even a bit scary. But embracing the opportunities for learning that go hand in hand with exploring new relationships can also be fun and exciting, especially if each of you recognizes that both of you likely are feeling some version of the same jitters. The best antidote for anxiety of any kind is exposure to that which we fear, probably in a gradual way that feels natural to you.

6. *Go slow.* One implication of the earlier point is that there is no rush in forming a new partnership; a relationship you cultivate over the span of a year is far more likely to be fitting and solid than one that rushes toward commitment in a few months. Especially because widowers are commonly more eager to remarry than widows, recognize that you might need to be the one who gently applies the brakes so that you can let a bit of the illusion that accompanies early romance to fade, permitting a clearer view of the partner and the relationship in the long haul.

7. *Do some guilt busting.* Before dating, you might consider writing an AfterTalk letter to your husband, letting him know how you are feeling about opening to a new relationship, affirming your love for him and asking his counsel. Listening for his voice within you, wait a day or two and then write back a letter as if from him in response. Many issues can be cleared up through this practice, which might of course extend through multiple rounds of exchange. Talking to others who are also widows, and especially those who have recoupled, can also help you sort through guilt, the "stigma," if any, that you encounter in being a widow and other obstacles that can get in the way of exploring new intimacy. And though you might well not need it, remember that a good counselor can also assist you with feeling your way through this form of reinvention of your life if other supportive figures seem hard to come by. Drawing on some or all of these supporters along with your own resilience, there is every reason to hope that you can write a new chapter in your relational life, one that brings its own meaning and satisfaction, even as you continue to cherish the previous one.

—Dr. Neimeyer

## Children and Remarriage

*Dear Dr Neimeyer,*

My husband passed away a few years ago when my children were very young. I was fortunate enough to find a wonderful man and remarry. He has embraced "our" children as if they were his own. My problem is that I am very conflicted. I want my children to grow up knowing about their "first" father,' but am concerned that by doing so I am undermining their relationship with their new father. One child was old enough to have memories of her first father; the second wasn't. All of this is tied up in my own continuing grief over the loss of my first husband and an underlying irrational guilt about remarrying. Therapists I've seen haven't offered any useful guidance. Can you help me?

**Nicole**

*Dear Nicole,*

Unfortunately, not all therapists are comfortable with grief, whether because they received very little training in dealing with the uniquely difficult challenges loss presents or because they mistakenly assume that working on issues of love and loyalty in a relationship can only be done when both partners are living. In fact, as AfterTalk demonstrates, nothing can be further from the truth, as we are quite capable of accessing the voices of those we have loved and lost as we also negotiate the inevitable changes in our lives.

So how might you do so? One place to begin would be by consulting your first husband in the matter through an AfterTalk letter. How might he advise you to handle this, balancing your understandable need to keep his stories alive with your children's readiness for a second father who loves them in his own way? What special memories would he want you to share, and what new exploits of the children with you and your current husband might he appreciate hearing about as they grow toward the young people and adults they will one day become? Fortunately, we have room in our hearts to love more than one person at a time: just as we don't have to stop loving our parents to marry or to withdraw affection from one child in order to have another, so too we can continue our bond with a previous partner while also opening our hearts to another. Embracing both husbands conveys this vital lesson to your children, as you teach them by example that carrying forward a legacy of love can enrich, rather than threaten, the present.

—Dr. Neimeyer

## Turning Over a New Leaf

*Dear Dr. Neimeyer—*

My husband died just over a year ago, so on January 1 I will start my second year without him, and I am not looking forward to it. It's not that I am immobilized by grief, as I have gotten better across the months in that department, and actually feel pretty good and function pretty well when I am visiting our children across the country or traveling with friends. It's just that I feel lost and listless at home, even though there are 100 things I need to be doing—from cleaning out closets through straightening the garage to finding something to do with my time. But it all just feels overwhelming, and so I just watch TV or curl up in bed. My friends tell me I have to stay busy, but it's not that easy.

So my question is, do you have any practical advice for me so I can turn over a new leaf in the year to come?

**Phyllis**

*Dear Phyllis—*

There's a reason for the season, as they say, as the dawning of a New Year, if approached thoughtfully, can signal a time of renewal. It sounds like you have processed your grief and retained a capacity to live well and stay connected to others—at least when not at home. So perhaps with the turning of the calendar page you can also, as you say, turn a new leaf and cultivate the new shoots of possibility that may be germinating beneath it. Here are a few principles to guide your practice as you do so:

1. *Reinvent your world.* As your home seems to be your "Twilight Zone," consider brightening it in some way. You might literally introduce translucent and airy window treatments, for example, or experiment with new lights in the rooms in which you spend the most waking hours. Change things up: rearrange the furniture to create a different feel to the space, paint a room. There are home designers who specialize in working inexpensively with what you already own to create a fresh environment that can surprise and delight by configuring existing furniture and decor in different ways. It can be surprising what a difference a modest change in our living space can make.
2. *Invite people in.* Especially if you try any of the previous tips, but even if you don't, have a few friends over for hors d'oeuvres or desserts to "reclaim your space" for the life you want. Perhaps you can even throw a "house rewarming" party, after the chill cast over the home by your husband's death. Set a trend with this, perhaps rotating monthly among

the homes of those in your friendship circle and rebuild bonds where these have grown frayed from neglect.
3. *Set process goals.* Life requires maintenance, of course, and not all tasks are as potentially eye-catching as remodeling your living room. So when tackling that garage or closet, or even the routine and "invisible" tasks of cleaning bathrooms, paying bills and the like, set a timer or play a series of favorite songs to mark 15 or 30 minutes, during which you'll stay on task, giving yourself permission to discontinue when the time is up. You can always return to the task the next day for a similar interval until the job gets done. Setting this sort of "process goal," rather than only giving yourself "credit" for completion, can help you side-step unfair self-criticism and overcome task avoidance as you make incremental progress.
4. *Track your successes.* Many of us keep a To-Do list, but the problem is that as the list becomes long, our feeling of being overwhelmed grows large. And this is understandable: if we were presented with a warehouse full of food that we had to eat in our lifetimes, most of us would give up before taking the first bite! Instead of listing everything that needs attention, keep a list of tasks accomplished, and post it on the refrigerator or in some other prominent space. The results can then serve to encourage rather than discourage future initiative.
5. *Live your values.* The idea that "staying busy" is good for grievers is only a half-truth. As with psychologists who recommend "behavioral activation," everything hinges on what you get active doing. Random behavior doesn't make for a meaningful life. Nor is generic advice (get some exercise, go out with friends) specifically helpful to us when we are trying to figure out what kind of life might take shape in the emptiness created by loss. So begin with some inner work, perhaps in meditation or contemplation, perhaps in journaling or conversation with a counselor or trusted friend. Ask yourself: What matters to me? What excites me, stirs me, feels like time well spent? What are my ultimate values, and how can those inform my choices? Perhaps you value altruistic service to others: What volunteer organization reaches out in a way you can support to those in need? Perhaps you value learning: Is there a book club or Meet Up group you can locate on the internet to share ideas about works of creative nonfiction or to go on educational outings? Perhaps you value creativity: What art classes are offered in your area? In other words, connecting scheduled activities to deep interests can help you begin to reconstruct life in the wake of loss in a way that reorganizes your life and time into a satisfying, even if different, form than before.

—Dr. Neimeyer

LOSS OF A HUSBAND

## How to Start Life Over

*Dear Dr. Neimeyer,*

I'm pretty sure this question is a common one, but how do I know if I am moving through grief the way I should? I lost my husband last winter. In some ways it feels like yesterday and in others a lifetime ago. I still miss him so much. He was only in his mid-forties. I miss the life we had and I miss the future we planned. I function and I go to work, but life seems dull and empty. I look for joy, but it's hard to find. A laugh here and there, but an underlying sadness is there.

I don't know if I can ever love someone else again, and I don't know if I want to be alone the rest of my life. So, how do I move forward without my best friend? It's been a year and a half and I am still so lost. He was my world. We couldn't have any children as I was a little older when I married. Anyhow, it's just me, and my Mom lives with me, who I take care of. I am thankful for her, but all I have been doing is spending every weekend with her, doing nothing but watching TV on the weekends. How in the world does a 51-year-old woman start her life over? I was so happy being married, so happy being with him. Now I feel so vulnerable. How do I take any steps to find my new path? I know this is a lot of questions! I just plain miss him and I still cry and long for him.

**Vanessa**

*Dear Vanessa,*

Much as is true for you, many bereaved people start to reflect on their progress through grief as they negotiate the difficult second year following their loved one's death. In some ways basic life functioning might be restored, but life often seems to have lost its luster, and especially for those who don't have the necessary structure imposed by child care, life can feel like a purposeless drift, as we feel that we have lost our mooring in the safe harbor that our relationship to the deceased once provided. The fact that your husband died in what should have been the prime of life can worsen this problem, as you might feel out of synch with the rest of the social world, filled as it seems to be with other married couples, whereas you, as you say, have lost the partner who was "your world."

Of the many questions that percolate up from this difficult transition, the very first you ask is how you can know whether you are moving forward in the way you should. Ironically, perhaps, the specific qualities of the grief you feel might give the truest answers to this question. That is, when you pause to really sort through your feelings in the aftermath of this loss, some are likely to clearly announce themselves, while others might whisper their presence. Sitting quietly, in a place you will not be disturbed, and with some Kleenex handy, try closing your eyes and going to a quiet, meditative place in your mind. Slow your breathing, and invite yourself to turn your attention inward, to your body, to the place you feel your grief. Then, after a few minutes of quieting and centering your mind in this way, just ask yourself, *What have I lost?* Wait for the answer to come; it might come quickly at first: "My husband . . . my marriage . . . my best friend." Whatever comes, welcome it with a simple, "Thank you." Then ask yourself again: "What have I lost?" Very likely more will come. Repeat this procedure, waiting quietly for the less obvious answers to arrive. After 5 or 10 minutes, you should have a fuller inventory of what your husband's death means to you.

Then, in a second step, repeat this procedure, substituting the question, *How would I like to change?* Whatever comes ("I want to embrace joy." "I want to have another best friend." "I want to be braver."), welcome it with a simple "Thank you," and repeat the question. Again, in 5 to 10 minutes, you will have the outlines of a plan that addresses your deep needs.

The final step is to begin to implement the plan in action. For example, you might have identified at Step 1 losing "your best friend," the one you counted on as a companion in joy and sorrow. In Step 2 you might have sharpened this by realizing that you want to change "to feel more active, more engaged," rather than accepting a weekend of TV as a passive default option for killing time. Recognizing this, you are in a better position to recognize that you need to restore a vital sense of connection to others beyond your mother in a way that invites you back into a world from which you retreated. Perhaps a meet-up group in your area for weekend exercise, eating out, discussing a book, visiting a museum, working on a political campaign, etc., then could be a relevant way to begin to foster this change and move forward differently.

In short, your feelings (of aimlessness? boredom? frustration?) have functions: they could tell you much about what you need to once again find a life of meaning. Listen to what they have to tell you and teach you, and then seek practical steps to move in that direction, in essence by reinventing the next stage in your life. Pursued wisely and with courage, there is every chance that this path will lead to meaningful relationships and reopening to a world that will welcome all you still have to give.

—Dr. Neimeyer

**Quilting a New Life**

*Hi Dr. Neimeyer,*

My husband of 40 years died three years ago after a very short illness (cancer). Never sick. We had no children, just our beloved pets. He was my life, soulmate, my everything! When he died, I died a little too! I guess my question is, will life get better for me? A little more happiness and less sadness. I miss my husband so very much. Thank you for your time.

Sincerely,

**Johanna**

*Dear Johanna:*

I am sure that your way of expressing the personal dimensions of this loss—that when your husband died, you died a little too—will resonate with many readers. Especially when much of the fabric of your life was woven together with his, it must feel like when he was torn away so suddenly, your life was ripped apart as well. Mending the fabric of that life is no easy task.

And yet it can be done. Perhaps your grandmother once sewed quilts, saving fragments of previous garments, blankets or tablecloths to piece together with a new and secure backing in an artful and practical fashion. (The internet will contain thousands of images of the remarkable comforters that result.) Like quilting, in grieving we commonly find ways to configure a new life pattern out of the pieces that remain of the old—those roles, activities and people that have long given our lives meaning and that can do so again in a new configuration. And, of course, your relationship with your husband can be very much a part of this.

You might start in an AfterTalk fashion, by writing a letter to your husband about your hope for a life with more happiness and less sadness, as you now move forward into the third year after his death. Then you might consider writing a "Dear Johanna" letter back to you from his perspective. What might he tell you about the dependable personal strengths on which you could draw? About the goals you once held together that you might now pursue for you both? About the people who love and need you, providing a strong sense of validation for the woman you remain? And what new pieces might he suggest you add to make the quilt of your new life both beautiful and serviceable?

As you imagine or reimagine this changed life, give yourself a nudge to "just do it," acting on intentions to make them real. And consider telling your husband about these concrete steps beyond your "comfort zone," just as you also recruit others in this effort by making plans that involve them. Step by step, a life of meaning and even happiness can emerge, even if it is different in important ways than the one you lived before.

—Dr. Neimeyer

## Advice on Moving Forward

*Dear Dr. Neimeyer,*

I lost my husband of 46 years 19 months ago. I married him when I was 19, so I went from my parents' home to being married. I have never been alone. There is sexual abuse that happened to me, and I always knew that if I had not married my wonderful, kind, sweet husband, I probably would have taken my own life. He was the only one that ever truly loved me. He had never been sick a day in his life and then was diagnosed with a brain tumor and died five months later. It was a horrible five months, as his personality really changed and he became increasingly angry at me. He told a cancer therapist he had no love, passion or caring for his wife anymore. I thought I would die on the spot! We had a wonderful marriage, and when he was in a coma-like state for five days, the only words he said were my name and "I love you." He and God knew I needed to hear those words before he died.

My question is: How do I go on? I have cried every single day for 19 months, and just recently had two days where I cried all day. I don't have a lot of friends and I just moved a block from my daughter. I have two children on the East Coast that I don't get to see but a couple times a year, I thought being close to my daughter would help, but she works and has a little girl, so she is busy. I do get to watch my granddaughter, who is seven, during the summer. My husband and I watched her every day from the time she was six weeks old until she started kindergarten. Our children were the most important thing to my husband and me, but they all have their own lives. I am devastated and can't seem to move forward. I see two therapists, take a lot of medication and go to grief support groups. What else can I do?

Thank you,

**Dina**

*Dear Dina,*

When we have known early hurt and betrayal as you have described, trust and intimacy can feel dangerous, and for good reason. Given this, it is impressive that you opened your heart to your husband as you did and enjoyed 46 years of loving connection to someone who seems clearly to have reciprocated this special bond. To lose it is no doubt grievous, and to have to contend with the painful memories of his seemingly retracting that love is complicating. So what now is needed to contend with these twin challenges?

One step is like the one you took when you nudged yourself to move beyond the fear and embrace him to begin with. That is, caring connection is the surest cure for loneliness, and active engagement is the remedy for ruminative grief. You sense this yourself as you reach out to care for your grandchild, although with the blossoming of her life to include other friendships and activities, more is needed than this. It seems clear from your letter that you need what most of us need—not merely someone to care for us, but also someone for whom we can care, or some purposeful activity about which we can care. Start by identifying your signature strengths, core passions or key values, and ask yourself what person or cause, perhaps of a volunteer nature, could give them expression. As you engage these people and things, you lessen your dependency on your family and begin to put down stronger roots in new soil.

Working with your therapist on the hurtful memories of your husband denying his love for you—itself a probable side effect of his brain tumor—could make sense, perhaps consolidated in an AfterTalk letter to him about the experience, combined with your writing a letter back from him about his true feelings. In this, you might reflect on what he would tell you is precious about you and how you might now engage those special gifts beyond the family circle, and even beyond the support groups that can also have their role. It is not a matter of replacing him, but rather of reclaiming those parts of you that constituted the person he loved.

—Dr. Neimeyer

## The Gifts of Grief

*Dear Dr. Neimeyer,*

It's been a year and a half since my husband died of cancer. I'll soon be a relatively healthy 70. He would have been 74. I am recovering but wondering if the grieving process brings any gifts or lessons other than the arduous rebuilding of myself as a person living alone.

**Lee**

*Dear Lee,*

Your very question suggests its own answer, as you make clear progress through an arduous transition toward a life that is rebuilt along different lines but retains its value. There indeed can be gifts of grief that come into focus in this process, though they are commonly revealed only as months meld into years, just as you seem to be recognizing. And although these gifts are as individual as any given in the context of a specific and special relationship, there are certain themes that are nearly universal.

First, the individuality of grief—as we mourn in our own personal, familial and cultural ways for this unique person—ensures that some of the unsought gifts or benefits of loss will take on different forms for different mourners. Some may encounter a kind of gift in the ending of a loved one's protracted suffering or in the lifting of the heavy burden of caregiving they willingly and lovingly undertook. These compensations for the loss may be relatively immediate, even if they are initially offset by the great pain of losing the loved one. Others become more tangible over time, as when we witness a child or grandchild grow to share distinctive interests, traits or talents of the deceased in a way that emerges more visibly as he or she matures. As our own sharp pain subsides, we may better note and value these living legacies.

Second, research and everyday experience also make clear that some of the gifts of grief are quite general, in the sense that they are shared with many others who have integrated the hard reality of loss in their own lives. Clinical investigators often call this posttraumatic growth, which can take the form of greater compassion and altruism in relation to the suffering of others—initially others who share a loss similar to ours, but typically evolving toward empathy for others suffering from a much wider set of circumstances. Alternatively, we can find reserves of resilience in ourselves that we never recognized, and perhaps even the seeds of long-dormant interests that might be cultivated into new and valued forms of engagement with new people and projects. Yet another expression of growth might be the deepening of our personal philosophies or spiritual beliefs, as we wrestle with the problems of death and impermanence in intimate terms. And perhaps most subtly, we may find that we come to appreciate the preciousness of life and cherish the moments of meaning that we encounter or create day by day, rather than merely taking life for granted. It might seem ironic that such gifts come wrapped in grief, but they seem to open only for those willing to do the arduous work of uncovering them as life is reconstructed, one day, week and month at a time.

—Dr. Neimeyer

# 4
# LOSS OF A WIFE

### Deep in Grief for a Wife Recently Passed

*Dear Dr. Neimeyer,*

My wife, Lisbeth, died just one month ago, and I am deep in grief. For more than 40 years, we did everything together, and she was my best friend. Even when I did things with other people or on my own, I came home and told her about it and enjoyed it again and more in the telling. Now, life just seems hollow and empty. Please tell me I can again find some joy.

I'm a professional actor, so I am used to working hard to develop a new role. But the two grief therapists I consulted so far, though sympathetic, said that I basically just needed to wait to feel better. But as a "doer," it just doesn't feel right to me to do nothing and wait for time to heal the wound of this loss. So I started doing some research on the internet and found AfterTalk, and you. Just as you suggest, I started writing to Lisbeth and have poured out my guts to her in four letters so far. It feels better to give voice to my feelings, and I did have one kind of mystical experience when I was lying in bed one night where I felt a sense of her presence, even though I'm not completely sure what to make of it. But I just thought I'd write to see if there is anything else I can do that would help me get on the right track. I just feel so sad and alone.

**Bob**

*Dear Bob,*

First, I take the depth of your grief at this early point to reflect the depth of your love; it's hardly surprising that just four weeks after the death of the partner who meant everything to you that you feel the deep mourning and loneliness you describe. But this doesn't mean you are powerless in the face of this bereavement, as I join you in believing that there are constructive steps you can take that can gradually help return you to a place where joy and hope are again possible. Like a role on stage or film that you work long and hard to perfect, the new role in life you are being cast into now will take time and practice to feel natural, but with effort and courage, it can be realized, one step at a time.

One such step is suggested by the writing that you've already begun. Understandably, it sounds like your first correspondence with Lisbeth has been to voice your deepest feelings of grief, and perhaps even despair—an emotionally honest description of the magnitude of your loss. But here is my recommendation and challenge: just as you would share with Lisbeth in life the events of your day, whether accidental encounters that brought a smile or difficult achievements experienced with pride, try sharing now with Lisbeth not only your pain but also the flickers of pleasure or purpose you might invite through your daily choices. Strike out in new directions: visit a new cafe, take in a show, try something difficult. Connect with people: strike up a conversation with a friendly stranger, do something for someone who needs it, catch up with an old friend. Each of these things will probably require you to give yourself a push, as grief tends to be an energy-sapping, self-isolating emotion. But as you say, you are a doer and are used to working hard to take on a new character. As you do that now, in a sense relearning yourself and the world in the wake of Lisbeth's death, tell her about it in your daily or periodic letters. Take her not only into your grief but also into the changing life that you are working hard to make real. And as you do, take time to savor how she would feel about your small joys and accomplishments, and with this, realize that her love for you is with you still.

—Dr. Neimeyer

## Seeking a Reason to Live

*Dear Dr. Neimeyer,*

My wife of over 50 years died a little over a year ago from a stroke. I have talked with my pastor, a psychologist, my family and friends, and it seems nothing helps me. I was her caregiver for about eight years, which given the opportunity I would do it all again. I am so proud of that. I know she is well and happy and with God. Still I grieve for her and yearn to just to be able to touch her velvet skin. I am worried about harming myself if I don't come out of this. I know it would be a terrible sin, but as others have said, why do I want to live? My life here I feel ended the moment she went to heaven. My question is: Where do I go from here?

**Gary**

*Dear Gary,*

You are right: your life, as you knew it, did end with your wife's death. And the burning question, "Why do I want to live?" insistently seeks an answer.

To go on without an answer is unthinkable, and yet the meaning of your previous life seems to be undone by this loss. So how might you find meaning in the life you have now?

First, you clearly seem to be a person of faith and one who is integrated into a church community. If so, I presume that there are many other older widows and widowers in your congregation who have lost spouses and who faced similar challenges in finding new direction in a changed life. Might you invite some of them out for coffee and have a chat about what worked, and what didn't, in handling this difficult transition? Might your church, or another in your denomination, even offer a support group for widowed persons where you could find guidance and understanding?

Second, you devoted yourself to caregiving for your wife for many years, and no doubt developed not only skill but also compassion in doing so. Are there others in your community who might similarly benefit from your occasional care? Extending this part of the story of who you have become in relation to your wife in the service of others who need care or their families who need respite could in an important sense honor the special person for whom you cultivated this part of yourself.

Finally, you mention your pride in relation to your wife, which she no doubt felt and appreciated during your life together. What now might you do that she could take pride in as you find a way to move forward in a life that was precious to her? Sometimes the question of finding meaning in life is not answered with a single, grand answer; sometimes it comes in a hundred little installments. To find them, you might ask each day, "What is one small thing I can do today that would make my wife proud?" Then do that thing—perhaps it is organizing your study, planting a flower, venturing out of your home, lending a hand to a friend or neighbor—and then have a private conversation or symbolic correspondence with your wife in which you tell her about it. In this sense, perhaps she can return some of the support that you generously provided her for many years, as you move through a difficult period of your own.

—Dr. Neimeyer

### Yearning for Her Presence

*Dear Dr. Neimeyer,*

As a former student of yours many years ago I have a deceptively simple question. My wife passed away less than 3 months ago. I have not felt her presence since I watched her pass away. The analytical side of me says that death may in fact be final, but the spiritual side holds on to hope that there is something after this world that I won't understand till I am gone. Unfortunately, in the past I was put under for surgery and I fear that it was an example of what life means when you cease to be.

What is the best way to reconcile my conflicting beliefs in order to understand my grief?

**Rodney**

*Dear Rodney,*

You are right that the question you ask is deceptive in its simplicity, as it bears on subtle understandings of the relation between emotional and cognitive "knowing," or what philosophers call "epistemology," as well as our human capacity to grasp ultimate reality, or what philosophers term "ontology." As a psychologist, I won't try to resolve either of these thorny questions, but instead address briefly what is most compelling in the context of your very personal loss, namely, how you might invite more of a sense of your wife's presence into your ongoing life and how you might reconcile this with an analytic part of you that wants this to "make sense," even if the evidence for an afterlife seems equivocal.

First, let's acknowledge what we do know: as human beings, we are wired for attachment in a world of impermanence. Although everyone and everything in our lives that matters to us will pass away, at least in an earthly sense, we are constituted to strive to sustain the bonds we build with cherished people, places, projects and even possessions, even when they are lost to us in concrete terms. In the context of bereavement, this takes the form of a natural tendency to find comfort, security and meaning in the continuation of the relationship with those we have loved and lost physically, whether we do so in a spiritual sense (as in believing in an afterlife of renewed connection), in a psychological sense (as in opening to internal conversations with the loved one in our minds and hearts) or in a social sense (by memorializing them and sharing stories with others that give testimony to their continued relevance to a larger community). People differ in how they experience such connections, and not all need to feel a mystical sense that the loved one is tangibly with us, although this too is common, especially when our bond to the person in life was strong. You might find, for example, that spending time in places that were special to you and your wife, writing an AfterTalk letter to her and pausing to sense her response or performing some form of ritual of remembrance, however spiritual or secular, all could help invoke her presence more tangibly for you. The book series entitled *Techniques of Grief Therapy*, though written for professionals, suggests dozens and dozens of tools for fostering this sort of healing bond.

Second, given how prevalent across cultures and human history some form of continuing bond is following bereavement, how can we square a heady belief that doubts the legitimacy of the continued spiritual presence of the loved one with a heartfelt hope that it is possible? One response would be to accept that our humble attempts to grasp the complexity of life and the natural (and supernatural?) world are inevitably incomplete and that our best efforts after understanding leave much that is a mystery. Perhaps in light of this, we can live more comfortably with ambiguity and even inconsistency, acknowledging that our perspective as individual human beings situated in a given culture, place and time will allow us to grasp some things, but not all things—at least in this one, short lifetime. If you cultivate a connection to your wife that survives her death, whatever form this takes, I trust that you can allow yourself to find comfort and affirmation in that special bond, even if you also allow your intellectual curiosity to continue to engage that mystery.

—Dr. Neimeyer

## A Fear of Loss

I lost my young wife after 20 years of marriage. Since then I feel like I've moved on; I found a new wife whom I love completely. We've raised terrific children. My problem is that I have an irrational fear of loss. At least once a day I obsess about losing my new wife, our dog, my closest friends and especially our children. I am consumed with anxiety that I can suffer another great loss at any moment. I resist becoming close with anyone new in my life for fear that they will die. I lose sleep over this. When I try to close my eyes, I imagine something terrible is about to happen to someone I love. If my wife doesn't call in, I imagine that the police will be knocking on the door to tell me she was killed in a car accident. When the kids fly anywhere, I cannot sleep until they text me that they've arrived safely. I wasn't always like this. I became this way after my first wife's death. I've taken several prescribed medications for depression or anxiety, but none make this problem go away. I am fine with the deaths of elderly relatives; it's untimely death that obsesses me. I'd appreciate your thoughts.

**Harvey**

*Dear Harvey,*

It sounds like the premature death of your young wife was traumatic by any account, and perhaps more so if her death came suddenly or violently, such as through the sort of accident you imagine might take from you others you love. In view of this, it is not surprising that you are hypervigilant regarding the safety of all those for whom you care greatly; in a sense, life has cruelly taught you that the fear of catastrophic loss is in this sense "rational."

But this is not to say that it is benign. As you clearly acknowledge, the anxious preoccupation with further loss through death carries real consequences for your health, as your sleeplessness attests. Just as seriously, your wife, friends and children are likely to be feeling constrained or even suffocated by your need to ensure their safety, perhaps at the expense of their freedom, spontaneity and autonomy. Ironically, this can bring about innumerable losses that are quite real in their own right, as they may begin to respond to your vigilance with anger and avoidance, or perhaps in the case of the children, with fearful or phobic narrowing of their lives as a way of managing a world that they have been taught is unpredictably dangerous. The sad result can be damaging to the very people and relationships you most want to protect.

Trauma-based learning of the kind you described is not simply something you can talk yourself out of or have medicated away. It requires "unlearning" in the only school that can effectively teach the lesson: the school of experience. This means that exposing yourself, one step at a time, to the situations that you fear for yourself or others can help you begin to challenge the obsessive equation of living and traveling freely with deadly danger, but without the magical "solution" of having loved ones text you that they are okay. It can help to have someone to support us in this hard work, whether the feared situations we need to master are ones we approach in action (e.g., visiting rather than avoiding places or circumstances associated with your wife's death) or only in imagination (e.g., with detailed mental imagery of your children taking a flight). In seeking a therapist who can provide structure and support for these brave but important steps, ask for someone familiar with "exposure" treatments for anxiety. Ultimately, your family and your health will thank you for it.

—Dr. Neimeyer

## Inconsolable Grief

*Dear Dr. Neimeyer,*

My wife of almost 35 years died suddenly four weeks ago. Yes, she was ill for many years but I took care of her full time including doing her dialysis at home, running her feeding tube every night and doing everything in the house, as she was unable to do those things due to her various illnesses. Despite her illnesses she had been doing well until the day she suddenly died next to me in her sleep.

We were ALWAYS together. We lived and worked together and literally were never more than a few feet apart for the last 27 of our years together. She was my whole life and my whole reason to live. She made me what I am. I am nothing without her. The pain of losing her and our whole way of life is unbearable. I cry all the time.

All I ever wanted was to be married and have one person to be with all the time. We didn't have children, so we could just focus on our very special marriage. Now I am alone and have no reason to go on. I can't stop grieving for my wife.

I guess my question is, why should I go on? I see no life for me now. I wish I had died with her. I never planned on being without her. I need a reason to live. Can you give me one?

**Samuel**

*Dear Samuel,*

No, I cannot give you a concrete reason to live; no human being can engineer that for another, however much we might want to. But I can stand with the side of you that hopes for such a purpose, for some way to fill the terrible void created by your wife's loss—the part of you that wrote this letter. So, joining my hope with yours, let's see what now is possible.

First, any compassionate response to your pain would have to validate your profound grief, so fresh and raw, scarcely a month after your wife's death. No doubt most of us who experience so recent and anguishing a loss would identify with your sense of desolation and questioning, and all the more so given the deep and dense bonds of connection you and she shared. Your grief is in proportion to your love, and when she was everything to you, of course it would feel that everything has been taken away. So I would hope first that you might accept that psychological reality and be caring and generous to yourself now, exactly as you would hope that she would be compassionate to herself had you been the one who died first.

Second, consider the essential roles she played for you: the attentive presence, tuning in to your feelings, perhaps talking things through. Especially because you turned to her so completely for these basic functions that all human beings require, you likely feel like a ship without a rudder or anchor for navigating the stormy waters in which you now find yourself. Psychologists speak of the profound way grief challenges our "emotion regulation," the gale force angst that surrounds us, without the safe harbor once provided by the very relationship we have lost. In mourning such a loss, we need to find another haven, even a temporary one, to ride out the storm.

In your case, with seemingly all or most of your ballast once provided by your wife, it may be especially wise to seek such a haven in an attuned relationship with a counselor or therapist—perhaps especially a woman—who can help you orient to this changed world, find the landmarks and, with support, begin to rebuild. Like reconstructing a storm-battered city after a hurricane, this is not something accomplished in a month or two. It begins with psychological first aid, continues with support from others and gradually takes the form of a new life, livable in its own terms.

Third, however, this new world need not be so completely different from the one now lost in a physical sense. As you ruminate about what you have lost, I would also invite you to meditate on what you have retained. Certainly, your professional skills as a healer persist, and perhaps even were sharpened by your attentive care for your wife for so many years. What other lives might be touched, saved or transformed by your efforts? And equally fundamentally, consider the gifts that your wife left for you, engendered by decades of loving interaction, even in the midst of her illness. What did you learn about yourself, the world and suffering nobly that you might draw on now and deploy in the service of others? Might you write an AfterTalk letter to her enumerating all she gave you and that she would want you to use rather than discard as if it had no enduring value? And imagine her response to your letter, fully acknowledging your pain, but also affirming your worth: How might she ask you to care for yourself in your suffering now, as you long cared for her suffering before? In these important senses, and in the invisible cloak of care she would ask you to wear and draw close, she can remain a key part of your support team, even as you gradually open to other relationships that can take on meaning in their own way.

In sum, be gentle with your tears as she no doubt would be, hold her close now in the lessons about love and life that she taught you and reach toward renewed reasons for living that honor this bond, even as you revise it with the help of a caring professional and others. And—perhaps with the supportive structure of AfterTalk as well as others who care for you—keep her apprised of the progress.

—Dr. Neimeyer

## Writing to a Deceased Wife

*Dear Dr. Neimeyer,*

I've been reading your column for some time now and trying to follow your advice about confronting rather than avoiding my grief through writing on AfterTalk to my dear wife, Dorothy, who meant the world to me before her death two months ago. We did just about everything together for decades, and even the things I did on my own were better because I could tell her about them when I got home. Now everything just feels so empty, and the pain of missing her has been so intense that at times I just have to wail in my home when I'm alone.

But I've always been tenacious and have been trying to take your advice by writing those letters to her using AfterTalk. And let me tell you something: the first ones were just awful! I told it like it was, because I would never lie to her, and told her how very much I missed her, and that I didn't know how I could go on without her. I cried. I even wailed through the first couple. But I stuck with it. I also reassured her that even when I was a mess emotionally, I was still making myself do what I needed to do, taking care of myself physically, pushing myself to work and sometimes even to go out with a friend. And gradually, it's been getting better. Today I wrote her, and even though I told her how much I missed her beautiful smile and always seeing her when I came home, I didn't wail. I didn't even cry. In fact, I found myself laughing later with friends—real laughs, not having to force it. So I'm telling you, I think it's working.

Here's a story I think you'll appreciate. Once when I was cooking a nice Asian meal for Dorothy, I burned my stomach badly with some hot oil, and had to go to the hospital. The doctor prescribed a special kind of burn ointment that I had to apply every day after showering and washing the wounded area. And let me tell you, every time I did that treatment, for a long time it hurt like the devil—just to have to expose the wound, clean it and reapply the medicine. But I made myself do it, and soon it began to heal. Today I'm fine, I don't even have any scars. I think your grief therapy is like that.

So here's my question: Do you think that I'm on the right track? And if so, what should I do next?

Yours,

**Enrico**

*Dear Enrico,*

You're not only one tenacious guy, but you are also a great storyteller! Your analogy of grief therapy to the burn treatment you received is the perfect metaphor for what you are doing: fearlessly exposing the wound, cleaning it and applying the treatment. And pretty clearly, you are healing a bit more each time, as wailing softens to crying, crying mellows to equanimity and equanimity makes room even for laughter. Grief can be a roller coaster with its daily ups and downs, but when faced with courage, the climbs are steadier, the valleys less steep, until you can finally step off onto firm ground.

And so you ask what to do next. My answer is "the next hard thing." Ask yourself, "What do I need now, and what now am I ready to tackle?" One possibility, now that you are facing your grief—and recovering a sense of connection to Dorothy without the pain being the only bridge—is to try writing back from her to you. What would she say about your current efforts, and successes, in managing your grief as you are? What counsel would she have for you?

A variation on this is to push back out into the world a little harder. Go someplace you've been avoiding because it was a place you shared with her, but make it someplace that feels manageably uncomfortable, not overwhelming. Then come home and write Dorothy about it. Naturally, across time, you'll find other audiences for your stories too, as you have in sharing them with me. But Dorothy can remain a part of that audience, as long as you want her to.

—Dr. Neimeyer

## Caregiver's Guilt and Regret

*Dear Dr. Neimeyer,*

My wife has been gone for several months, but I can't seem to stop thinking about her and focus on my life now. It's not her death that troubles me as much as her life in her final couple of years. She had increasing dementia at the end, and I frequently misunderstood her behavior as intentional or just thoughtless, though I now recognize that many of the things that frustrated me were the result of her disease and the problems of memory and speech that it caused. But I am left with the guilty feeling that I was often mean or cruel to her in the course of my caregiving, which became more and more intense as the disease progressed. I guess that I was also bitter and disappointed, as that wasn't what I imagined our retirement years would be. But now she is gone, and I don't know how to "fix it." I'm open to any ideas you have about how I can make this better.

**Theodore**

*Dear Theodore,*

Intensive caregiving of the kind you describe can be isolating and exhausting, and made all the harder by the recognition that our best efforts will not turn back the clock and return our loved one to the person he or she once was, in view of the advancing disease process that dementia entails. And the reality of medical systems in our country means that respite care that gives caregivers a break from their 24/7 responsibilities is both rare and costly, contributing to the well-documented prevalence of caregiver burnout, especially when families are small and dispersed over great geographic distance. All of these factors make it difficult to give an optimal form of loving care to our family member, especially when the signs and symptoms of dementia are so easily misread as willful carelessness or lack of concentration, particularly in the early stages.

So what now might you do with the preoccupying thoughts and feelings that you are left with, all this time after your wife's death? Here are a few ideas:

1. *Seek understanding.* Do some research into accounts of other caregivers who contended with similar struggles during the time of their loved one's illness. Many will have experienced some version of the struggles you did and discovered affirmative ways through the maze of stresses and emotions these engendered.
2. *Reach out for mutual support.* In many places, including the Web, those who have been caregivers meet virtually or face to face to seek and offer

help to one another through a difficult passage. Going beyond reading the accounts of others to sharing your own could help break down your isolation, normalize your feelings and help rebuild ties with a community that understands what was uniquely hard about the living loss with which you and your wife were trying to cope.

3. *Ask for your wife's forgiveness.* In an important sense, you continue to carry your wife's presence within you, and it is with this internalized image of her that you need to make peace. In the midst of her disease and your exhausting caregiving, neither of you was in a position to extend compassion consistently to the other and acceptance of your respective insufficiency to meet the other's needs. Now, however, you are better able to imagine and perform a healing dialogue with her, allowing the loving and contrite part of you to address the loving and wise part of her. This could be done, for example, through an AfterTalk letter in which you express your guilt and wish for how the caregiving could have gone, as well as your sentiments regarding how you would like to move forward with her memory and presence in your life now. Writing back from her in response, you could lend her your pen or typing fingers to say what she would have said, not at the depths of her dementia, but instead from a place of clarity and caring. Such correspondence can be deeply healing and go a considerable distance toward completing the "unfinished business" left by complicated circumstances at the end of life.

—Dr. Neimeyer

## A Sudden Death

*Dear Dr. Neimeyer,*

I lost my wife after 43 years—she fell over dead one day a year and a half ago. I can't get over it. What's going on, and what can I do about it?

**Gordon**

*Dear Gordon,*

The sudden loss of such a long-standing and central relationship can have a heavy impact in virtually every area of our lives, from challenging those basic rhythms of daily living associated with regular breakfast, lunch and dinner times, through costing us companionship in home and leisure, to depriving us of a conversation partner with whom to share our most intimate concerns and hopes, as well as the events of ordinary life. These impacts can be especially heavy for men who are widowed, as our wives are often the ones who ensure that our homes are functional and welcoming and that our social connections to others in the family and beyond remain in good repair. Without this caring and organizing presence, we can feel even more radically alone and bereft of much that is familiar and comforting. As a result, our lives as well as our emotions can feel out of control, and we may respond with rumination and self-isolation, which only makes matters worse.

In view of this, it may be too much to expect that you will just "get over it." What you can learn to do is to live with the loss and make good decisions in light of it. Start with the question "What have I lost?" and then stick with it until you can give at least 10 brief answers: a regular bedtime, healthy meals, social contact with friends, visits from the kids, someone to share the hard things, a reason to live . . . you get the idea. Rank these in terms of which are most urgent and which are most important. Then start thinking creatively on your own, with someone who cares about you, or with a counselor, about how you can take steps to meet these needs. You'll likely find that some things are simpler than others—go shopping with a friend or family member for some healthy, easy-to-prepare food; establish a regular time to wake up and turn in; join a "meet up" group that shares your interests. Other things will be harder, especially if you are retired and lack the clarity and purpose of meaningful work—establishing significant goals, finding a role that connects you to community, learning ways to move from rumination to action. Sometimes a counselor can help with the latter, as can support groups of other widowed people.

Above all, avoid the trap of sitting back and waiting to feel better. Very likely, action will precede motivation, not the other way around. Defining what you have lost, what you need and what you can do about it can begin to renew your sense of pleasure and purpose, leading to a life that is different from the one you and your wife shared for many years, but one that has meaning nonetheless.

—Dr. Neimeyer

## Grieving and Sleep Problems

*Dear Dr. Neimeyer,*

I'm in my late 60s, and for most of my life have slept pretty well and had plenty of energy to tackle the day. But since my wife died 14 months ago, I've had a real problem sleeping. I get tired but [lie] awake with my mind churning, and usually watch TV until the wee hours before falling asleep exhausted, only to wake up early and unable to get back to sleep. As a result I start the day feeling beat and nap when I can just to get through what I need to do. At least I am retired, because I don't think I could keep my concentration in the kind of demanding sales career I had for many years.

In most ways I feel like I'm doing alright under the circumstances, even though I miss my wife and the life we had together. I stay active socially and can't say I'm really depressed. But I just can't seem to get my sleeping on track, and it's really starting to affect me some days, like when I fall asleep in church or catch myself nodding off behind the wheel. My doctor wants to give me sleeping pills, but I hate to take medicine I may not really need and have heard that it can have bad effects in the long run. What advice do you have for people like me?

**Dave**

*Dear Dave,*

An old professor of mine who studied sleep once called it "the gentle tyrant: the behavior before which all other behaviors lie down." That is, even though it involves inactivity, it is ultimately supremely powerful—we can't ignore its demands, and when we fail to meet them, we notice its "tyranny" in the price we pay in other domains of our lives.

Certainly, the degradation of your concentration, wakefulness and energy in the context of a sleepless bereavement provides evidence for this argument. And research also suggests that disrupted sleep greatly exacerbates stress and its serious effect on our wellness, leaving us more susceptible to diseases of all kinds, including heart problems. So the issues you raise are serious, even if they are often overlooked in discussions of the more emotional impact of loss.

And so what might you do, beyond the short-term expedient of sleep medication, to reset your biological clock and help ensure a more restorative nightly slumber? Health psychologists suggest the following principles of "sleep hygiene" as essential practices to manage this crucial dimension of your day more effectively:

1. *Cut the caffeine.* Faced with chronic fatigue, it is easy to fall into the habit of taking a second, third or fourth cup of coffee or other stimulant (tea, caffeinated colas, energy drinks) to perk us up throughout the day, only to pay the price at night with "early insomnia," in the form of lying awake for hours, followed by a fitful and shallow sleep, waking fatigued and starting the cycle all over again in the morning. Though individual caffeine sensitivity varies with our body size, physiological makeup and history of consumption, a good rule of thumb is to limit coffee to one cup in the morning and no more than one additional stimulating beverage in the early afternoon in order to wind down as bedtime approaches and move toward the bedroom in a less activated state.
2. *Avoid alcohol.* Another "behavioral backfire" that we can suffer when struggling to sleep is attempting to induce it with a couple of stiff drinks before calling it a night. While this might indeed help us fall asleep,

it also has the unintended and often unrecognized effect of disrupting deeper levels of sleep that are most restorative, leaving us sleeping more fitfully and awakening less energized. If this becomes a habit, of course, we can find that the "cure" becomes worse than the "disease," in the sense that we can develop alcohol dependence and the many psychological, social and medical problems that come along with it. Perhaps for men especially, alcohol abuse can also greatly complicate adjustment to bereavement.

3. *Set a schedule.* You know yourself pretty well, I imagine, and can estimate the number of hours of sleep you need to function well, even if these tend to decrease in number across the years. If you need seven hours, say, make a point of going to bed at the same time each night and getting up at the same hour each morning. Routine can be your friend and a shifting schedule your enemy in training your body when sleep is called for. Even if you don't feel sleepy, head to bed at a decent hour and set an alarm to wake yourself up at the same time each morning. Then, if you find yourself lying awake for more than 15 minutes, get up and do something: wash the dishes, read a magazine. Fifteen minutes later try hitting the hay again. Gradually more regular sleep cycles will become a rhythm, just as they likely were during your years of employment. Research has documented that one of the secondary losses following the death of a partner is the disruption of our daily rhythms and activities, often requiring conscious efforts to re-establish them.

4. *Reserve the bedroom for rest.* Though this seems obvious, the ubiquitous presence of electronics (TVs, computers, tablets and smart phones) in our lives can easily leak over to the bedroom, eroding the natural boundary between mentally activating functions and restful ones. Less recognized is that all of these devices electronically stimulate the brain in ways that are incompatible with sleep, so that what we assume will be a way of "winding down" actually can function as a means of "gearing up." Instead, keep the bedroom as the sleeping chamber it was designed to be, and ease into sleep with a good old-fashioned print book or other nonelectronic activity (such as gentle stretching, meditation or journaling). Your sleep-ready brain will thank you for it.

5. *Watch out for the nap trap.* Though we seldom recognize it, daytime naps are the enemy of nighttime slumber. Instead, consider the drowsiness of a napless afternoon as a precious resource that will help induce sounder sleep a few hours later.

6. *Get a move on.* Build some exercise into your day in a way that respects, but gently challenges, your current state of fitness. For many people a brisk evening walk of 30 minutes can discharge nervous energy and induce "healthy fatigue," while also delaying sleep until the appointed hour. How

much is enough and at what level of intensity can be something to consult about with your doctor or trainer, but attempting to get 10,000 steps a day (easily measured though any of several fitness monitors) can be an appropriate fitness goal for many mature adults. Along with eating a balanced diet a few hours before bedtime, managing your activity in this way can pay dividends in your health as well as in your adaptation to loss.

Finally, beyond sleep hygiene guidelines, be alert that sleep disorders can be both a symptom of and contributor to prolonged grief. After a few weeks of practicing the ideas outlined here, you should find a significant improvement in your sleep. If not, you might find consultation with a counselor or therapist worthwhile to check on whether there are other dimensions of your grief that warrant attention, even if these are not so clear at this point. Ultimately sleep is just one essential part of a healthy lifestyle, and adapting to the physical absence of a loved one can challenge us in many ways, some obvious and some subtle, as we strive to rebuild a healthy life in the wake of loss.

—Dr. Neimeyer

## Parting With a Loved One's Belongings

*Dear Dr. Neimeyer,*

My wife passed away two years ago. We were both in our middle 60s. I want to resume dating, but female friends tell me I need to remove all traces of my wife from the apartment before I do so. I have not been able to part with anything since she died. Her closet and drawers are still full of her clothing. Family photographs are on every wall. I am convinced I want to get on with my life but feel paralyzed whenever the idea of parting with her belongings comes up. Is this common? What's holding me back?

**Jerry**

*Dear Jerry,*

In Buddhism, the "Middle Way" refers to a path to enlightenment that steers between two extremes, such as self-denial and self-indulgence. Avoiding a choice between such radical opposites, in this view, is the noble path that leads to right understanding and right action.

But one need not be a Buddhist to recognize the wisdom of this perspective. To remove all traces of your wife from your home and your heart, your closets and your conversations, would be to erase a vital part of your life story, the personal history that makes you, you. Surely a relationship based on love and openness would not demand such relinquishment of your identity, as if the years spent with your wife could simply be edited out of your life, like the pages of so many chapters cut out of a novel. On the other hand, the futile effort to freeze time suggested by your inability to release anything associated with your wife suggests that you are not yet ready to make room, literally or metaphorically, for another relationship.

What, then, is the Middle Way in this situation? Perhaps it would involve a careful, unhurried sorting of your wife's possessions: Which are genuinely cherished mementos for you to hold close? Which might become precious "linking objects" to your wife passed on to others who love her—perhaps your children or grandchildren, her siblings or her friends? And which might become legacy gifts for those in need given in your wife's name, perhaps to a charity whose work carried meaning for her? Taking time to sift through such possessions, whether on your own or with a close family member, can itself be therapeutic, often giving rise to meaningful conversations with yourself in a personal journal or with the trusted person who joins you in the task. The important thing is to give such work the time it deserves, with no hurry to "get rid of" anything: some belongings will obviously be keepers, while others can clearly be gifts, and those in between can simply be placed in storage for later sorting. The first step is the hardest, and you may find that the process comes to feel right as you make decisions of which your wife would approve. With each such decision, you will be honoring your love for her, as you also make room for a new relationship.

—Dr. Neimeyer

## Ready to Love Again

*Dear Dr. Neimeyer,*

I am a widower (although I don't like this moniker) after more than 30 years of marriage. I don't understand why "widowers" are not in the highest demand. We have proven our capacity for commitment, as well as have tons of experience in child rearing, relationships and the refinement of how to love a woman. If not, we would be in the divorced category. I fulfilled my marriage vows and am willing to love and be loved again.

It seems by most articles I have read that many men are in denial that their wonderful wife is gone and not coming back. So, it's hard for them to think of doing it again with a new leading lady and a few prop changes. I am not one of these men.

**Kent**

*Dear Kent,*

I clearly hear your readiness to open your heart and life to a new love in a way that draws on the lessons in living and loving that you learned in a long and satisfying relationship with your wife. The good news is that, statistically at least, you are in a better position than your female counterparts to realize that dream, if only because by the time we reach our 60s women outnumber men, and the ratio tilts more in your favor with each year that passes.

But of course, there are more than statistics at play in determining the prospects of remarriage. As you point out, many widowed persons are not yet ready for new intimacy or new commitment, and some will choose to remain single for the rest of their lives. Family reactions, as in the form of the reluctance of grown children to accept a "replacement" for their deceased parent, also can pose obstacles. So too can grief and trauma from the previous loss; some people, having struggled with the illness and death of their previous partners, may hold back from allowing themselves to love and become vulnerable to new hurt.

But for each of these cases, there are others in which people find love, companionship and meaning in a new relationship in later life, just as you are inclined to. When the time is right and you have made peace with your loss, open yourself to gain. Get in the social mix. Check out online dating after writing an honest "job description" for the kind of partner you want and the kind of partner you are. Join a meet-up of like-minded people. Take a dance class. Ask someone out for a coffee. You can find highly relevant counsel of a wise and compassionate sort in the recently published book by Gloria Horsley and her partner, Frank Powers, called *Open to Love*, covering all the ins and outs of senior dating. Above all, in a way that feels natural, even if a little anxious, stretch into possibility, but without the press to find "Mrs. Right" right away. After all, your history of loyalty to your previous wife across 30+ years suggests that you are likely to want to make a mutual choice that will endure for the long haul.

—Dr. Neimeyer

# 5
# LOSS OF A PARTNER OR CLOSE RELATION

**Lost in Limbo**

*Dear Dr. Neimeyer,*

Since my partner died three months ago, I feel totally lacking in any desire to be involved in life. I just want to let days slide past without going anywhere, doing anything, seeing anyone. Going to places we loved and knew is hugely upsetting; meeting people who ask how I'm doing reduces me to tears every time. . . . And I can't stop remembering his last month when we knew he was dying. The increasing vulnerability and fragility; the problems walking, talking, eating; the incontinence . . . all so undignified for a man who prided himself on his ability to help others and to always look his best.

I feel like I'm in limbo: somewhere between life and death. A big part of me wants to die; a much smaller part knows I need to get back into life. I am stuck and I don't know what to do.

Any advice or suggestions, please?

**Miles**

*Dear Miles,*

From your description of your life since your partner's death, I have the sense that you are adrift, without orientation or direction, and with little wind in your sails to steer toward any chosen destination. And that makes sense, as you have lost the moorings provided by the man you loved and seem to have no access to the safe harbor he once provided. Without him, even once-familiar destinations seem foreign, and venturing into them without his companionship becomes merely a reminder of all you have lost. However achingly common this might be in the early months of bereavement from someone who has been our soulmate, an eternity will not return him as a physical being who can provide the simple but profound reassurance of a human hug. Grief is the appropriate response to such a loss.

And yet, a small part of you is beginning to reach out, if only through your letter, in the hope of embracing a future that is different from the seemingly endless present. Let me speak to that part and offer a few ideas to consider as you contemplate not only what you lost but also what you are willing to change.

1. *Allow the tears.* When those who genuinely care ask the anxious question, "How are you doing?" respond with your emotional truth. You are unspeakably sad, disoriented, hurting. Let them in to the extent it feels safe. Express appreciation for their presence and willingness to listen, even if there are no easy answers. Accept the consolation and companionship offered by others who have known their own histories of loss, without need to compare them for their severity. We are soft bodies in a hard world and are all ultimately vulnerable to death and loss. Holding this reality together while still connecting with others in compassionate understanding is the truest gift we can give to one another at points of hard transition.
2. *Process the loss.* Even if your partner died a natural death, there is much in his dying that was traumatic, likely for him as well as you. Certainly, the haunting images of his being reduced by his illness call for attention, which entails the hard practice of calling them to mind, speaking them to another willing to hear and possibly even drawing them out as images on paper, however unartistic we may be. One thing we know is that attempts simply to avoid the troubling imagery have, at best, a fleeting effect, after which it returns with redoubled force when we let down our guard. This is not work for the faint of heart, however, and working with a therapist who is practiced in trauma interventions can be very helpful here. Integrating the story of the loss, in all its vividness and difficulty, will allow you ultimately to hold the story, rather than having it hold you. Seek a safe and therapeutic relationship that can help you toward this goal.
3. *Reclaim the world.* As impossible and unjust as it may seem, the world did not die with your partner. All that you loved together is still there, awaiting you, even if it is also now alloyed to pain. Reconnect, one step at a time, to the people, places and projects you shared. Go there. Do that. Gradually increase your participation in these spheres of life, perhaps accompanied by a reliable friend. And as you do, you may find that your partner is still there, in a sense, cheering you on. Even in that most difficult final month, it is unlikely that he wanted you to die with him.
4. *Ask his permission.* Understandably, we sometimes feel that lessening our anguish is equivalent to weakening our bond to the one we have loved and lost, as if embracing life in its fullness would be a kind of betrayal. Question this logic. Did your partner require you to suffer as an expression of your love? If not, why would he do so now? Even acknowledging

the profundity of your grief, consider what his counsel would be, given his identity as "a man who prided himself on his ability to help others." What would he suggest that could help you now? As you meditate on this question—perhaps facilitated by an AfterTalk correspondence with him—allow his counsel to serve as a compass for you, as you invite him to be present to you in the steps you take from loss to life. As you do so, you will likely find many ways in which he will be with you as you continue your voyage, ultimately forming a safe inner harbor that you can carry with you into a world that still beckons.

—Dr. Neimeyer

## After Sudden Death of a Partner, Finding Meaning in Life

*Dear Dr. Neimeyer,*

Six months ago, my partner of 47 years died suddenly. We have no children and have always been very close and spent a lot of time together. This would have been our first real year of retirement together, and we were looking forward to growing old together, just enjoying our free time and everyday things. Now he's gone I can find absolutely no meaning in life. Every day I wake feeling panicky and dreading the day ahead. Throughout the day I'm hurt and upset over and over again at the thought of how he died, suddenly, and at what we've both lost.

I'm not lonely but completely alone. I don't want lots of people around; I just want him and the companionship we always had. Sharing news, a joke, gossip, a meal. I try to keep busy during the day but there's so little to do, and the evenings are unbearable, by about 8:30 I can't stand it any longer and go to bed. Then the next day I get up and have to do it all over again. What is the point?

People keep telling me I'll feel better in time, but I've spoken to bereaved friends and neighbors, and most of them don't feel better. One friend said 4 years after losing her husband she feels worse than ever. At 65 the prospect of years of this is unbearable, I just want to go to sleep and never wake up.

**Yvonne**

*Dear Yvonne,*

As you can well imagine, no simple advice can assuage the pain of losing a life partner who had become a soulmate, especially in circumstances like yours where no children or grandchildren exist to share your grief and potentially provide supportive lifelines to reconnect with life in the ways that remain possible. Just as you imply, the loneliness you feel in the wake of this unique loss is not simply a social loneliness that calls for "staying busy," helpful though that may sometimes be, but rather is a form of emotional loneliness that reaches much deeper into our hearts and souls, from which we are not easily distracted. The "panic" that you feel is also very real, stemming from a kind of separation distress that nearly all bereaved persons feel when they lose someone who was their "secure base" in the world, the person to whom they would naturally turn for consolation, comfort and care.

So, what might you do to recover a life that, as you say, has meaning? Here a few suggestions, offered in full recognition that that there is no simple prescription for rebuilding life when the one we had was lost.

1. *Watch for the small changes.* Being as honest with yourself as you can be, do you notice any improvement in your sleep, any recovery of a capacity for positive emotions, any return of hope in the six months since your partner's death? This is not to say that you "should" be feeling greatly better—relearning how to live after devastating loss can be a much longer process than that sentiment suggests. But if after half a year you see no signs of improvement in any quarter, then you may be headed into a form of "complicated" or "prolonged" grief that time alone will not heal. Seeing a therapist who specializes in bereavement care could then become a high priority.
2. *Stay engaged.* This implies something more than "staying busy," although both involve pushing yourself to go beyond the self-seclusion and shutdown that might seem like a temporary refuge from the pain. Instead, real engagement implies involvement in activity that matters. If it seems that "nothing matters" after your partner's death, that may be much of the problem, calling for a sincere effort to connect to people, projects and places that carry meaning for you, either by rediscovering those that once were a source of joy and purpose to you or by discovering new ones. What values, causes, communities of belonging or interest helped give value to your life and your partner's? What might he suggest you do, were you to invite his ongoing advice to you? How might you tap into these sources of meaning now, and who might join you in this project?
3. *Choose life.* Your passive death wish—to go to sleep and never awaken—is common in complicated grief, as it also is in depression. But it is also concerning. If you seem to be frozen in your adaptation to this deeply unsettling transition, consider consulting a physician as well as a therapist, adding possible antidepressant treatment to your grief therapy. Countless others have been helped by the right combination of the two and have resisted the siren song of suicide to create the safe space needed

to put down new roots in the soil of a new life. Like any transplant, this one needs careful cultivation to be successful; a neglected plant deprived of water and nutrients will surely wither. Reach out for professional as well as social support to give yourself the care needed to again thrive in a changed world.

—Dr. Neimeyer

## Cancer Death of a Boyfriend

*Dear Dr. Neimeyer,*

My boyfriend died very recently from cancer. We never had a chance to say goodbye. How do I move on from the feelings of did I do enough and is he okay with things between us? I keep thinking I should have done more. Thanks for your help.

**Charlene**

*Dear Charlene,*

When love is cut short by loss, we are left with many unanswered questions, and often many unspoken feelings. In fact, research suggests that the closer the relationship, the more likely people are to report unresolved relational issues, sometimes called "unfinished business," with their loved ones at the end of life. For obvious reasons, when the death is relatively sudden, with few opportunities perceived or taken to talk through the difficult topics and make peace with what you had and what you didn't, the distress about such issues is greater. In fact, our studies suggest that even under normal circumstances, nearly half of bereaved people acknowledge regrets, many of them, like yours, about missed connections or the failure to make sure all was well in the relationship as the loved one reached life's end. In the pandemic era, one study we did even suggested that such unfinished business was literally universal—literally all of the hundreds of people who participated in the study acknowledged regret, guilt, shame and related self-critical emotions given the impossibly difficult circumstances in which their loved ones died.

At the same time, your use of the present tense (*Is he okay with things between us?*) suggests that he has a kind of continuing existence for you, perhaps of a spiritual kind. If so, does your faith in his existence include the sense that he can hear your earnest entreaty, prayer, apology or even simple attempts to continue the conversation with him? If he is a sentient being who is still attuned to you, then consider speaking aloud or on paper what remains to be said, what you wish you had expressed at the time of his illness and how it is for you now. Perhaps the Private Conversations function of AfterTalk could provide a safe place for this kind of dialogue in written form. Then, giving yourself a day or two to let this potentially emotional communication settle, consider writing back as if from him, growing quiet to sense what he might say. In this way, perhaps even more than during the time of his terminal illness, given the fogging of his attention with pain-regulating drugs and the impersonal press of a hospital ward, you might find that the conversation you yearn for is still possible, though in a nonphysical form. Take time to finish the unfinished business between you and then move on to thinking creatively about how you might create a life in which he would wish to intangibly accompany you with pride and pleasure.

—Dr. Neimeyer

## A Veteran and a Partner's Suicide

*Dear Dr. Neimeyer,*

My partner committed suicide in front of me last February. He asked me to hold his hand. I always promised I'd be there for him, regardless. But this was something I couldn't imagine.

Because we lived in the South, and his family [was] in the Northeast, we were on our own. I called his family for support two weeks prior to his death, as they never visited, only to get excuses why they couldn't come down; I even offered to pay for the travel. It didn't happen.

After the death, because we'd never had a Civil Union, I was treated no better than a roommate or friend. His mom, during our 10 years, referred to me as her "adopted son" and often stated I was the best thing to ever happen to him, but gave me no recognition as his spouse, although, throughout his suffering, I was the only one there for him, ever. Yet now, I didn't mean anything to anyone. The police couldn't even talk to me.

I've lost my job, lost our house and had to give away most of our belongings as I couldn't stay in the South financially and had to move north to stay with family until I figure out what I'm supposed to do with my life.

On top of it all, as I am a veteran, the VA is my health provider and have offered minimal help: I've talked to 10 people from the VA, explaining in full the details of my situation. It seems that if you're not suicidal, they're very lax about helping you.

I can't stay with the family forever but draw a complete blank when I try to think if starting my life from scratch. I'm afraid to get involved with someone new in case they die. Life without love is just existing. How do you overcome the fear of loss?

**Brad**

*Dear Brad*—

Your story sadly illustrates how the death of a loved one can bring with it a cascade of losses, some visible to the world and others invisible. In particular, it summons up the idea of disenfranchised grief, a concept formulated by my friend and colleague, Ken Doka, to describe a response to bereavement that is unrecognized, unsanctioned and without broad social acknowledgement and support. Originally offered as a description of social responses to the death of an ex-partner following divorce, disenfranchised grief is, if anything, even more acutely relevant and anguishing in a case like yours, where a committed same-sex partnership of years may be dismissed as irrelevant by authorities, caregivers and even the deceased partner's family. The result is a kind of double loss: first of a man you deeply loved, and the second of even the social, legal and economic status of being his survivor. As you tragically note, this can set in motion a litany of losses (of home, income, social networks) that deepen the original wound, massive as it is, and militate against healing.

In your case all of this is further compounded—and perhaps partly caused—by the traumatic nature of your partner's death by suicide, a manner of dying that remains stigmatized, often horrific and commonly associated with social avoidance at best and social blaming at worst. As survivors at different geographic and emotional distances from the deceased struggle with the question of why he died as he did, it is all too tempting to attribute responsibility to those who were closest to him—in this case, perhaps to you. At a time when you yourself must be struggling with many questions—Why did he end his life so suddenly and violently? Who am I now in the shadow of this loss?—you are also likely struggling to manage the sights, sounds and sensations associated with the scene of the death and your helplessness to avert it. In addition, you are trying to sort out what this means for your attachments to others, including potentially other romantic partners. This is difficult emotional work in the best of circumstances, and your uprootedness and relative isolation surely make it more difficult still.

So, what to do as you pick up the pieces of a life shattered by disenfranchised, traumatic loss? First and most basically, seek others who can stand with you in the pain and complexity, without recoiling or blaming. Might there be a gay men's grief support group available to you in your community or online? Friends or family who would draw close in compassion, rather than distance in disdain?

Second, find a good therapist, one who respects same-sex partnerships and is familiar with trauma interventions and grief therapy. The surest cure for disenfranchisement is to rebuild a social (and professional) network that acknowledges the gravity of your loss and is willing to join you in finding new direction through it. If the VA doesn't provide that—and as a care system more oriented toward dealing with the wounds of war and deployment than those inflicted by suicide, it may not—look elsewhere, including at resources offered by the *American Foundation for Suicide Prevention* and the *Alliance of Hope*. As you say, life without love is merely existing, and you deserve the recognition of and support for your loss that would once again allow you to move toward living and loving fully, even beyond this trauma.

—Dr. Neimeyer

## Loss of a Beloved Uncle

*Dear Dr. Neimeyer,*

I just lost my uncle, and I can't even see a picture with him in [it] without breaking down. He and I were very close, but I didn't even get to go to his funeral. I feel like I let him down by not going. The last time I saw him was the day before the accident. I couldn't visit him in the hospital because I'm not really his family. And then my aunt told me he was brain dead and they were cutting off life support, and I couldn't be there. I didn't even have a chance to say goodbye, and it was all so sudden that I didn't know what to do. Then it was decided that his funeral would [be] held at some bar, and I'm underage. And now I feel like I'm never going to be able to come to terms with the fact that he's gone. How can I do that without having been able to tell him goodbye?

**Meghan**

*Dear Meghan*

From what you say you enjoyed a very special, perhaps almost father-daughter, relationship with your uncle, one whose warmth and meaning were not fully appreciated by others. And of course, in a moment of crisis and loss, when they too are losing a unique person in their own lives, other adults in the family may find it especially hard to think through the unintended consequences of their decisions about end-of-life care and memorial services on others. This is part of what is meant by the concept of "disenfranchised grief," a grief that is unseen, minimized or discounted by others. Like disenfranchised citizens at an earlier point in our political history, it is as if you didn't get a "vote" and had no say over how or even whether to connect with your uncle and others in those critical moments of transition. I can easily imagine that this deepens your sense of loss by adding lost opportunity to express love to all of the other things that seem to have slipped away with your uncle's life.

But with some creativity and courage, perhaps you can craft a way to not only say "goodbye" to your uncle but also to say "hello" again. In our best understanding, those who have experienced brain death cannot literally hear or process the words of love being whispered to them, though they may have great meaning to the speaker. Similarly, might you find a way, in a letter that you write and perhaps send to the heavens in a ritual fire, to affirm your love for your uncle, just as if he could read it with pleasure and pride? Could you share a cherished story about him with your friends on your Facebook page, and in this way help keep those stories alive? Might you find times in family gatherings to share both the sadness of his dying too soon and the treasure of your having him as long as you did at a time when they could better hear what he meant to you and share with you what he meant to them? Could you find a photo of just the two of you, perhaps from the time that you were small, and post it on the wall of your bedroom or your wall in social media? In all of these ways and more, we can honor those we have loved and lost as physical presences in our lives, while still holding them close in many ways that matter.

From your description of your relationship with him, I imagine your uncle would be deeply touched by your love and loyalty.

—Dr. Neimeyer

### Feeling Abandoned by a Friend

*Dear Dr. Neimeyer,*

The wife of a close friend of nearly 50 years passed away from ALS [amyotrophic lateral sclerosis]. We spoke each week at least once, and I visited her when I could. I actually emailed her more toward the end since she [no] longer could speak. The bottom line was that she asked me a few months before her passing to promise I would stay in touch with my friend, to which I replied, "Hey, we've been friends forever, so why wouldn't I!" But their marriage wasn't the best, and she had other illnesses over time that her husband was very squeamish over. Weekly I'd ask how "he" was doing, to which he'd always reply, "Hey, I'm not sick, she is!" But toward the end he said after work he just wanted to keep driving and not go home, which I sympathized with. Finally, at her funeral, his out-of-state daughter reiterated her mom's comments to me to "promise you'll keep in touch." Odd, I thought. But as time passed, we spoke about finances, went out for a few beers and then bang, I'd call and get no call-backs. I'd send holiday cards, leave email, but nothing. It all came to nothing. I wasn't the only one he "abandoned," it was pretty much everyone. It's been like 10-plus years now. I guess it's done. I just want to know what it's all about!

**Ken**

*Dear Ken,*

There are two basic ways to cope with adversity in general, or loss specifically. The first is to integrate it, move toward it, find a way of managing the troubling feelings and experiences and make peace with them. The second is to avoid the troubling event, segregate it and cut off from it and the people, places and projects that remind us of it. Of course, adapting to the illness or death of a significant person in our life customarily involves some measure of both: we need to acknowledge the hard parts if only to figure out what to do with them, and we also need "time out" from constant confrontation with the loss, if only to remind ourselves that life continues. But problems can arise when we rely so heavily on one of these coping styles that we exclude the other.

Much about your friend's situation suggests that he was primed to follow the path of avoidance. Both his wife and daughter must have sensed his tendency to cut off, or they would not have been so insistent that you take the initiative to stay in touch. His confession during the illness that he didn't want to go home, but instead to keep driving, signals a similar tendency—however understandable—to move away from, rather than toward, a painful encounter. And his failure to return calls or email, likely to not only you but also to other friends and family, followed in a similar vein: avoid the people whose very presence served as reminders of the loss, and in doing so step away from the troubling feelings they evoke. To sacrifice so much of one's life and relational world is a big price to pay for the fragile protection afforded by avoidance, but it is a pattern many people, and perhaps especially many men, display when they can't figure out how to tolerate, understand and address the difficult feelings associated with loss.

—Dr. Neimeyer

# 6

# LOSS OF A PARENT

## Grief and Depression

*Dear Dr. Neimeyer,*

I assumed I would always know what my dad would say if he were here today. We were best friends, and he was very, very outspoken. Without blinking, I feel in sync with his priorities. Yet lately, I've been wondering how he would respond to something. I'm not the type for séances, so the question is on hold indefinitely, but maybe I can explain it to you.

Approximately two years after my father's death, I was diagnosed with depression. It took me months to communicate what I was feeling. I've been relatively articulate since I was a young child, but I had no words. Finally, I explained that the pain was so large; describing it was like trying to fathom the size of our planet—beyond my capacity.

I took that diagnosis seriously, and I worked really hard to be happy again. However, I always looked at this as short term. I mean to say: I thought that the whole depression thing would go away after some time passed. After all, this was because my dad died, right? It was tragic, I was traumatized, but we all move on.

When I got better, I really thought that I had been right, and this was over. Now, I see that I was just having a particularly good run of it.

Things changed sophomore year of college when I got depressed again. It wasn't as bad as the first low point, but it hurt in a different way. I guess I thought I would never be in that place again. I thought I was done staring off into the distance, hearing the faint muffle of a psychiatrist tell me, "Caitlin, it sounds like you're seriously depressed."

Returning to the present pondering, I am in a good spell, but I live in fear of its return: the private, ugly beast in my mind.

This summer, I've been thinking. If this depression will continue beyond the immediate aftermath of my dad's passing, is it possible that it was here before he was on his deathbed?

I am reminded of one afternoon in my freshman year of high school. I was schlumping in bed after school, as I tended to, when my parents walked in. My mom said she was concerned that I was lethargic. I didn't know what the word meant, so naturally, I thought it was a fatal disease. When explained to me as being chronically tired and lazy, I scoffed at it. I'm not lethargic—I'm a teenager!

Unbeknownst to me, earlier that day, my mother had expressed concern to my father that I was depressed. He scoffed at that. She's not depressed; she's just a Dillinger [the name of our family]! Well, I can't argue with that one. I am certainly a Dillinger. Now for the real inquiry: Was my Dillinger Dad depressed too?

He had told me stories of rough teenage years, times he was miserable, but he never made a big deal of it. He barely accepted psychiatric medication when he was fighting and losing a battle with stage four colon cancer. My mother knew my father since they were 12 and 15, respectively. I think if you asked her, she would say yes, my dad was depressed at times in his life.

It's hard to imagine how my dad would advise tackling a problem that he never acknowledged himself, but I often wonder if he could've helped me through this having, albeit unknowingly, been there before.

**Caitlin**

*Dear Caitlin,*

Perhaps your father would tell you not to make the same mistake he did. Ignoring depression—a vulnerability to which can indeed be passed down through the generations—doesn't make it go away. Only awareness, skillful management of one's actions and choices, the support of relevant others and often appropriate professional care can do that. Although a gritty attitude of determination to keep moving through the darkness plays a part in this adaptive response, it is often not enough on its own. What is necessary is understanding "the ugly beast in your mind," in all of its complexity, and then trying earnestly to address the needs implicit in it. Without wanting to oversimplify what can be a complex and multidimensional problem, here are a few tips on managing what seems to be a recurrent life challenge:

1. *Figure out what you are dealing with.* This is harder than it sounds, as depression often rolls up like a fog bank, making everything it envelopes hazy and indistinct. But by exploring the feeling rather than merely trying to banish it, we can often get a sense of its meaning and origin. Does it indeed feel like yearning and aching for a lost loved one? Anxiety and paralysis in the face of looming demands? Retreat from the world in the face of a sense of failure or shame? A response to loneliness and the craving for deep companionship? A sense of being stuck, having made life choices that seem to have led to dead ends, with no apparent way out?

An utterly mysterious cycle that sets in at a similar time each month, or each year, perhaps as days of sunlight grow shorter? In other words, "depression" is not one thing, but many, and discerning as clearly as we can its meaning and origin gives us a much clearer idea about how to address and assuage it. Without this, it is like shooting in the dark.

2. *Take action.* Depression tends to shut us down—mentally, emotionally, behaviorally and socially. Resisting this pull toward inertia and inactivity—which only compound the original problem with many others—can begin with active reflection. This can take the form of personal journaling or honest and sustained conversation with a counselor, therapist or someone else we trust and who cares about us as we look for themes and triggers in our depression that give us a better sense of what we need. Activating ourselves—especially in directions that address these needs—is a crucial step in managing our mood.

3. *Don't go it alone.* As implied earlier, depression can isolate us from others, at the very time we most need their engagement and support. We sometimes back away from people when we feel this way in order not to burden them, but this often only compounds their sense of helplessness to assist us. Instead, move toward others, reaching out with a specific request or invitation—to talk, have lunch, take a walk or simply to unwind together—and balance this with genuine offers to do things for others. Remaining engaged in the give and take of the social world can go a long way toward mitigating the sense of solitary confinement in the prison of our depression, directly addressing some of the sources of mood disorder and mitigating others.

4. *Acknowledge biology.* Some forms of depression clearly arise from life events—like the death of a loved one, the breakup of an important relationship or an experience of failure in some important life domain—while others are more mysterious, seeming disconnected from any clear cause. But both ultimately are registered in changes in every part of our lives: in our daytime activities and in our sleep cycles, in our mood and in our actions, in our brains and in our bodies. And for some, a biological disposition toward or expression of depression may be fundamental and require specialized intervention to supplement our own psychosocial efforts in the form of light therapy, medication and other treatments. Antidepressant medication in particular is rarely a panacea for depression, but it is an essential part of the answer for many and something worth discussing with a trusted physician. Much more help in this area is available to you than was available in your father's generation, and the loving part of him would unquestionably have wanted you to take advantage of it.

—Dr. Neimeyer

## Not Permitted to Grieve for a Dad

*Dear Dr. Neimeyer,*

I was not permitted to grieve for my Dad when he passed over five years ago because of his wife. I asked her if I could pick the casket out with her and be involved in the planning of his funeral. She said no and went ahead with it. Dad and I were always close (also with my sisters). This woman he married did not like Dad's love for us. So she did everything she could to keep him away from us for the three decades they were married. I have a lot of anger toward her. I still feel I need to grieve. Dad's will did not go through probate; that was planned by her so that we couldn't read it. We had to ask her lawyer. My lawyer did find a way. This woman told me after Dad passed that she got everything. . . . I didn't ask her that. My sisters and I are in Dad's will, but we know nothing will become of that, which isn't the important part . . . the fact that she lied was. We do not speak to her since Dad passed, nor she to us. How do I grieve for Dad? I have thought about this a lot. Then I thought that I didn't need to, because I have Dad in my memory. I can't get over feeling like I want her to pay for this. This story of what she did is a long one, but I think I am making my point. Please help me.

Thank you,

**Eileen**

*Dear Eileen,*

Grief can be complicated, and more so when the relationships we lost and the ones with which we are left are complicated as well. As you describe it, it is almost as if you lost your father twice—once to a marriage that inserted distance between a father and his daughters, and again at the point of his death over five years ago. And compounding these relational losses are others, such as loss of representation in his will and the tangible validation of his love for you that that would have provided. I can well imagine that leaves you with a great deal to sort through.

In such cases, many people find it helpful to identify what is grief and what is not grief, in the sense that the emotional tumult in which we are left can represent a mixture of different feelings that jumble together, and even block the resolution of each. It can be helpful, then, to ask first, "What is my most vivid feeling?" From the sound of your question, it sounds as if the answer would be anger—especially directed at the woman who seems to have taken your father away from you in life, and now again in death. Acknowledging this, you might then ask, "What else is there? Is there a feeling beneath the feeling? What would be there if the anger weren't?" What might come through would be a purer, perhaps even little-girl-like grief, for a father you lost too soon and too finally. Just sitting with that sadness, that yearning, might begin to clarify the muddle of emotion: the primary emotion of grief and yearning and the secondary emotion of anger. Each may carry with it distinct associated needs. In the first case, you might need to find ways to honor your father's contribution to your life or communicate with him about your disappointment and perhaps even your sense of abandonment, as through an AfterTalk letter. In the latter case, you might need to find productive ways of acknowledging your anger and safeguarding your boundaries in relation to his wife, without letting that feeling lay claim on even more years of your life. If this work is hard to do alone, a capable therapist can assist with both steps. You deserve to access the best of your past memories with your father without having those sallied by the anger and to reclaim a future beyond its resentment-filled grip.

—Dr. Neimeyer

### Finding Her Dad's Body on Father's Day

*Dear Dr. Neimeyer,*

Do you think that because I found my dad's body a few hours after a normal visit that could be a reason I'm having such a difficult time now with his death? Today is five months, and I can't stop crying. I lost my dad on Father's Day, and it was so unexpected.

My mom passed away more than 20 years ago when she was 52; I was 28. My only sister passed away at the age of 40; I was 37. Now I'm 51 and my dad is gone. All three were unexpected. My dad is the only one I found dead.

Sometimes it seems like it's so fresh and then I think it's been five months and I don't want time to pass. I feel all alone even though I have a great husband. Make any sense?

I'm sure people are sick of me being sad. How can I move past all these tragedies and stop being so sad?

**Mimi**

*Dear Mimi,*

Your sad experience illustrates two components of grief that can complicate our adaptation after a loved one dies: the difficulty of processing the "event story" of the loss itself and of reorganizing our life story in its aftermath. As you imply, shocking encounters with the death, such as your unexpected discovery of your father's body, can prompt intrusive, even traumatic, imagery that comes to mind unbidden in quiet moments or at night, bringing with it an array of troubling feelings, from horror to helplessness. At the same time we are also struggling with the deep sense of separation that follows in the wake of the death, which certainly can be made worse by the history of other losses that precede or follow it, deepening our sense of aloneness in the world. Your story, sketched briefly in your question but lived out across many years, contains features of both these challenges: the trauma of the death scene and the corrosive loneliness that followed.

What can you do, you ask, to "stop being so sad"? One response, ironically, is to allow the sadness, to embrace the reality that the grief you feel might be appropriate a mere four months after the loss of yet another member of your nuclear family. However, if this sadness truly seems to be invariant or even worsening across time and you find yourself unable to take a "time-out" from the grief in order to connect in hope with other relationships, then personal or professional grief therapy might be helpful.

Assuming that your grief is significant but not life-threatening, I might advocate that you specifically set aside times to journal about the loss and about the special gifts that each of your family members gave you (in the form of shared experiences, a sense of being loved and lovable, a transmission of values, etc.). In this, your goal would be to acknowledge fully and deeply the truth of your grief, but also to leaven it with the enduring contributions each special person made to your life, which you will carry forward into a changed future. In this way despair can mellow into nostalgia and appreciation and be borne less heavily.

Second, if the troubling memories of your discovery of your father's body continue to haunt you in the months to come, consider going back to them, consciously and by choice, perhaps even returning to the place where you found his body, and imagine vividly what you wish you could have done if you were there with him, unable to save him, but able to provide comfort and companionship during his passing. Perhaps you would have held him, expressed your love, and wished him well on his journey. The idea is to build up a healing image that competes with the horror and helplessness of the original one, in this way "staring it down," and recovering a sense of loving connection.

In both cases, it is important to feel safe and supported by relevant others—perhaps your husband, a close friend or others in a bereavement support group. But if either the reflective or active processing of the loss feels like too much to manage alone, look for a good therapist who is familiar with grief and trauma interventions, who can help you pace this work and address the feelings, thoughts and images that arise for you as you do so. With each step forward in these directions the path should become a little easier, allowing the grief to mellow to something more sustainable, while making room for you to reinvest in other living relationships.

—Dr. Neimeyer

## A Long Delayed Grief

*Dear Dr. Neimeyer,*

It's been 11 years since I buried my mom and dad, and I've never been able to accept or deal with their deaths; and then in February I lost my final grandma, so there's been some issues with family since, and I have left and never looked back; but I still haven't dealt with or even accepted the passing of my mom and my gram. How do I start grieving? I can't even talk about them in counseling. I'm at a loss of what to do.

**Robin**

*Dear Robin,*

It sounds like you have lost not one but three anchor points for your life, and with them three caring relationships that could have provided a special kind of security in a larger family system that feels much more conflicted. Sorting through what all three meant to you, and perhaps your mother and grandmother especially, would therefore seem to be a priority. However, your comment that you "can't even talk about them in counseling" suggests the value of a few "conversation starters" to open the door. Here are a few ideas along those lines:

1. *Introduce your loved ones.* Tell your counselor a bit about each of them, something of an appreciative kind. Perhaps you could bring in a cherished memento of each to stimulate your comments. What kind of people were they? What were their special qualities? Their idiosyncrasies? Their signature strengths? What was special about how each related to you? What did they see in you and want for you? Just like we might introduce living loved ones in conversation to someone who was interested to meet them, so too we can introduce those who have died but who are still part of our lives in emotionally relevant ways. This often strengthens us to look for ways to draw on our relationship with the deceased to adapt to our lives now, as well as to identify particular feelings or issues that require more attention in therapy.
2. *Open the family album.* If a spontaneous introduction seems too daunting, bring in some family pictures and use them to describe the people and relationships to your counselor. Do you remember your loved one at the age depicted in the photo? How did he or she change across time? As you look at the person's face or eyes, what do you see there? What would those eyes or that mouth say if that person could see you looking back on them with love and grief so many years later? Going deeply into the relationship with this person—especially when the photo captures the two of you or the

broader family together—can strongly concentrate the emotions, which can help your counselor identify a "growing edge" that can be acknowledged, validated, explored and ultimately transformed in healing directions.
3. *Share a memory.* Whether with the counselor or someone else, speak your loved one's name and tell a story about them that means something to you. This need not be long . . . though it could be. The key is to challenge the regime of silence that seems to have descended on all three relationships, which not only blocks you from processing your loss but that also dishonors them by banishing them from acknowledgement in the world of the living. Reclaim the relationships, and make them part of your present and future, as well as your past.
4. *Explore the loss and discover the gain.* Ironically, when we avoid discussion of the dead to avoid the short-term pain of doing so, we suffer a kind of double loss—losing the other to death and then suffering the death of their story as well, including how it remains interbraided with ours. Articulating and exploring the unique dimensions of each life and loss, in contrast, allow us to realize what we also have retained in the form of the many gifts they gave us, whether of our interests, our culture, our values or our basic sense of self. Discovering just how much of us was shaped in each relationship can make it clear that we carry them forward in our lives—lives that they helped shape and sustain. And this is how it is, generation after generation, as we are touched and transformed by our parents, grandparents, mentors and friends and then pass it on to others. Opening to speaking of such things is the first step to accessing them in a vital, living way, one that takes grief as a transition toward a changed connection.

—Dr. Neimeyer

## Loss of Both a Husband and a Father

*Dear Dr. Neimeyer,*

It's been around two years now since I lost my husband and my dad a few weeks apart. The grief is still so debilitating I can hardly get up in the morning. I see a therapist, but it doesn't feel like it's helping very much. I attempted to take my life earlier this year, spent some time in the hospital but now am back to work and expected to function as a supervisor again. I live in a pretty small town and am unable to find any grief support groups. I don't know what else to do to get out of this dark place. Can you suggest some books or material I can read to help begin to move forward, please?

**Dolores**

*Dear Dolores,*

Though we all wish it were otherwise, the sad truth is that time alone does little to heal the wounds of grief; it is more a question of what we do with the time that matters. And from your brief letter, it is clear that you have tried to do much to surmount the pain of your double loss, from your desperate attempt to end your life to your determined attempt to return to work and your interest in reaching out to groups and for readings that might provide support and compassionate counsel. I want to join you in these latter, more constructive efforts.

Of course, your first priority needs to be safety; if you do not survive, then there is no life on which to build. This clearly needs to be a central focus of your therapy with your current provider or another to help address the psychic pain, despair or aloneness that has driven you toward suicide. Beyond reducing risk through limiting access to means of self-harm (safely removing firearms from the home, entrusting potentially lethal medicine to a friend or relative), it will be critical to identify what, for you, can begin, even by small degrees, to restore hope. Perhaps this might be as small as learning some new skills for combatting the escalation of overwhelming negative emotion through mindfulness or moderate exercise or taking steps to complete one or two of the tasks on a neglected and similarly overwhelming to-do list. Likewise, anything that enhances reasons for living—such as strengthening important relationships, grounding in a faith tradition or personal philosophy or undertaking meaningful projects—can help you both defend against despairing impulses and rebuild a life of meaning.

Second, it is clear that you need to work on your grief per se, not only generically on depression or engaging your work (though this also is important). In this, your impulse to find mutual support from others like yourself could be a relevant step, even if this means planning a weekly visit to a nearby community that offers support that yours does not. There are even weekend or week-long grief retreats that could be specifically healing, for a tiny fraction the cost of psychiatric hospitalization. Alternatively, or additionally, I would encourage you to search on the internet for online support forums for people with similar losses, which should be abundant. Increasingly therapists and counselors also offer consultation and therapy in online environments such as in videoconferencing, which can be as effective as face-to-face sessions. Importantly, this would let you find and work with a truly expert provider specializing in complicated grief, just as you would consult a medical specialist rather than a general practice family physician if you were facing an equally life-threatening medical condition. Your profound and prolonged grief needs to be taken no less seriously.

Finally, hold a magnifying lens over the grief itself. What feelings and needs, specifically, do you find threaded through the fabric of your bereavement?

If loneliness, you need to find not only activity companions but also good listeners. If hopelessness, you need to connect to people and stories that can speak of moving through similar darkness toward the light. If spiritual struggle, you need to read books in your faith tradition that ask and answer the hard questions of where God is in your suffering. If self-criticism, you need resources that help you view your self-talk in a more self-distancing perspective and find ways of moving toward less harsh self-judgments. And if resolution of unfinished relational issues with your husband or father, you need to find ways of addressing them with the help of a therapist skilled in facilitating symbolic conversations with the deceased or helping you find a secure base in your continuing bonds with these figures (with AfterTalk conversations playing a potentially useful role here) or with others in your lives. In other words, whether you examine your grief with a group, with a therapist or through the lens of self-help books or grief memoirs you can find on sites like Amazon or Open to Hope, the crucial thing is for you to safely examine what your grief tells you about what you need to find or change to not only manage your pain with self-compassion but also to reach toward a changed but meaningful life in the future.

—Dr. Neimeyer

## Unable to Talk About It

*Dear Dr. Neimeyer,*

I had a significant bereavement over two years ago when I lost my father to cancer and Alzheimer's and am still unable to talk about it or face it in any way. I have emotionally disconnected from my grief. It overwhelms me at times, but this is so unbearable that I shift back into my comfortable place of denial. I would like to understand how I am able to stay in the left side of my brain (with regard to this trauma) for over 2 years now! Is this a normal part of the grief process to avoid anything that triggers the associated emotion? I cannot talk about it, look at photos or listen to music. From the standpoint of my work life and my parenting, I look like I'm functional, but I feel constantly keyed up and anxious, and am especially short and annoyed with my mother, who sometimes mentions my father, leading me to snap at her.

I do not understand this. My father was always the key person in my life, always gentle and loving and wise. So, it makes sense that I would grieve him. But I am concerned that I hardly feel my grief, just a kind of tension, and it does not seem healthy to continue in this state. Can you help me understand myself and what is happening?

**Rachel**

*Dear Rachel,*

As I read your words, I conjure an image of someone whose stoic avoidance of grief-related emotions and perhaps circumstantial "triggers" gives way at times to a great welling up of pain, which itself makes processing and integration of the loss of your father nearly impossible. It as if the surge of grief that rises up when you are reminded of him trips a kind of "circuit breaker" to prevent system overload. This works—after a fashion—but just as you sense, it doesn't address the basic problem, which is the need to find some safe way to revisit the time of his illness and make sense of what must have been a confusing and anguishing series of losses, as you gradually lost your father both psychologically and physically. As you do so and manage to take in the reality of his death more fully without going into a state of high alarm, you likely will also be able to access more of those loving memories of your father and carry him with you in the ways you can now—as a kind of inner mentor, perhaps, or a secure base who reminds you that you have unique value and worth.

But how might you do this? Perhaps the best way would be by working alongside an experienced grief therapist, one who is informed about both trauma and attachment. Working from this perspective, he or she would likely seek safe ways for you to introduce your father by sharing some stories that convey his special place in your life and then gradually begin to introduce the story of his illness and passing, doing the latter in a kind of slow-motion detail. Here the goal would be to confront the painful reality of his dying and to receive support for managing any difficult emotions this entailed. Working together, you would probably also systematically begin to approach, rather than avoid, the photos, music and even conversations with your mother that open the door to the grief, if only initially for several minutes at a time. Like physical exercise, where one builds strength step by step in weight training, running, etc., you would likely find that your adaptive range and comfort increase as you do so.

From your act of reaching out to me, it seems clear that you are nearly ready to undertake this work and begin to process a loss and the associated grief that has been tensely held at bay for so long. It would be a privilege to be the therapist who works alongside you to find ways of moderating that pain and working with the meaning of this heavy loss, which for too long has left you in limbo.

Dr. Neimeyer

## Blaming Herself for Her Mother's Death

*Dear Dr. Neimeyer,*

How do I stop blaming myself for my mother's death? She was 85 and 18 hours away from heart valve replacement, doing well, ready for it. She was told to walk some before surgery, and her last walk was fatal. I think I could have stopped her from overdoing it, but I wasn't there. Other family was at the hospital with her, and I was to stay the last afternoon and evening with her. I took some time to paint my toenails and take care of a few other things before leaving for the hospital. If I had not done those minor things, I could have been there and feel like the course of the day would have been different. This is hard for me to get out of my head.

**Carrie**

*Dear Carrie,*

Psychologists have a name for the kind of repetitive and self-accusatory thinking that you find "hard to get out of your head"—rumination. This sort of obsessive, circular thinking, while punishing and even anguishing, makes a kind of sense if we understand it as an attempt to comprehend a seemingly random and unnecessary loss—even if we do so at our own expense. And so what might we do to shake this pattern and the sense of corrosive guilt to which it gives rise? Here are a few alternative responses that other bereaved people have found helpful:

1. *The path of logic.* Though seemingly plausible, the persuasiveness of your ruminative self-accusation relies on a delicate series of unsubstantiated assumptions. Did your mother indeed "overdo it," or was she within the minimal levels of cardiac stress prescribed by the physicians? Could you have detected it if she were not? Were other family members grossly negligent, or were they attentive, just as you would have been, but sadly paid the price for their attention with their presence to her dying? If you had not taken a bit of time for self-care and instead have been held up in traffic or at the nursing station, would you have held yourself accountable in the same way? Looked at closely, much of the tissue of which self-blame is made is insubstantial stuff indeed and falls greatly short of what would be required to establish guilt in a fair court of law.
2. *The path of compassion.* If your sister or teenage child had been accompanying your mother on that final walk or stayed home for a time taking care of themselves and daily tasks, would you be constantly attacking or accusing them of malfeasance as you are yourself? Would you berate them or lament their negligence in their presence as you do with yourself? That is highly unlikely. If anything, you are likely to feel compassion and empathy for the hard position they were in. Why then torture yourself with hurtful barbs that you would spare another person you love?
3. *The path of humility.* Though we sometimes would like to believe that we can control life's negative outcomes and spare those we love misfortune and even tragedy, life teaches us relentlessly that such control

is elusive at best, and utterly illusory at worst. However attentive and careful we are—even to the point of obsessiveness—many or most of the outcomes are beyond our limited control, and in the end death will come to all. This truth asserts itself more and more forcibly as we (and our loved ones) reach venerable ages, as did your mother. Viewed in this perspective, the lessons of loss teach us the folly of grandiosity and acceptance of our simple human condition. Coming to terms with this, and even embracing this truth, can allow us to ask, "What now is mine to do? Where can I contribute, if I relinquish the grandiose illusion that I can protect my loved ones from all suffering?" The answers, while humbler, can move us to make differences in the ways we can and ultimately to accept that there are other outcomes that elude our inherently limited ability to predict and control the precious lives that are ours . . . for a time.

—Dr. Neimeyer

## Both Parents Died a Year Apart

*Dear Dr. Neimeyer,*

What are the effects from parents who have passed away? Mine both had cancers, and they both passed away a year and a half apart. It has caused me a lot of grieving, crying, a lot loss of memory, forgetfulness, anger and not wanting to move on. It's been very hard for me. I am the youngest out of the four, and they say the youngest one takes it the hardest. It is true. I still can't move on.

**Julie**

*Dear Julie,*

The death of a parent—much less both parents in quick succession—can be uniquely difficult, as we may lose that special sense of a "secure base" in a relation with those who may have loved us well for our entire lives. No one again will ever know us as they did, nurture us through our tender years, take pride in our growth and development and, in the end, perhaps also accept our caregiving of them as an extension of that same bond of love. Some research suggests that such a bond may be particularly intimate for the "baby" of the family, whose last position in the birth order can lead parents to take special delight in his or her birth or life.

And yet, part of the pain such loss brings may come from how we approach bereavement. When we view it merely as loss, the abject absence of loved ones, and feel the press to "move on" in a way that implies leaving them behind, our hearts logically resist this requirement. On the other hand, when we ask ourselves, "How can I continue to live my love for my parents now, in their physical absence? What do they now require of me? How can I help keep their stories alive?," we can view their long and strong participation in our lives as sources of inspiration and their place in our hearts and in our lives with others as a continuing resource. As loving beings, how did your parents move forward themselves following the death of *their* parents—your grandparents? Every generation learns and relearns this lesson: How do we redefine connection to those who have gone before, as we live deeply and meaningfully with those now living beside us, in a way that prepares for those who will come after? Suffering is a part of this lesson, but so too is embracing its significance.

—Dr. Neimeyer

## Still Waiting to Grieve Her Death

*Dear Dr. Neimeyer,*

My mother died over six years ago, and I'm still waiting to grieve her death and not feel numb towards her passing. Both my father and I cared for her for a long time. I lived several hours away from my parents, but the doctors would call me all hours of the night concerning my mother's emergencies, as my father was partially deaf and at the time at the beginning stages of dementia. While taking care of her for almost 15 years and working a full-time job (which I hated) I slept maybe three hours a night and was myself very emotionally and physically sick and worn down by my mother's indifference and outright nasty behavior towards me and my father. Those years I cried myself to sleep wondering how my life would go on as I would miss my mother so much and missed and wanted the person back that she used to be (we once were close). I myself was shocked that when she did die, as I just went through the motions of arranging the funeral without a single tear. I thought I must be in shock and once everything was taken care of, I would break down and cry. That has never happened. Those close to me tell me that I grieved my mother's death while she was still alive. Is this so? How could this be since I was so afraid of losing her? Is it because she suffered so much and now I don't have to be witness to not only her suffering but also how badly she treated me and my dad? My dad passed away three years ago, and I miss him terribly. My priest told me that they are both at peace and together, and my comment to him was, "I hope she's not driving him crazy up there as she did down here." As I am writing this, I know I sound very angry towards her. And I am.

**Fran**

*Dear Fran,*

"Absent grief" following a significant death can mean many things. As you imply, it can reflect numbness and disbelief, especially when the death was shocking and sudden, as research indicates is more likely following violent loss. Alternatively, it can represent simple resilience, as when transitory sadness soon gives way to practical efforts to get on with life, especially when we find the death an easy one to accept because it seemed timely and perhaps even merciful. A third possibility is that absent grief could follow the loss of someone we feel we "should" be grieving but in fact aren't—especially when the relationship was less close than others might assume given the nature of the kinship connection. And finally, numbness and minimal grieving can stem from our tendency to mute feelings of all kinds, especially when some of these are difficult to acknowledge and are socially unacceptable. Although it is hard to say which of these explanations might fit best for you without the benefit of a more substantial conversation, your letter suggests that the second of these formulations is more plausible than the first, the third more likely than the second, and the fourth the most probable of all. That is, while your mother's death might have brought relief and your love for her might have dimmed across the years, your understandable anger at her and the long and difficult final years of your life as a family could have made it hard to acknowledge or express feelings of any sort after her death. Until now.

And so what now might be done about this anger and the other possible emotions that could arise when it is explored or expressed? Here are a few ideas:

1. *Go to where it hurts.* If the most accessible emotion you have about Mom is anger—at her distancing from you, mistreating your father or demanding what you were unprepared to give in your own state of illness or depletion—then give that anger or resentment voice. Write her an AfterTalk letter in which you name and claim the feelings you likely suppressed when she was alive, and probably since. Then sit with this for a day or two and write back as if from her, restoring a potentially healing dialogue with your "inner mother."
2. *Hear from the mother you fear, and the mother you need.* As part of this restored dialogue, try writing back from two different perspectives: first from the mother you knew in that demanding last chapter of her life, as she seemed self-absorbed in her own suffering, and then from a more compassionate and engaged mother, perhaps the one you knew in earlier times. Then ask yourself, "Which of these can I live with?" Choosing what we attend to in others gives us more freedom to sculpt our own realities now.
3. *Listen for the feeling beneath the feeling.* As you process the anger, it is likely to recede in its vividness, making way for subtler emotions, and perhaps

more vulnerable feelings that it eclipsed or covered. Might there be sadness or grief lurking beneath the rage? If so, welcome it in, and seek a way to give it a place. Perhaps a special ritual of remembrance performed privately or with others who understand would let you memorialize your mother's constructive role in your life, as well as acknowledge the hard and disappointing parts. Life is rarely simple, and it can be helpful to find an audience—in therapy or in our natural support system—for the whole story.

—Dr. Neimeyer

### Struggling With the "What Ifs"

*Dear Dr. Neimeyer,*

My father had schizophrenia, and I am so proud of how he managed his illness. He will continue to be an inspiration to me, and I do direct my son, who struggles with mental illness, to Grandpa's example. My father found that walking cleared his thoughts and decreased the symptoms of depression. My Dad walked miles every day. My Dad's greatest fear was losing his ability to walk. Sadly, that became a reality for him four years ago. We did not get a diagnosis as to why he lost his ability to walk until June two years later. Chronic inflammatory demyelinating polyneuropathy. Unfortunately, the diagnosis came too late. What I am really struggling with is he took the initiative to go to the hospital during a long holiday weekend four years ago. He was suicidal and he needed to know why he was having trouble walking. My husband and I drove two hours to that hospital, and we were reassured by the hospital staff that they would keep him until the team could assess him the Tuesday after the long weekend. Unfortunately, they discharged him the holiday Monday before the team was back to assess him. My Mom and brother and I are really struggling with this. His next admission to the psych unit was that fall, and the psychiatrist was wonderful, explaining to my dad and the family that his inability to walk was not due to the side effects of the meds, and the CAT scan of his back did not show any reason why he could not walk. He suggested my Dad see a neurologist. Unfortunately, the hospital did not have a neurologist, and due to other health issues, we were not able to get my Dad to a community neurologist until a year later. I am really struggling with the "what ifs." What if he saw the psychiatrist during his admission first admission four years ago and we were given that information then? Would he have gotten the diagnosis sooner? Would it have been lifesaving for him to have received treatment sooner? My Dad was someone who had a heart for others suffering with mental illness. He would walk to the hospital and sit on a bench and feed the birds. Apparently, mental health patients at the hospital would visit with my dad on that bench, and he was a support to them. I keep thinking that I need to follow up with the hospital regarding that admission four years ago. Not really to complain, but rather in honor of my father, to explain the importance of that admission and to hopefully help other seniors struggling with other health issues who also have underlying mental health issues. I feel like I may not have peace unless I do follow through with this. What do you think?

**Carol**

*Dear Carol,*

Nobility comes in many forms in life, perhaps especially when we witness others who surmount or manage great challenges across a lifetime, as it seems was the case with your father. His ability to live with chronic mental illness, but to do so in a fashion that provided inspiration and support for many testifies to the reality that each of us has something unique to offer when we live responsibly and with compassion. I hope that sharing this vignette of your father's life helps convey this meaningful message to many readers.

How tragic, then, that your father might have died of what was an avoidable and undiagnosed condition. Medicine is as fallible as any other human endeavor, and the venal realities of contemporary healthcare institutions ironically can make it more so. A death under these conditions of ambiguity leaves many questions unanswered and often prompts surviving family members to engage in what psychologists call "counterfactual thinking," meaning that they—like you—may find themselves "rewinding the tape" of events associated with the illness and imagining different possible scenarios that could have led to a better outcome. Often this takes on the form of assigning responsibility for critical actions (or inaction) to oneself or others, stoking the fires of guilt on the one hand and anger on the other. Yet in their extreme forms, these emotions may simply contribute to depressive self-criticism in the first instance or a dynamic of accusation and defense in the second. In a sense, both of these alternatives compound the problem of the death rather than resolve it.

Fortunately, your closing thoughts suggest a way between the horns of this dilemma, one that collaborates with hospital representatives rather than one that confronts them with their failure. As the issue of the unavailability of the diagnostic team and the premature discharge seems to have been more administrative than medical in origin, perhaps the appropriate person to contact would be a patient care representative who can hear your complaint and ideally respond constructively to it. Improved care for those with similar conditions would seem to be something your father would have appreciated, just as any other support you can offer to people with mental illness—either directly or through an advocacy or service organization—would honor his legacy of compassion and engagement.

—Dr. Neimeyer

## A Bedroom Shrine for a Departed Father

*Dear Dr. Neimeyer,*

My question is regarding my mother. We lost my father very unexpectedly this past summer, and she is having a very hard time with his loss, as we all are. My question is this: Is it good for her to have her bedroom looking like a shrine to him, so that whenever she looks anywhere in the room, she is reminded of him and starts crying? I don't know what's best at this point. Thank you for your help!

**Dara**

*Dear Dara,*

"What is best at this point" could have less to do with the number of months that have passed since your father's death than with where your mother is in the course of her grieving. It sounds as if she is both striving to maintain his possessions just as they were after many months and also experiencing great pain rather than a sense of consolation and closeness to him when in their presence. If so, then it could be that she is reaching for some way to restore a sense of secure connection or attachment to him . . . but that "freezing" his room is not meeting this need. In this case it could help to consider what steps could be taken to reduce the discrepancy between her inner and outer world, psychologically and practically.

First, let's consider her inner world. How could she be encouraged to develop a more secure bond with her husband, one that can survive his physical death? Many people feel a greater connection when they spend a bit of time each day or each week writing a letter to their departed loved ones—perhaps a letter that not only laments their deaths but that also updates the deceased on the writer's ongoing life. Others find that natural conversations that mention the loved one, share a memory or consider what he or she would do when faced with a particular problem or question helps to convey the idea that the deceased is still, in a sense, part of the family and not someone whose very name is banished as the family moves forward. If your mother feels that she is the only one who is "loyal" to your father, she may hold fast to his possessions all the more tightly, whereas if she feels that others also welcome his "presence," she might be more comfortable with allowing her relationship with him to evolve in new and less physical directions.

Second, let's consider her outer world. The idea of creating a shrine to a loved one is not at all odd when considered historically and across various world cultures. Indeed, it is far more common than the alternative of "cleaning out" all mementos of the loved one, as is often practiced in the contemporary Western world. But a shrine that honors the departed is typically something a person visits, not something in which one lives. For example, a small altar with a few cherished photos of the loved one or special mementos is often placed in the living room of Asian homes, perhaps with candles that can be lit as one spends a few minutes a day praying or having an inner conversation with the person before moving on to other valued people and projects that are also part of life. Arranging such a space together as a family with your mother's participation could contribute to her feeling less alone in her grief and allow her to begin to change the space she now maintains for him by contributing to the family altar. Rearranging articles in the room or establishing what my colleague Darcy Harris calls a "grief drawer" of cherished reminders that she can open and visit at times, but also close, can be further steps toward allowing the room to evolve, and allowing her grief to evolve with it. Embracing change while honoring bonds can be a natural process, as families find a way of moving into a meaningful future in which all those they have loved can continue to play a part.

—Dr. Neimeyer

## Slipping Back Into Grief

*Dear Dr. Neimeyer,*

I've been in a strange place recently and wanted your help in understanding what is going on. My father died suddenly four years ago when I was in college, and because he had always been the "perfect dad," an outdoorsman, civic leader, friend and role model to my brother, my sister and myself, we all missed him terribly and sought support from one another and, in my case, a very helpful grief counselor. For me, the counseling was so helpful in encouraging me to write to my dad to express my feelings for him and about the loss and to affirm through my interest in art and photography what he meant to me in my life. I think the fact that I was in college, far away from other family and the community that knew my dad, made this especially helpful. I then went on and completed college and started in my career in my own small office. I have a picture of all of us as a family on my wall in my new space and even used some of my dad's tools in building the shelves in the office, using skills he once taught me.

The strange thing is that I've been crying a lot lately, even though I thought I had been doing well for the past two years. I find myself thinking about how my dad didn't get a chance to see me graduate or blossom in my work, as he is also missing my brother's recent marriage and my sister's pregnancy and expected birth of a baby boy who will share his name. It's like I'm slipping back into grief, but I haven't been able to see my grief counselor to discuss it because he has since moved out of town. So, my question is, is this normal, or do you think I should seek therapy with someone else?

**Mara**

*Dear Mara,*

Nothing you describe impresses me as unusual for a sensitive young woman who deeply valued a loving father and who understandably misses him grievously as you encounter the inevitable "marker events" that complete one life stage or are the harbinger of another. What could be more natural than looking for his proud smile at such points of transition, as you must have seen it on countless other times? And its absence as a physical expression of his validation of you as a growing woman and professional must be wounding, making each step over a new life threshold feel just a bit hollow. Grief is an appropriate response on such occasions, not a sign of incomplete "grief work" or regression.

And yet steps forward need not represent steps away from your dad. Even in the hammer and drill you hold as you build your shelves, you literally are using tools he passed on to you. And I have no doubt that in that photo on your office wall he is smiling down on a daughter whose achievements validate his dreams for you . . . even if he cannot acknowledge that in words. Indeed, it is our common (but not inevitable) destiny as fathers to die before our children realize their full potential, and to have the sense that they will survive us in a way that affirms our hopes and values is as much as any of us can ask. So, my counsel would be to honor your father with your tears of love from time to time, as well as with your actions and accomplishments. Of course, grief therapy remains an option if your sadness and separation distress prove persistent or progressive across a period of months. But grief alone is not the problem—only losing oneself or one's direction when it becomes unremitting. As you and your family continue to provide support for one another through parallel life passages, you may discover that you have now become the witnesses to your ongoing emergence into adulthood, and that process may be made sweeter by conjuring the image of your father's pride as you do.

—Dr. Neimeyer

# 7

# LOSS OF A CHILD

### Preparing for the Anniversary of a Daughter's Passing

*Dear Dr. Neimeyer,*

How do I handle the one-year anniversary of my daughter's passing, which is coming up next month? She left three babies behind, and I found her in her room with the boys with her. Luckily, they were sleeping. But I can't get that vision out of my head! I cry, I laugh, I cry! I am scared of what the day of the anniversary is going to have in store for me. I am broken, confused and lost. What can I do to prepare for that terrible day?

**Doreen**

*Dear Doreen,*

As difficult as the anniversary of the death may be, both research and practical experience suggest that the anticipation of the anniversary may be worse, as the fear of not knowing how the day will go can spawn anxious rumination that can preoccupy us for weeks. What, then, can we do to cushion the blow that the fateful date represents? In addition to cultivating self-compassion and planning to do something that is self-nurturing and soothing, you might consider some form of *ritual of remembrance* to mark the occasion.

Anthropologists teach us that rituals of transition, across cultures and religions, tend to include three basic elements. Adapting these to the anniversary of a death, these might include three "*Re-*" functions:

1. *Recognition of the deceased.* Consider doing something that honors your daughter: light a candle for her in a prayerful or meditative moment; write an AfterTalk letter of appreciation to her and read it aloud or post it to other readers; place a special picture and remembrance of her on your or her Facebook page. The key here is to take a symbolic step toward recognizing and perhaps circulating her special qualities as a

person in a reverential or loving fashion, recruiting an appropriate audience for its performance.
2. *Reconstruction of your identity as a survivor.* This could involve reflective writing about who you were to your daughter as a mother, who you are now in the midst of your mourning and who you hope and strive to be three years in the future, when you will have integrated this loss and found new meaning in its aftermath. By linking past, present and future in this realistic but hopeful fashion, you can begin to create a vision statement for a changed life. Sharing this with others in a ceremonial fashion can help set an intention to live into this future in a way that might make your daughter proud of you, while also recruiting social support for the changes you are attempting.
3. *Reaffirmation of the community of concern.* By arranging to come together with those who know and love you and your daughter, perhaps by extending a simple invitation to participants who wish to do so to share a recollection of your daughter, a hope for you or simply a poem or thought that in some way touched them, you place your own grief and theirs in the healing circle of your mutual concern. Perhaps a tone can be set through a candle lighting, as noted earlier, a shared meditation or two minutes of silence or playing an evocative piece of music. Afterward, people could be invited to briefly speak or share, or simply to "hold the silence" respectfully for those who do. Consider creating a place in the day and the ritual for the children: even a preschooler could be invited to draw a picture for his mommy or dictate a letter to her. Sharing a simple buffet meal in the home together following the ceremony can suggest a natural reintegration into life and reaffirm that each of you—including your daughter—continues to have a place in a living community.

—Dr. Neimeyer

## Does Time Heal?

*Dear Dr. Neimeyer,*

My 27-year-old son died almost two years ago. The first year was hard, but I mostly felt in a fog. Now it seems that fog is lifting, but this second year is proving to be a lot worse than the first. I am remembering more about the death and funeral and still cry almost daily. People tell me time will heal this sorrow I feel, but I doubt it. Do you find this to be a usual progression when one is dealing with the death of a child or loved one?

Thank you.

**Katia**

*Dear Katia,*

Like our own breath on a mirror, the fog of early grief can soften the hard images it buffers, and in this sense protects us for a time from the sharper pain that may come. But the surreal quality of living in a familiar world made strange by the death of our loved ones typically gives way across the weeks or months to the harsher and unavoidable recognition of the keenly felt presence of their absence. In our research as well as in our practice and personal experience, we observe just what you are talking about—that negative feelings like depression, yearning and sometimes anger all show a visible up-tick as we approach the second anniversary of the death, which can leave mourners feeling like they are going backward instead of forward.

But sometimes this is what is required to place us in a position to change how we are living our loss. As the fog begins to dissipate, we may feel more exposed and vulnerable, but we also may see with painful clarity what now needs attention. For example, the prominent images of your son's death and funeral may loom large, inviting closer processing. Some traumatic grief therapists, for example, join with clients in doing a kind of slow-motion replay of the critical scenes of the death, staying with them and breathing through the hard parts rather than trying to escape them or push them away. Often this gives rise to important questions about the feelings, intentions and motives of the deceased; of relevant others involved in the dying; and perhaps in our own hearts and suggests further work in the form of journaling and writing letters to (and from) the deceased, as in AfterTalk, to help us make some sense of a seemingly senseless loss. This can be hard work to undertake alone or even in a support group, and it is for this reason that the series of books on *Techniques of Grief Therapy* (published by Routledge) has been developed to help counselors find the tools to support bereaved parents and others in sorting through anguishing stories of loss and finding some meaning in them that makes living with the loss more bearable.

So, while time alone may not magically heal the wounds inflicted by a tragic or premature death, what we do with the time can help. As we integrate the loss more fully, it does not so much fade away as step into the background of our lives, allowing a fuller and more positive engagement with our present and future, as well as our past. Every bereaved parent knows that the grief does not dissipate like the protective fog you described, but many can also tell you that lives of purpose and even pleasure can come into focus and help balance the burden.

—Dr. Neimeyer

## A Senseless Loss

*Dear Dr. Neimeyer,*

As I am approaching the second anniversary of my youngest son's death, I feel as if I will never know exactly who I am for the rest of my life. There are good days and bad days, and today is a bad one. It just cannot ever make sense to me—maybe someday, far away.

It's just so tough trying to come to terms with the senselessness of it. I was his mom for over 25 years—and now I'm wondering what happens from here? A definite piece of my life puzzle is gone forever.

**Kaitlin**

*Dear Kaitlin,*

Your image of the "puzzle" of your life, missing the prominent piece that was your son, is so evocative: it captures the sense of fragmentation of a once-coherent picture of your life, like a jigsaw puzzle that has fallen to the floor, its pieces scattered, and at least one seemingly lost for all time. Surely many bereaved people, and bereaved parents especially, must feel this kind of brokenness and senselessness following an irreplaceable loss and, like you, are left wondering what sense life makes, what sense *they* make, in its aftermath. And despite the cultural adage that time heals all wounds, this is often simply not true when the death is premature, violent or unexpected; in fact, research indicates that a worsening of many grief-related symptoms is a common phenomenon as the second anniversary of the death approaches.

And yet, there may be ways to respond adaptively to a grievous loss, even when one cannot simply banish it or "get over it." One place to start is by attempting to conserve, rather than relinquish, your valued role as a mother, not only in relation to your living children but also in relation to the son who is with you in spirit. Though it might seem paradoxical, it can be worth asking yourself, *How does my son need me to be a good mother to him now?* Might you play a central role as the loving custodian of his memory, someone who helps keep his stories alive in the world? Would you do so by sharing the proud, loving or funny moments that otherwise might be eclipsed by the dark memory of his death, or fall silent through the awkward avoidance of others? Are there aspects of his legacy you could extend, perhaps in the form of acting on his behalf to support people or causes he cared about? Might caring for yourself, as he might have cared for you as he grew to maturity, become a way of "channeling" his love for you? Might you even consider writing a symbolic AfterTalk letter to him about such questions and then write back a response from your "inner son" to the letter from a lost and grieving mother?

In any of these ways, you will be turning from the sometimes-futile effort to find meaning in his senseless death, and instead give attention to finding renewed meaning in your life now. And a part of this can involve crafting a new puzzle piece to fit in the hole, one that helps you rebuild, rather than relinquish, your identity as a mother to a precious boy who was taken from you far too soon.

—Dr. Neimeyer

## Death of a Teenage Daughter

*Dear Dr. Neimeyer,*

My teenage daughter Daniella died in a car accident almost two years ago, and even though I have been able to go on raising my other two children and working in my office job, I continue to feel a great deal of grief and also some irrational guilt about her death, because I gave her permission to go out with friends on the night she died. My husband is also visibly sadder and quieter since her death, and although he tolerates my leaving her room pretty much as it was when she was living, I know he would prefer that we do something with her things and move on. My friends are obviously uncomfortable when I bring up Daniella in conversation, and I know I should be getting over this by now. My question is: Is there something wrong with me, and what can I do about it?

**Anna**

*Dear Anna,*

There is nothing wrong with being a mother who continues to love her child intensely beyond her death and who wants to preserve a sense of connection to her in tangible and conversational ways. As human beings we are wired for attachment to those we love, and the caregiving bond between a parent and child is what allows our children to grow and thrive with a secure sense that they will be cared for and supported in confronting life's many challenges. It is hardly surprising, then, that this urge to care for your daughter survives her physical death, even if it must now somehow accommodate the reality of that death and change the form in which you express it.

For example, rather than eliminating all of your daughter's belongings from the house, might you make some of them, along with one or more pictures of her, part of a shrine that honors her memory and continued presence for you? Of course, this sort of shrine need not be frozen in time, as in many cultures such places that honor deceased loved ones might change with the seasons of the year or the seasons of our lives, as through decorating them with flowers or different memorabilia over time. You might find that doing so frees you psychologically to then begin—perhaps along with your husband and other children—sorting through Daniella's things and deciding which to pass on to others, which to display and which to put in storage.

Finally, as implied by the shared activity of sorting and remembering noted earlier, finding conversational and social spaces that are "safe" for including Daniella are also important. For good friends, simply thanking them for allowing you to speak of your daughter in natural ways may be enough, even if that conversation is filled with sadness as well as love or pride. But many bereaved parents also find benefit in online sharing and memorialization of their children (as in the *Open to Hope* site), writing symbolic letters about residual issues like guilt to their children in AfterTalk or connecting with other bereaved parents who respect and value the natural importance of a continuing bond, as in the mutual support provided by the *Compassionate Friends*. In short, although there is nothing wrong with your urge to maintain a loving attachment to Daniella, there is much that you can do to cultivate it in a form that is sustainable, even beyond her physical life.

—Dr. Neimeyer

## Feeling Misunderstood

*Dr. Neimeyer,*

I stay so angry at people that expect me to be over my son's death eight years ago. What can I say to them? They act like I have failed or just want attention. I hurt terribly.

**Bette**

*Dear Bette—*

No doubt it is hard, if not impossible, for someone who has not lost a child to imagine the pain of doing so; thinking back, perhaps it would have been unimaginable, even to you, a decade ago. The death of a child, as you have tragically learned, is not merely something a parent "gets over." It might be more accurate and compassionate to say that the goal is learning to live with the grief rather than trying to "move on" without it.

But this does not mean that incapacitating depression and persistent anger need to become a life sentence. I recently had the pleasure of talking with the national director of The Compassionate Friends, the global support network for bereaved parents, who is himself a bereaved father. In the course of our conversation he noted that in his many years of experience with the organization, approximately one-third of the parents he has met remain stuck in a complicating, life-limiting grief, seemingly indefinitely; one-third mourn their child acutely for a significant period but ultimately find a way of bearing their grief more lightly and adapting to their changed lives; and the remaining one-third ultimately show impressive "posttraumatic growth," valuing life, family and relationships more keenly, living with enhanced purpose and clarified priorities and engaging in altruistic projects to help others who suffer adversity, and especially the adversity of the death of a child. In other words, quite different paths open to different people who have had similar losses.

If you find yourself in the first group and feel profoundly misunderstood by people around you, you might find solace and wisdom in the presence of other parents who have known analogous losses. Especially as you share your experience with "veterans" who are a number of years out from the loss, as you are, you might find not only support for your loss but also inspiration for how to accommodate it with less anguish and perhaps even growth through grief. Coming to know others who model that hoped-for outcome can help make the impossible seem more possible.

—Dr. Neimeyer

## Spouses Grieving a Daughter's Death Differently

*Dear Dr. Neimeyer,*

My daughter passed away four years ago. My husband and I grieve so differently. I find it difficult to feel supported by him because I have always needed to talk about my grief while he rarely talks about his. When I cry, he doesn't know what to say and doesn't really offer the support I need and want. I attend support groups, bereavement camps, etc., alone because he won't even consider joining me. He misses her so much, but I worry that he isn't getting the support he needs. I also worry about us because we are handling this so differently. How can we move forward together? Should I be concerned about the way he is grieving?

**Lorinda**

*Dear Lorinda:*

The tragic death of a child often reminds us of a basic truth: that just because we've had the same loss, we don't necessarily have the same grief. Our grief is a function of who we lose, how and when we lose them . . . but also of our unique relationship to them and our own particular ways of coping with adversity. Nowhere is this clearer than with many mothers and fathers mourning the loss of their child.

Although there are of course very great differences in grieving styles within genders, there are often subtle differences between them as well. Like you, many women (and plenty of us men) display our emotions readily and prefer to talk with others who we hope can hear what others cannot, with no press to offer simple solutions to complex problems. But many men (and women) tend to be more stoic and self-controlled and orient to finding solutions as quickly as possible, especially when someone they care about is clearly distressed. When these two styles come together in the same couple, the result can be misunderstanding, and a kind of pursuer-distancer dynamic can worsen the pain of the shared loss.

So, what to do about this? One strategy is to put your husband's coping in context. How has he dealt with other significant setbacks, stresses and losses in life? Is his response similar, but simply more intense, in the wake of your child's death? How did the two of you coordinate or tolerate your coping at these other times, and how did it ultimately work out for you both? Sometimes complementary rather than similar styles serve a family well, letting one person attend to the emotional agenda of others (such as their other children or parents following the loss) while the other takes care of the practical necessities to keep life going.

But sometimes the distance between partners can be anguishing. In such cases, my colleague, Laura Hinds, suggests that they find a "grief spot" in their home—perhaps a basket or box with two parts in the child's bedroom or other private place—in which each person can, every day or two, leave a brief note or small gift for the other in some way related to the loss. The offering need not be large to be big in its impact. For example, you might leave a short love note or description of how you are feeling for your husband or the sort of small present that only you could give. He would then reciprocate with a note or offering to you. At least for the first few weeks, both partners would commit to check the "grief spot" at least every other day and *not to talk about* what is left there. This code of silence is important, making the small exchanges "safe" (especially for your husband) and special—they are not merely more demands for conversation. This sort of exchange, practiced with love across the early months of grief, can gradually meld into greater closeness and perhaps more feeling-oriented conversation when the grief becomes more manageable.

—Dr. Neimeyer

## Cycling From Depression to Mania

*Dear Dr. Neimeyer,*

Following the death of my 22-year-old daughter of a drug overdose two years ago, I, of course, have struggled with my grief, but also had two very distinct periods of depression, each approximately six months long, filled with classic symptoms of lack of energy to do anything; loss of interest in food, sex or social life; general self-neglect of my self-care and appearance; and a sense of cutting off from my husband. The symptoms seemed to come on suddenly and then turn off just as suddenly. For example, this last time they came on in the midst of an otherwise enjoyable vacation in the late summer and persisted until the middle of last month, when they lifted in just a day or two. Of course, I am still very sad and miss my daughter, but more or less returned to full functioning. In part this might be a result of my taking Prozac that my doctor starting prescribing to me three months ago.

What is even harder for me to understand is that this last time I seemed to pop up into what might almost be called a super-normal mood: I have been filled with energy, have started a lot of new projects at home and at work, don't need as much sleep (even compared to my life before my daughter's death), have started to play a musical instrument and take lessons for the first time and am making more friends. On the downside, I confess that I tend to get irritated at people who can't seem to keep up with me, and my husband says I talk too much and too fast. He thinks I seem manic. I don't have a history of bipolar disorder, but I guess I have always been kind of an "on or off" person, with not much in between. Now, though, it seems more extreme.

So my question is, could this be a result of the grief, or what? I'm kind of liking all the energy I have now—it sure beats the depression—but I don't want to drive people away or burn myself out.

**Sandy**

*Dear Sandy,*

Your rich description of the months of darkness does indeed seem to point to a textbook case of depression, even if the clarity of the entrance into and exit from each of the two episodes is sharper for you than it would be for many people. I also appreciate the way in which you yourself can distinguish between the grief over separation from your daughter and the symptoms of your mood disorder, which seems to have a seasonal affective disorder (SAD) quality in its onset and offset. Because SAD can carry some important treatment implications, it is something worth evaluating with your physician as a factor that can further complicate your bereavement.

As to the mystery of your current "super-normal" mood, again the feelings and behaviors you describe do suggest a hypomanic upswing in mood rather than simply a return to your emotional baseline. A serious loss like that of your daughter under tragic circumstances can indeed trigger both mood disorders (like a collapse into depression) and susceptibility to bipolar disorder if the mourner has a propensity for that (as your description of your usual "on-or-off" personality style might suggest). Again, this is something that deserves closer consideration by your physician and could be clarified by a family history (that is, a discussion of whether other blood relatives, and especially parents, grandparents or siblings, displayed signs of mania or bipolar disorder, whether or not this was diagnosed or treated). However, another strong possibility is that the antidepressant medication you were given might require adjustment in type or dosage, or the addition of another medication such as lithium or Lamictal to help stabilize your mood or reduce the risk of future episodes of cycling through extreme highs and lows. So, a conservative recommendation would be to begin by consulting your physician about your current symptoms and whether they could be linked to your medication regimen.

Finally, as important as medication may be in your case in treating your depression and moderating your current tendency to cycle too far in the opposite direction, remember that your own self-awareness and the observations and support of people who care about you also play a crucial role in restoring emotional balance in the aftermath of trauma and turbulence. Having an open dialogue with your husband about your concerns and his, and perhaps even bringing him into consultations with your doctor, can add helpful perspectives on what you need, as well as demystify for your husband some of what you are going through. Each of you has suffered a greater loss than any parent should have to bear, and experiencing greater tension or distance from one another can only compound this tragedy.

—Dr. Neimeyer

### Harder in the Second Year

*Dear Dr. Neimeyer,*

I'm grieving more in the second year after my son's passing. I am embracing the passing and think of him often, which I learned from the grief class I attended last year. He died so young from a pancreatic cancer. Should I return to this class? I feel otherwise pretty good—missing my little granddaughter and her Mom who moved to another state after he died for several good reasons, which were partly economic.

My son was also a close friend to me. We shared many things like the love of music, etc. I feel a need to look at their wedding video—maybe seeing him "alive" and talking and moving about might be comforting. What do you think?

**Eva**

*Dear Eva,*

Just as you have described, our research also points to a resurgence of grieving early in the second year following bereavement, at a time when our own shock and numbness may have worn off and the high levels of social and ritual support for the loss have fallen away. This in itself is certainly not a sign that your grief is problematic or complicated, especially because, as you say, you are "feeling pretty good" in other respects. However, it is always appropriate to seek a circle of caring others who can listen compassionately and offer perspective on our bereavement, as your grief class seems to have done for you. In return, you might also bring a helpful perspective to the group based on your own experience a year or more beyond the loss, rather than in its immediate aftermath. Among other things, your story might help others struggling with loss to recognize the normality of grief across a longer period of time, especially following the death of a child, as well as offer counsel about what has helped you manage this loss in a way that does not undermine your life.

You also ask about reviewing the wedding video of your son and his wife, now moved far away with your granddaughter. In an important sense, it is less a question of *whether* you watch it than of *how* you watch it. Would it represent a futile attempt to turn back the clock and retreat to the past or an attempt to refresh your memories of him as a person, to appreciate his vitality and uniqueness and to seek ways of carrying him forward with you as an inspiration or in appreciative stories you share with others? Likewise, viewing this poignant moment in your son's and his wife's life story could merely reinforce the tragedy of a life cut short or deepen your wellspring of compassion for his partner and little girl in a way that prompts you to stay connected with them in a loving way as they reorganize their lives. In all of this, you may well find that more positive possibilities open in the second year of bereavement than in the first, as you seek ways of moving forward with your son's presence in a new fashion.

—Dr. Neimeyer

# 8

# LOSS OF A SIBLING

### A Son's Anger Over His Sister's Death

*Dear Dr. Neimeyer,*

My 18-year-old son lost his sister (age 10) two years ago as a result of cancer. He had a very close relationship with her and was and still is devastated as he grieves for her. He has so much anger around her death, but he won't ever talk to me about his grief. He lashes out at me frequently, and we are having a hard time getting along. He has seen a therapist and seemed to open up to her about his loss, but he is still so different and angry around me. He is in college now and is doing well, but I am worried about him. Our relationship has changed, and I don't know how to help him. Is his anger normal?

**Stella S.**

*Dear Stella—*

For an adolescent to be angry following the death of a sibling would surely be a common response to the violation of his world brought on by a cruel and unfair loss. But cancer and other serious illnesses do not play by the rules, and the persistence of your son's anger across a period of years poses the very real risk of further loss—in this case of the close and loving relationship you likely once had with him and want to have again. What, then, might you do to repair your mother-son relationship in the shadow of this shared traumatic loss? Here are a few ideas:

1. *Do a self-assessment.* Although your son's anger is his own, take an honest look at what you might be doing or not doing that he could be reacting to with his outbursts. Might he see your attempts to approach him as too intrusive? Too blaming? Too mollifying? What might others—perhaps a good friend or your spouse—candidly say about how you have responded to your daughter's death? Might she or he see any shift in your behavior toward your son that he could see as provocative? It is always easier for us to see another

person's contribution to a conflict than it is our own, and only a strong effort toward empathy can help us override this built-in tendency and view our behavior through their eyes. Ultimately, the goal here is to see whether you might be making some unintended contribution to the breakdown in the relationship, so that you can be more empowered to make changes.

2. *Look through his spectacles.* As an extension of the previous point, try to imagine the unique meaning of your son's relationship with his sister and what her illness and death meant to him. What did she give him that no one else did, and who was he to her in turn? Did her death signal the loss of innocence, of safety, of trust in adults (and parents) to protect and care for those who are young and vulnerable? Did a part of him seem to die with her—perhaps his youthful playfulness or his own big brotherly sense of power to shield her from harm? Understanding these deeply personal meanings of the loss, and the feelings associated with them, might help you read beneath the secondary, defensive emotion of anger to the primary emotion of hurt or fear that lies beneath it. And this could help you relate to him with compassion and clarity when he responds in externalizing, impatient or blaming ways.

3. *Consider family therapy.* Even if your son's anger is linked intimately with his grief, he is part of a family system decimated by the same loss, and how each person deals with it has a great impact on others. Meeting together with a therapist who really understands family systems, communication patterns, roles and structures and how death affects these can go beyond the impact of individual therapy in healing the wounds in family relationships originating with a shared loss. Most basically, such therapy can help family members speak to what they felt and needed at the time of their loved one's illness (often healthy children feel neglected by parents who are preoccupied by the needs of the sick child), as well as now. In this process, misunderstandings can be addressed and the shifting needs of the surviving child as he or she grows toward greater maturity (sometimes all too quickly) can be understood and met more clearly. Your son's ability to succeed at college despite his loss is surely a good sign, and finding ways to validate his resilience and respect his grieving style while also rebuilding your relationship is both feasible and important.

—Dr. Neimeyer

### After a Long Battle With Cancer

*Dear Dr. Neimeyer,*

My only sister died three years ago after a long battle with cancer during which I was a primary caregiver. She was like a second mother to me since she was 16 years older than me, and I cannot say what a profound effect her loss has had on my life. Since she died, our mother has been diagnosed with Alzheimer's, and she is deteriorating. I have tried to take care of her but have become extremely withdrawn, as being around family and friends tends to make me very uncomfortable now. Feeling bad for my mother, I planned a birthday dinner at her house tomorrow. Now I just do not feel that I can make myself go. It hurts me to see my sister's family without her and to see her grandchildren with another woman. It hurts to see that my mother has forgotten her. Would it be okay if I were to set everything up for the dinner and just not attend at the last minute? I have a great desire to withdraw from my family permanently, as being with them now, experiencing the hole that is left where my sister used to be and dealing with my mother's illness just hurts far too much.

**Nita**

*Dear Nita,*

Although much of the social world may not understand the true meaning and impact of these twin losses for you—of your sister to cancer and your mother by degrees to dementia—it sounds like you have experienced the collapse of two of the major pillars that have anchored you for a lifetime. Just as you imply, it as if you have lost your mother twice. Add to this the heavy demands of caregiving for both, and it is easy to understand that you feel depleted and reclusive and feel the urge to recoil from gatherings that only make the past and present "holes" in the family that much more visible. It is a natural human impulse to draw back from that which causes pain and to hunker down in a place of refuge.

And yet, it is important to consider the long-run costs of this form of self-protection, in effect providing a thin buffer from your grief at the cost of shrinking your world further and leaving another hole in your family where the third crucial "mothering" figure—you—used to be. To recognize the cost of this sort of retreat from pain, imagine that someone you know and love, perhaps a daughter of yours, were to break an ankle, and rather than following a painful but necessary course of physical therapy to return to full functioning over a period of months, chose to withdraw to her bedroom, avoid the prescribed weight-bearing exercises and allow her leg to atrophy to the point of becoming a permanent handicap. As her caring mother, would you support her retreat into a crippled and isolated life, or apply a gentle and compassionate press to help her return to functionality and a broader world of family friends and meaningful relationships? What advice would your mother and sister give you if you were this child? Though life would be easier if it were otherwise, reaching through grief to reengagement with life often requires persistence despite the pain, rather than avoidance of it.

As you gradually take steps to reengage them rather than to abandon them, your sister's children and grandchildren may one day thank you for it.

—Dr. Neimeyer

## Coping With Multiple Losses

*Dear Dr. Neimeyer,*

Why is it so hard? I lost my sister in the spring, then my husband a month later, then my son two months later. It's been a losing battle. I just don't know how to handle this.

**Paulina**

*Dear Paulina,*

When a person has a litany of losses in such close succession as you have suffered, another loss is upon you before you can even grieve the one that came before, and the result can be a kind of fog of grief, a blur of pain and longing that is hard to sort out, and harder still to adapt to. And to make it worse, the losses may include the very people we would naturally turn to for help and support with the other deaths. It is hardly surprising that such bereavement overload can challenge the coping capacities of even the most resilient people and put us at risk for a long and complicated course of grieving.

One small but useful step in such cases can be to "comb through the losses" in order to disentangle the associated grief. Just as one might do with tangled hair, the solution is not simply to cut it off, but instead to tease apart the different strands of feeling and meaning associated with each loss. With a box of tissues handy, write the names of each beloved person across the top of a page of paper, drawing a column beneath each going down the page, with their names as the headings. Then, on the first row, write in a few words a description of what was special to you about each person in the column below his or her name, perhaps "my closest ally when I was small," "always gave me strength and made me feel safe" or "sweet and funny." Then, on the next line, describe your relationship to each person, such as "co-conspirators against our parents," "understood each other without speaking" or "I was his caregiver when he was ill." Continue in this way, adding other rows that seem important to you: my main feeling in relationship to _____, what I would say to _____, who best understands what this death means to me, what would help now with this specific loss _____. The themes are up to you, but be sure to include this final prompt last, as it will often suggest a practical step you can take to address the unique needs you have in relation to a particular grief strand—perhaps to have an AfterTalk conversation with your sister, to visit a place with a good friend you once enjoyed with your husband or to direct to another child in your larger family system some of the loving attention you once gave your son. Gradually, this can help the strands become less tangled, and the way forward through each loss can become clearer.

—Dr. Neimeyer

## Loss of All Parents and Siblings

*Dear Dr. Neimeyer,*

I've lost all my parents and siblings. Each one I've grieved and tried to move on, but now that I've lost my last remaining family member, my sister, five weeks ago, why do I feel like I'm grieving for them all now? I've never felt so lost and alone now that I've lost all of my family.

**Devorah**

*Dear Devorah,*

When we lose the last member of our family of origin, we may lose the most relevant cast of characters of our childhood, all of the witnesses to a unique world of our youth—a time that defined us and that will not come again. And with the loss of siblings we lose the people who know us most thoroughly, across the years, jobs, roles and relationships, those few who have followed the thread of our life for nearly its entire course. As long as one person remains who stands in this unique relation to us, we may feel seen, understood, known. But when that person is lost, the enormity of our aloneness can rush in all at once—indeed, we may lack even the very person we need to understand our unique grief.

And yet, for better or worse, every family will encounter such a moment of transition, when only one member of the nuclear family remains. How we cope with that inevitability if we are that lone survivor will depend on who we are and who we love: we might draw on our personal or spiritual beliefs, as well as our network of extended friends and relations, to seek a sustaining web of meanings and bonds that supports us in our grief and helps us find a potentially redefined meaning in our lives. A woman experiencing a similar position to yours wrote me just a few days ago, saying she felt like "The Last of the Mohicans," referring to the James Fenimore Cooper novel about the lone surviving member of his Indian tribe during the time of the Revolutionary War. But the protagonist of that story found new (and heroic) meaning in forging new bonds with American settlers, even as his people migrated, developed new ways of life and blended into other tribes. Perhaps this is the challenge for us as well as we address the questions: To what am

I now committed? To whom do I now belong? How best can I represent my people in a changing world? Confronted with courage and compassion, we can find answers to these questions, and in so doing reestablish a world of meaning that has been shaken by loss.

Dr. Neimeyer

### Self-Medicating After Brother's Death

*Dear Dr. Neimeyer,*

I think my adult son is "medicating" himself with alcohol to try to deal with his brother's death two years ago. He's an adult, and no one can make him go to his doctor or a counselor. He has a good job that I fear he could jeopardize. I know that there is also guilt involved with his brother's death. Is there anything we, his family, can do?

**Cyma**

*Dear Cyma,*

Sadly, bereavement can sometimes present us with two problems for the price of one: not only does the death of our loved one usher in a profound sense of anguish and grief but this understandable separation distress can also be compounded by the less-than-optimal ways that we respond to our pain. Unfortunately, attempting to anesthetize the hurt by turning to alcohol or other drugs is a common response, bringing in its train other losses—financial, relational, health related and occupational. The result can be a downward spiral that affects not only an individual mourner but an entire family system. Your description of your son's coping style conjures just such a worrying image.

What can you do as you seek balance on this slippery slope? A starting point may be recognizing that your son isn't the problem; the problem is the problem. That is, distinguish between the suffering human being who is your son and the alcohol that is beginning (or continuing) to undermine his life. Adopting a loving, nonblaming, but actively concerned stance can be the crucial first step to take as a family, so that your approach to him is not characterized by anger that merely pulls for a defensive response on his part.

Second, consider the history of his relationship with alcohol, since it is unlikely to have begun with his brother's tragic death. Typically, people cope with loss as they have coped with other major stressors, for better or worse. This means that if your son has long turned to drinking to deal with troubling circumstances or reversals, the course of treatment is also likely to be long-term, rather than a "quick fix."

Third, pull together as a family, organizing an "intervention" in which people join in a compassionate confrontation of the alcohol abuse, speaking deeply of your love for your son, as well as your concern about the impact of his drinking on him and the rest of you. As each of you is likely to experience your own profound grief about the death of his brother, acknowledge and express this, emphasizing some of the ways you have tried to cope with his death. And then offer concrete alternatives for treating both the alcohol abuse (and participation in an Al-Anon group can be quite helpful in this regard) and the grief, seeking a specialist in your area who is familiar with complicated bereavement. In consultation with these resource people, you can better find a way forward through a personal crisis that carries implications for you all.

—Dr. Neimeyer

## Anxiety and Depression

*Dear Dr. Neimeyer,*

I lost my older brother just a few weeks ago. I feel so sad and depressed. Plus, I have major depression and an anxiety disorder; panic disorder too. Could losing my brother make me have [a] lapse back into a deep depression again?

—**Rita**

*Dear Rita,*

The short answer to your question is "Yes, certainly." Good evidence exists that people who have a history of anxiety disorder and panic—particularly linked to fears of abandonment—are more susceptible to complicated and prolonged grief, just as those with a vulnerability to depression are likely to have a further episode of depression triggered by bereavement.

But depression and grief, while they may co-occur, are not the same thing, and it is important to distinguish them, as each may carry different implications for treatment. Although sadness is certainly a part of both, it is also a natural, nonpathological response to bereavement, and even an adaptive one, giving us time to retreat from the world, signal to others our need for support and reorganize life goals in light of the loss. When it merges into a prolonged, persistent and anguished preoccupation with the death or the deceased to a point that interferes with our functioning, that's another matter. But even this form of life-vitiating grief is distinct from depression in many respects. Rarely in grief do we become morosely focused on our own worthlessness or low self-esteem or struggle with frequent thoughts of suicide; at most we may wish that we were reunited in an afterlife with our loved one. Depression also tends to have a relentless and pervasive character, saturating every moment of life, whereas grief tends to come in waves, with periods of relative clarity, focus and even pleasure being interrupted, often unexpectedly, by significant resurgence of longing. Depression commonly undermines our ability to complete activities of daily living, such as routine household chores, meal preparation or self-care, to a far greater degree than does grief, which typically allows us to "go through the motions" even when we don't feel like it.

As someone having long experience with depression, you know best how it intrudes into your life—and what medical, psychological and social strategies are most effective in helping you manage it. For example, if one of the telltale signs of depression for you is agitated and disrupted sleep, appetite disturbance or lack of energy, then medication could help restore each of these functions. Likewise, "behavioral activation," pushing yourself to move into the world and tackle manageable tasks step by step, can help structure your day and reinforce your self-esteem, while availing you of the social support of others. Challenging unrealistic negative thoughts or developing strategies to resist depression, almost as if it were an opponent, can also be helpful. But whatever your approach to self-management of your depression, your sense of empowerment will grow as you make progress, and as the depression retreats, those challenges that are unique to the grief (e.g., making sense of how or why your brother died, what his death means for your life now or how to continue a constructive sense of connection to him) will become clearer. Sometimes the grief too can be complicated, but it is more easily addressed—even by grief therapists—when the fog of depression begins to lift and the mourner is better able to confront its unique challenges.

—Dr. Neimeyer

### Grieving Daily for the Loss of a Brother

*Dear Dr. Neimeyer,*

Is it normal that five months after my brother died I'm still crying every day and everything reminds me of him?

**Meika**

*Dear Meika—*

Across the course of a normal lifespan, our siblings will be the longest intimate participants in our life stories, sharing our childhood and much of our adult years, typically into old age. Premature loss of a brother or sister denies us this form of special companionship, and its impact on us is too little recognized by the social world. Your question about whether significantly grieving the loss of a brother is "normal" just five months after his death suggests just how little validation and understanding we often receive for so substantial a loss, to the point that we begin to question our own responses.

Beyond mere reassurance, however, I would hope to offer you some possible pointers in moving forward in your bereavement. One idea is suggested by the very phrasing of your brief question, as you note that "everything reminds me of him." Can you actively open to, rather than avoid, such reminders, drawing on them to invite in special memories of him for which you feel gratitude, or using them as portals for accessing some of his signature strengths, qualities as a person or values in a way that might provide inspiration for you? Can you allow the reminders to connect you to the joy, warmth or mutuality that you shared with him, rather than only the great sadness of his absence? This is not to propose a simple answer to a disorienting grief, but only to suggest that daily reminders ultimately can be used to connect you to his spirit in ways that are appreciative and sweet, as well as sad. The tears that come with that subtle shift might then become cleansing rather than bitter and open onto vistas of positive emotion as well as negative.

—Dr. Neimeyer

# 9
# COMPLICATED RELATIONSHIPS

## Mourning a Former Spouse: Disenfranchised Grief

*Dear Dr. Neimeyer,*

My ex-husband and I were married for 25 years, together 28. We raised four children together. He was charming, sociable, affectionate, intelligent and silly. We enjoyed numerous good times. Toward the end, however, he became abusive and I made excuses to stay. After he took out his anger on one of the children, I could no longer remain married to him. He was arrested, and an acrimonious divorce followed. I subsequently remarried, had nothing to do with him and am quite content. Upon hearing that my ex died of cancer last February, I reacted viscerally, which surprised my husband. I had to handle some of my ex's legal affairs, as he never remarried. Occasionally since then, I get flooded with memories of him and the good times we shared. It's almost haunting. I am saddened he is missing the wonderful events in our children's lives. Do people mourn their divorced spouses years after remarriage?

**Carla**

*Dear Carla,*

Just as you so poignantly describe, people can indeed mourn lapsed relationships, even when we ourselves have chosen to leave them, and when our ex-partners die, we may grieve again, and more profoundly, for what may amount to a double loss. It was precisely this experience of grief over the death of a divorced partner that led my colleague, Ken Doka, to formulate the concept of "disenfranchised grief," a form of mourning that is considered illegitimate or invalid by the larger world, and perhaps even by the mourner herself. After all, if we left the partner or he or she left us, what reason is there to mourn? Is the partner's death even "worth" the pain? Does our grief threaten the partner's current mate, if there is one, or our own? Such grief is therefore complicated by a variety of factors, including the incomprehension or disapproval of others, our own tendency to criticize ourselves for our feelings or simply the "invisibility" of our grief to the social world. There are few seats reserved at funerals for ex-spouses.

And yet, viewed compassionately, such feelings as those you describe are fully understandable. There were no doubt countless moments of mutual love and joy and the enduring legacy of your shared children; however, these brighter times might have darkened as the years moved forward. In my therapy with clients in your position, I encourage them to tease apart the "two spouses," the younger one whose marriage was predominantly hopeful and positive, and the later one that came to exemplify something quite different. Then, in separate choreographed conversations in counseling, or perhaps in an AfterTalk letter to each, I prompt them to express their clear feelings of love, grief and regret to Partner 1 and their anger, disappointment and resignation to Partner 2—with the clients, of course, ultimately being the authority on what emotions, declarations and questions are appropriate to each. Finally, as ex-partners are often excluded (or exclude themselves) from memorial services, it can be useful to create a private ritual of resolution that acknowledges the loss—perhaps in the form of visiting a place once significant in the relationship for a walk-through and private reflection or a symbolic ceremony of release witnessed by others who would understand. In either case the goal is to validate the grief as real, even if also complex, and in this way to counter the disenfranchisement that denies the legitimacy of the loss.

—Dr. Neimeyer

## Which Mother Am I Writing To?

*Dear Dr. Neimeyer,*

I've been a fan of AfterTalk and your column for some time. I have used AfterTalk's "Private Conversations" to talk with my deceased father for years.

My mother died two weeks ago. I am starting to gel my "Conversations" to my mother in my head. Here's the rub, and the challenge: Which Mother am I writing to?

Am I writing to the loving, easygoing mother who I knew most of my life, the one who got all my jokes . . . ? The one who laughed with me till we cried? Or am I writing to the sharp-tongued mother who when influenced by one toxic family member fueled negativity and upset?

I am at peace with my relationship with my mother. She lived with me and I was her primary caregiver. But each time I start to write, both personalities come up in the "conversation."

**Laurie**

*Dear Laurie,*

As you might already anticipate, the question of whether you should write to the "good mother" or "bad mother" is an unambiguous "Yes!" That is, it sounds like you have much of importance to say to both figures: much to affirm and appreciate with the former, and much to redress with the latter. Separating these "two mothers" in your mind can be a crucial first step to recognizing and validating the quite different grief you might have with each.

How might you do this? As there seems to have been a shift in your relationship with your mother over time, you might begin by reviewing an old photo album of those early years, especially looking for pictures of little Laurie and her mother together. What feelings and stories come to mind and heart as you hold these images and ask silently or aloud, "Who *were* you?" "Who were *we*?" Let the answers come, perhaps with tears, and commit them to paper or screen in a heartfelt letter to that mother, speaking to what she meant to you, and means to you still.

Then, on another day, review pictures from later years, after the shift. This time ask, "Who did you *become*?" "Who did *we* become?" "And why?" These answers are likely to arise with a different feeling tone and with very different stories of disappointment underpinning them. Write these too in a second letter, acknowledging the unresolved relationship issues, the unfinished business, the hurt, the protective pulling away.

Differentiating each "mother" in this way, you might then see if a bridge of integration might be built between them, without forcing it to be so. To do this, read one letter aloud, pause and then read the next, just holding them in the same field of awareness with no pressure to make them one. Instead, you might hold one letter in each hand, hands separated by a meter in front of you as you sit, eyes closed. Then, very, very slowly, almost imperceptibly across the course of 20 seconds, bring your hands holding the letters together, a centimeter at a time, until they meet, and both hands hold both letters together. Note what feeling, if any, arises in you as you do this. You might find that a shift is sparked that is hard to anticipate, that leads naturally to a further question: "How can I grieve you now?"

—Dr. Neimeyer

## Finding Safety in Isolation

*Dear Dr. Neimeyer,*

I lost my husband one year ago. My biggest problem is our children live so far away and only visit once a year. I feel so isolated because they are so busy with their lives and I am not included. One daughter will call weekly, and the other daughter very rarely calls to check on me. I was a caregiver for my mother for six years, and two weeks after her passing my husband became ill and I cared for him for six years. So, I became isolated from my friends and groups I belonged to, to lovingly care for my husband for he could not be left alone for very long. I am finding it very hard to stop crying and to reconnect with the friends from six years ago, for they have moved on without me. I do stay busy with projects by crocheting, and I donate to the homeless and nursing homes. But this is done alone, and I am not sure I want to reconnect with the friends of the past. I feel safe just staying home alone. Is this normal?

**Bethany**

*Dear Bethany,*

It sounds like you made many sacrifices for those you loved, substantially setting aside your own friendships to provide care for your mother and then husband for a dozen years. And now, in the wake of their passing, you feel the price of that sacrifice in the loneliness that characterizes your daily life. Adult children who are busy launching or maintaining families and careers, especially when they are at geographic distance, often can't fill the void, and perhaps they, like your friends, became accustomed to your absorption in caregiving and reorganized their lives along more independent lines. Thus, your friends and family, like you, seem to have learned to adapt to greater distance, and it seems like a hard pattern to unlearn, despite its cost.

As you mention your altruistic activities on behalf of the needy, it seems that you have found several creative ways of continuing your caregiving but have redirected it to the homeless and elderly, in this way preserving a strand of consistency with a major source of meaning over the past 12 years. But as you imply, crocheting and donation do not necessarily offer human contact as compensation. As you further suggest, there might even be a part of you that has come to prefer the distance, despite the loneliness, as reflected in your comments that you are not sure you want to reconnect with old friends and that you feel "safe" at home alone.

So, what is to be done? At a practical level, of course, there are steps you could take toward a world that again includes deeper forms of companionship: participation in a support group for widows, "meet ups" with people who share your interests that can be found in every community on the internet, crocheting circles and volunteering time as well as material donations to needy groups. But a first step is to have a heart-to-heart conversation with the part of yourself that resists taking these steps, the part that feels "safer" not doing so. What does isolation keep you safe from? What is the protective function of distance? Might it minimize the risk of something even worse than loneliness, such as allowing yourself to care again deeply for others, only to risk losing them as well? If so, are there other ways of confronting this fear, without retreating into house arrest now and in the future? Compassionately inquiring into the meaning of your reluctance might yield candid answers that could let you understand your fear and find helpful and hopeful ways to assuage it as you reconstruct a life shared with others.

—Dr. Neimeyer

## Guilt and a Mother's Passing

*Dear Dr. Neimeyer,*

I didn't want to post this because I don't want my loved ones to know the guilt I feel about my mother's passing. But before my mom passed last year, I avoided her calls, as my sister said she was drinking a lot. We lived in different states. And she was drunk a lot when I talked to her. It was hard seeing her this way. We had a difficult relationship to start with. She was a teenager when she had me. Anyway, I have so much guilt and regret for doing this and not seeing why now. Turns out she had a painful cancer. No wonder she drank! I was able to say I'm sorry, but she really didn't know why. And I broke down to her. She wanted to be as close to me as I did her, but we let the world get in the way and now I can't ever get that back. I just am having a hard time forgiving myself and feeling I wasted so much precious time with her. How do I get over this, and will I ever get over this?

**Amy**

*Dear Amy,*

Your final questions are a good place to start, because I suspect that the question of *whether* you can move beyond this difficult and guilty place in which you feel stuck will have a great deal to do with *how* you attempt to do so. In other words, time alone is not likely to heal the wounds in your relationship with your mother, which you seem to have suffered long before her death. And sadly, death itself does not resolve the hard feelings that accumulate across a lifetime; it just makes their resolution something we have to pursue more consciously. Let me suggest a few ideas about how you might do so.

First, it helps to recognize that your guilt persists because your relationship with your mother persists, even beyond her dying. While this is a problem, it also suggests a solution, as you can seek resolution through working to make amends to her, just as you would have in life. You might start by talking about your feelings with her, perhaps through an AfterTalk letter, expressing some of what needs to he said about how the relationship was hard for you and also about how you wish you had been able to respond to its challenges better. You might also have questions to ask her that still require answers. Then wait a day or two, re-read the letter as if through her eyes and access her inner voice that you carry inside you to write a response as you expect or hope she would. Focusing lovingly on the mother who was striving to reach out to you, however imperfectly, may help you find this voice. What would she say to this daughter who also responded imperfectly to her overtures?

Second, consider how you might seek to grow closer to her over time, rather than only more distant. How might you invite further positive "inner conversations" with her, whether through AfterTalk exchanges or in the privacy of your own thoughts? What sorts of memories of her of a healing kind might you access and share with others? How might you take her with you into the world, perhaps by visiting places special to you both, that help restore a connection? How might you live in a way that would make her mother's heart proud of the daughter she bore and who has a chance to live a life with less pain and struggle than her own? All of these things are based on the idea that even though a person dies, a relationship doesn't die—it just changes how it is expressed. And great healing can come with living it well.

Finally, bear in mind that psychotherapy evolved, in large part, to help us sort out complicated relationships with our parents, even though the history of our troubled bonds might now be remote or the parent might no longer be living. This implies that you might readily find professional assistance in coming to better terms with a complicated life with your mother, both before and after her death. Time alone won't transform your connection with her, but working on your own or with others, you certainly can do so.

—Dr. Neimeyer

## My Husband's Daughter Accused Him of Molesting Her

*Dear Dr. Neimeyer,*

My husband passed away suddenly and unexpectedly over two years ago. I am in a lot of emotional pain, but that's not why I am writing.

Three decades ago my husband's daughter accused him of molesting her; this recollection had come to her, she said, during a course of psychotherapy. He said it wasn't true, and he did not exhibit any emotional overreactions or defensive attitudes; I had never had any reason or indication at all to think that he had pedophilic tendencies, and I believed him. It was during the height of the satanic ritual abuse panic, and his daughter's therapist was in the business of extracting these kinds of memories. A few years later she seemed to be coming around to the view that they were false memories.

Now, just this week, his daughter emailed me (we are not in touch) to bring this matter up again. When I asked her what had caused her to come back to this way of thinking, she went off in a diatribe to say that I had no idea how many people my husband had hurt, that she was being kind not telling me the true story, but she would, etc. I do not think any of it is true, and I certainly had found nothing in his papers, files, computer entries, souvenirs and the like after his passing to suggest anything untoward at all; not that I had been looking—this is only in retrospect. We had a very loving marriage, and he will be my partner as long as I live. But this situation is very hurtful to me, and I don't know why his daughter is invading my life in this way. I would very much appreciate your assessment and suggestions for how to deal with it and with my emotional responses to it.

With thanks and appreciation,

**Wanda**


*Dear Wanda,*

I can imagine that this accusation is unsettling in several senses, because of the corrosive conflict it introduces into your relationship with your stepdaughter, because of the way it assaults your deceased husband's reputation and perhaps, but not necessarily, because of any seeds of doubt it plants regarding his behavior in relation to his daughter years before you arrived on the scene. In a smaller but still significant way, it also might well undermine your faith in counseling to the extent that your stepdaughter's therapist could have inadvertently reinforced the apparent validity of memories of abuse that were vague or altogether imagined. This latter effect would be regrettable if it discouraged you from consulting with a therapist who could actually help you sort through this complicated family dynamic in which you might well feel caught in the middle between the living and the dead.

To seek clarity in the midst of this painful confusion, let's begin by considering the facts as best psychological science can establish them. First, there are few things as unreliable as eyewitness testimony, as any criminal lawyer can attest. Memories are not recordings of events as they happened; they are reconstructions in the present in light of current emotions and motivations. This does not mean that they are simply falsehoods or that people who report dramatic or traumatic events are maliciously lying—though of course, this too may sometimes be the case. More commonly, we as human beings tend to recall details that fit our sense of how something happened, selectively recalling details without consciously intending to do so in order to support their current story and then invisibly filling in the gaps with assumptions that we mistake for truths. This is so even when we are trying to recall in detail the specific actions that constituted our having breakfast this morning, and it is certainly the case when we as adults are attempting to reconstruct memories of events that occurred in our early childhood. Complicating this cognitive reality is a social one: remembering is an interpersonal process, one in which the questions, intentions and convictions of another can easily influence what we remember and what sense we make from it.

Now let's place this well-documented psychological fact up against another one: the best estimates of the occurrence of childhood sexual abuse suggest that perhaps one-third of all women have been sexually abused in some form in childhood, the majority of them by a family member. This sobering statistic means that the chances are good that if someone is reporting abuse, the claim should be taken seriously—even if not accepted uncritically. In legal arenas where such claims are investigated, careful protocols to establish the evidence for the accusation are followed, with the pursuit of evidence of wrongdoing sought in tangible form (photographs, videos), medical records (injuries compatible with the claimed abuse) and corroborating testimony (similar claims against the same defendant, as in recent clergy abuse scandals). Here, of course, you have found no such evidence in your own attempts to investigate your stepdaughter's claims, and no further legal action is in any case possible. So, the issue is necessarily one to be dealt with therapeutically, rather than in a court of law.

What, then, might be done? Very likely the answer will be different for you and your stepdaughter, just as your predominant emotional response to your husband's death has been different. For her, it sounds as if she will need to come to terms with a relationship with a father that was at minimum deeply disappointing and at worst actively abusive, and perhaps marked by a sense of abandonment if she blames him for leaving her mother if it were a case of divorce. Grief therapy could make a contribution to that by providing her a forum for safely venting her hurt, anger and resentment, while also reclaiming power to direct her own life as an adult, seek compassionate understanding for the little girl she was and to make wise and safe choices as she seeks out trustworthy relationships in the present. Note that such therapy would not require the therapist to have a "God's-eye view" of the reality of any abuse suffered but would instead work with the feelings and conclusions your stepdaughter lives with, as they are what constitute what is psychologically real for her. A skillful and compassionate therapist can be a great ally in winning freedom from the grip of events we can neither verify nor change.

But of course, for you, the process of grieving will be different. Your emotional pain is as real as your stepdaughter's, even if it is of a very different kind. You have every right to mourn the man you knew and loved, to contend with the loneliness of living without him and perhaps to work to come to terms with any human failings that he showed in his marriage to you, even if in other respects the relationship was a precious and unique one for you both. Grief therapy might therefore also be useful to you, helping you claim the legitimacy of your loss, while in effect granting your stepdaughter the right to her grieving process, as you also require her to grant you the right to yours. It would be an unfortunate further loss if granting this space to you both resulted in greater distance between you, especially if you once enjoyed a history of closeness that would gratify you both to reaffirm in the years that remain. But this more hopeful outcome would require the assent of both parties and a mature and compassionate stance on both sides to acknowledge that although you have had the same loss, you do not have the same grief.

—Dr. Neimeyer

## A Family Cutoff

*Dear Dr. Neimeyer,*

My husband passed away five years ago. It was right before our oldest son graduated from high school and our youngest son was eight. My oldest son graduated with a degree in electrical engineering last year. My oldest son, I believe, bottled up everything; he won't even talk to me or his little brother. My youngest and I went to grief therapy through a local hospice. It helped us learn that it is okay to talk about Dad. Also, that we would have good days and bad days.

What I would like to know is how do I communicate to my oldest son? He moved to another state right before the holidays without a goodbye or anything. I'm still his mom, I love him to the moon and back. Every time I think of him I hurt. I hurt for my youngest son too.

**Selena**

*Dear Selena—*

Your heartfelt anguish for what amounts to a double loss comes through clearly in your letter: not only has your husband passed away, the father of your children, but you also feel as if you have lost your older son, as he protectively withdraws from the pain to great geographical and emotional distance. It is hardly surprising, then, that you ache when you think of this young man, both for yourself and out of empathy for his younger brother.

In view of this, your apt phrase that you love your son "to the moon and back" is strangely fitting—even if that distant moon is in another state. Some things require considerable time and patience to resolve, and the distance that can open up between family members following the death of someone who might once have been the bridge is one of these. A first step, then, might be to take a fearless inventory of the reasons your older son might have pulled away: Is his style of grieving stronger and stoic, whereas your own and that of your younger son is more expressive? Did he feel overprotected by you as he headed into college and beyond? Did he blame you in some way for the death or cultivate anger over some circumstance associated with his father's illness or manner of dying? Understanding as best you can the reasons for his seemingly angry cut-off could give you a clearer idea of how to reach out to him, beyond reasserting your love.

Prior to writing or calling your older son, you might find it helpful to talk with a family therapist who specializes in loss who lives near you, who should be able to talk through the questions raised earlier, clarify your feelings about this apparent rejection and help you craft a style and strategy of response that is appropriate to the unique relational challenges that can arise in the wake of a death in the family. Most basically, however, you may want to extend love and understanding to him, with no immediate pressure to write or call back—merely an invitation to do so at a time that feels right to him. Be sure to express an interest in his life and include photos of you and his brother as an emotionally evocative reminder of the family that loves him still. Few such cut-offs last forever, particularly when the parent adopts an open-armed, accepting stance that makes it feel "safe" to return. With love and patience, I trust you will find your way back as a family to greater wholeness, even after this devastating mutual loss.

—Dr. Neimeyer

# Part 3

# HOW WE LOSE

As any reader of this book will recognize, grief is a function not only of who we lose but also of how we lose them. Ample evidence attests to the traumatic impact of violent deaths—such as by suicide, overdose, homicide or fatal accidents. But deaths by wasting illness and sudden deaths arising from natural causes such as heart attack or stroke pose their own great challenges for mourners, as they frequently impose the burden of caregiving on the one hand or deny mourners the prospect of tending their loved ones at the end of life on the other. Questions in this part of the book engage these issues, blending common complications arising from the circumstances of the death with distinctive features of the authors' relationship to the deceased.

Readers interested in further web-based resources relative to different causes of death are encouraged to explore the list provided by AfterTalk at the following link: https://www.aftertalk.com/grief_organizations.

# 10
# FATAL ILLNESS

## Loss of a Young Child to Autoimmune Disorder

*Dear Dr. Neimeyer,*

I lost my daughter, a 12-year-old, Melissa, three weeks ago today. Earlier this summer she was diagnosed with a rare autoimmune disorder but was in good health—at least we thought. But when she got her first treatment, within a week she was in the CVICU [cardiovascular intensive care unit] and then we had to make the heart-wrenching decision to take her off the machines two weeks later because her heart was severely damaged. My question is this: I have read about the steps of grieving, but I am so all over the place. I feel guilty, like I failed her as a Mom. I'm sad and have difficulty eating and sleeping. Is this normal for sudden loss and since it just happened? I do not even know what to do or how to grieve. I'm just so confused!

**Felicia**

*Dear Felicia,*

First, throw out everything you've read about "the steps of grieving." Your steps will be your own, not the idealized progression that begins with denial, advances to bargaining, shifts to anger, collapses into depression and then progresses toward acceptance. As you say, you "are all over the place," and the map you might draw of your grief journey will surely contain many strong emotions (like guilt, but also yearning, anxiety, despair and more), all in a confusing and unstable tumult of feelings. Your world has been violated, your daughter tragically taken from you and all others who love her. Profound grief is an appropriate response to such a loss.

So the immediate question is what you need now to weather this hurricane-force storm of anguish. To begin with, very basic self-care may be an early priority: eating even when you don't feel like it, getting some temporary help from your doctor to get some restorative nightly sleep, striving to find your way back to basic routines. In addition, many parents in the throes of anguish over losing a child find solace in one another's company, as they wrestle with similar questions and feelings and seek the companionship of the only people who really "get it"—one another. Groups like The Compassionate Friends, Bereaved Parents of the USA and similar mutual support groups that can be found readily on the internet can provide a great deal of tangible assistance and information that can reduce the confusion and sense of aloneness that mothers and fathers contending with this uniquely hard loss face. And if you find after some months that you seem to be heading in the wrong direction, in the sense of falling apart rather than gradually pulling yourself together, or if family relationships begin to suffer serious damage as a result of different ways of coping, then these same bereaved parents are often a good source of referral information to mental health professionals who can help you with the hard challenges of making sense of this tragedy and your life in its aftermath.

Above all, remember that you did not rob Melissa of the life she deserved; a rare and random medical condition did that. Your task now is to carry on for your family and for her, keeping her close in a heart that mends and enlarges to contain both life and loss, while still making a place for her.

—Dr. Neimeyer

## Ambiguous Losses: A Brother's Cancer Diagnosis

*Dear Dr. Neimeyer,*

Five years ago my younger brother, Eric, was diagnosed with cancer, though he was only 15 at the time. Our life as a family seemed to change overnight, as we all were faced with the fear of what this might mean, and my parents became totally absorbed in his chemotherapy, hospitalizations and care. As the healthy child, I understood, but I had to pretty much fend for myself as I finished high school and tried not to make many demands on my parents and to be helpful with my brother. Mostly I've done fine, but I miss the closeness we once had as a family, as everyone has been so focused on Eric's treatment, and I've sort of had to become an independent adult. Now I'm finishing college, which makes me anxious about what will come next for me, because school has always been my "safety zone." But I don't want to trouble them about it, even now that Eric seems to be in remission.

I'm not even sure that what I feel about loss of closeness or security is grief or not, because no one has died. But I guess I am just trying to sort out where I am now and what, if anything, I can do about it. Thanks for any thoughts you can offer.

**Sandy**

*Dear Sandy,*

One of the hard things about difficult transitions like the one associated with your brother's cancer diagnosis is that we have little language and few rituals to recognize them: unlike losses through death, where nearly everyone acknowledges our grief, offers support and joins us in memorializing our loved one, serious illness and other unwelcome changes often go unnoticed, or are even actively avoided as uncomfortable topics by those outside our family. For this reason, grief counselors often refer to these as "ambiguous losses" that commonly lack recognition or validation, though they are very real to those who suffer them. And among other reactions, they clearly can engender real grief.

In your case, like many siblings of an ill child, you seem to have encountered secondary losses that are easily missed or minimized by others, even your parents, as they mobilize to provide lifesaving care to Eric. In such a case, it is not surprising that you felt a loss of family connection, having had to deal with many smaller-scale challenges on your own without "burdening" your preoccupied parents. Now, as you face another major life transition as your brother's condition stabilizes, you have an opportunity to step back toward the family, perhaps especially during the coming holiday season. There is much to share and celebrate in Eric's apparent recovery and your pending college graduation, and finding understanding and hopeful words to secure once more bonds of love that were frayed by the illness may be the greatest gift you could give one another this year. Your ability to write me about this in compassionate rather than angry terms suggests you are ready to take this important step from ambiguous loss to clear gain . . . for all of you.

—Dr. Neimeyer

## Holding Onto Good Memories

*Dear Dr. Neimeyer,*

My 26-year-old son died seven years ago after a prolonged battle with a malignant brain tumor. I was his caretaker. He was my first child and my only son. Our relationship was magnificent. I cannot get a grip on the good memories. I am constantly thrown into memories of one of his grand mal seizures or the vivid memories of the day he died. How do I grab the good stuff? He was a very funny, very good man and extremely well supported by his community. I miss him so much. I have a broken heart. I do have both talk therapy and psychiatric care.

**Leah**

*Dear Leah,*

Even with the brief glimpses you offer of the course of this illness that you aptly describe as a battle, it is easy to imagine that you suffered keenly alongside your son as the whole family contended with this incurable form of brain malignancy. Although some of his symptoms likely were mitigated by treatment, it is clear that many were not, and the seizures you mention must have served as a vivid and traumatic reminder of the limits of medical care and your own ability to spare him the ravages of this illness. That he grew to be a decent and well-loved man, and one who cultivated a unique sense of humor despite the presence of the disease, speaks volumes about him, as does the obvious depth of your connection to each other.

And so, there is a kind of double tragedy in feeling as if the good memories of his quarter-century of living have died with him. Sadly, this is often the case when the manner of dying was traumatic, when visual images of what was witnessed or imagined overshadow memories of the life that was ended. In such cases more is needed than supportive talk therapy or antidepressant medication, though these may have a role. What is often required is a trauma-informed therapy, one that specifically helps the bereaved person take in and master the horrific imagery so that the warm, proud and loving memories can come through.

One such practice is called "restorative retelling," essentially a slow-motion review of the event story of the dying—and in your case, perhaps the terrifying imagery of the seizures as well. A therapist trained in this method of prolonged exposure can help you stand in the distress through the use of breathing exercises or other means of self-soothing, while you give voice to the visual, auditory and other sensory details of the traumatic and troubling moments in that account, sometimes doing so in 10- to 15-minute intervals that are repeated across sessions, and sometimes in one or two more substantial immersions in the story. The goal is to give voice to precisely the parts of the story that have been silenced in an attempt to protect others or the teller herself, rather than try to suppress them. A good deal of research suggests that such suppression actually makes distressing emotions and images all the more preoccupying, as they seem to press into consciousness with the demand for fuller processing.

Obviously, this approach, along with other exposure-based therapies like EMDR (eye movement desensitization and reprocessing), which requires holding the images in mind but not necessarily giving them voice, is strong medicine. As such, it is wise to be accompanied by a therapist to help prevent the feelings that are triggered from becoming overwhelming. Personal journaling about the painful details of the death, alternating with sessions in which the therapist assists with reviewing the written story, can also be valuable. But whatever your form of exposure to the trauma story, recognize that you are in effect clearing away the dark cobwebs of your son's death that currently obscure your view of his life, making room for the consolidation of healing and loving memories of him in conversations and rituals, as described in other discussions of "legacy projects" included in letters to other readers. In this way, if well accompanied, you can reach through the darkness toward the light and find a more sustainable way of holding him.

—Dr. Neimeyer

## Guilt and Grief: A Husband's Long Decline

*Dear Dr. Neimeyer,*

I am married to a man more than a dozen years older than I am, and through most of our four decades together he has been the strong one who has taken care of most things. Over the last decade he has had many surgeries. He has many different things wrong, but not one disease that says an end is near. He has had prostate cancer, surgery with that and then it returned, so radiation. He has had his hip, shoulder, wrist and just recently his knee replaced. His heart is always in a-fib [atrial fibrillation]. He is [in his] mid-70s. Since a few years ago, I have slowly taken over everything. And the things I cannot do are just not getting done. He thinks he is OK, but I have seen such change. I have lost a lot of my friends, because he will drink (only three or four drinks a day) and starts arguing and there is no talking to him or calming him in the moment. He has had three TIAs [transient ischemic attacks], so I believe he has vascular dementia. He is so medicated with heart pills, blood thinners, antidepressants. I know I am rambling, but I guess my question is, what do you do when you have someone who has many issues but not just one disease, and I feel guilt each time he seems like he is getting better, because I know it won't last long.

**Dolores**

*Dear Dolores,*

I am struck by the many losses you and your husband have had to face—of his health, one condition at a time, and of his ability to provide a sense of security to you as a strong and in-control life partner. Now, over a period of seven or eight years, so much has changed as his health has eroded, and with it your own responsibilities have grown in number and heaviness. Complicating all of this seems to be the sense that you have already lost much of the husband you knew to the fog of medication and alcohol, and perhaps encroaching dementia as well. In the face of all this, you could be forgiven for finding hope in his recovery difficult to sustain.

How might you handle this slow slide toward loss and the many very real losses you yourself have already sustained? One answer is to begin with self-compassion: your husband surely must be suffering the losses of his autonomy, competence and physical integrity, and each of these has ushered in equally substantial losses of freedom, security and more for you. If a friend were in your shoes, what might you do for her and what caring counsel might you offer? Ultimately this might include some form of self-care for yourself, so that you might also better provide support for your husband. For example, many cities have specific day treatment facilities that can provide respite care for families, engaging even cognitively challenged older adults in meaningful activities, while also giving family caregivers the hours off they require to restore some semblance of normality, friendship and practical functioning in their lives while knowing their loved one is in good hands. A further benefit of such a program would be its role in curbing your husband's drinking, which likely grows more significant in isolation.

Whether you seek respite through professional services onsite, in your home or from a friend, it could be valuable to consider what your husband needs as well. Though he might defensively put on a brave face—even belligerently at times—it seems clear that he is also suffering from the cascade of losses and what must feel like the growing specter of helplessness and death. Consulting a therapist together about how best to manage his illnesses, and perhaps even talking through healthcare decisions going forward, could help you both open communication about necessary things, ideally helping rebuild a sense of teamwork that you seem to have enjoyed for decades, as life now presents so many new challenges.

—Dr. Neimeyer

## Anticipatory Grief

*Dear Dr. Neimeyer,*

If you have been experiencing anticipatory grief for a loved one, once they die do you still experience normal grief? Or is it all combined within the anticipatory? I have a daughter who is a medical guinea pig, and as far as we can tell she is the oldest surviving person in Australia to have had corrective surgery on transposition of the great arteries. Due to the form of surgery we have been told that she will have a massive heart attack before she is 40, and she turns 30 this year. I have tried not to dwell on this too often, but as I am doing my degree for Counselling and I am covering the course of Grief and Loss it has been a constant with me.

**Victoria**

*Dear Victoria,*

What a hard path your family has had to walk for what I presume has been the majority of your daughter's life. And like so many families with a member facing a grave and uncertain health risk, it is very likely a path walked with great anxiety that spikes at times of symptoms, medical assessments and procedures and likely diminishes during periods of more normal functioning. But I imagine that it never truly goes away, hovering somewhere at the edge of awareness for you, for her and for others who love her, even during periods of relative calm. Susan Roos writes about this in her eloquent book, *Chronic Sorrow*, which describes well this normal reaction to an abnormal circumstance: a living loss without clear boundaries that continues to shadow one's life.

And of course, you are apt in describing your response as a form of anticipatory grief, as you acknowledge the hard reality that you could well outlive your precious child. As real as this grief is, it is unlikely to eliminate the grief that could follow her actual death, if indeed she does predecease you. It could, however, blunt some of the shock that complicates premature loss and, most importantly, prompt you now to treasure moments together, to speak honestly and compassionately with one another and other family members about things of importance and to generally strive to live in a way that minimizes regrets and missed opportunities. Our research and experience with families anticipating loss further teach us that those families who cultivate social support for their grieving, who are comfortable with intimacy and closeness, who are able to make sense of the loss, perhaps even in medical terms, and who draw on a consistent spiritual or philosophical frame of reference prior to the loss are at less risk of complicated grief during bereavement. Your outreach for support and understanding, evident even in your writing to me, suggests that you are pursuing a healthy path even in the shadow of a threatening illness.

Dr. Neimeyer

## Suicidal Thinking

*Dear Dr. Neimeyer,*

My attention was recently drawn to your website, and especially this section of it, and I now have a great desire to ask for your help.

My beloved husband wanted to die at home. We had been married for over 50 years, and he had suffered with lung cancer and eventually dementia for nearly seven years. With a little help, I looked after him at home, with the help of a nurse who I consider "midwifed" his last hours in his own bed.

I cannot get over my overwhelming sense of loss and grief, despite quite a lot of counselling. I always knew that my husband had rescued me from a childhood home of sexual abuse when I was a teenager, providing me with a sense of safety, reassurance and quiet steady love. I had a good life with him, with interests and hobbies outside my home, although I was almost his only interest. With his death I lost my sense of safety in life, and I know so clearly now that I just do not want to be alone. Mostly, I want to be dead. I have no religious beliefs and I find myself turning more and more to the idea of suicide, because although I have tried to make a new life for myself, I don't want one. I have children, who seemed afraid of their father's illness and did not help with the caring work when he was alive, although they visited regularly then. Now they seem to prefer not to visit, even when I suggest I would like some help, telling me that I can look after myself. And I can; I just don't want to.

How can I turn myself around now? Or rather, maybe, how can I make myself want to stay alive?

**Andrea**

*Dear Andrea,*

First, let me emphasize what should be obvious: that my necessarily brief answer to your overwhelming grief and growing suicidal resignation is no substitute for direct, face-to-face professional intervention and support. You refer to "quite a lot of counseling," and I am hopeful that you are still engaged in that and with a therapist you view is fully competent and trustworthy. If not, I urge you to find such a therapist in your community, as well as a psychiatrist skilled in evaluating and treating depression. It is clear that the loss of your dear husband has been devastating for you, and you need and deserve the same quality of care from a professional team that you and others provided to him during his own period of suffering.

Finding alternatives to the tunnel vision that leads to suicide as the only solution would be the first priority of such work, and you might well find that antidepressant medication makes a contribution to lifting the sense of hopelessness with which you may contend. Medication is surely not a sufficient answer to the challenges this loss raises for you, but it can make it possible to stick around long enough for the other answers to appear.

Second, much of your letter underscores the very special sense of safety and security your husband provided for over half a century, against the backdrop of a harsh and abusive childhood. No doubt that greatly accentuates the sense of aloneness you feel now. I will not trivialize the impact of the loss of his physical presence in your life by suggesting that you can find someone to "replace" him; we both know that such love is irreplaceable. But I would counsel you to look deeply within, in a quiet moment of radical honesty, and ask yourself the question, "What did my husband give me that has enduring value? What did our 50+ years of quiet, steady love install or instill in me that is with me still?" I very much doubt that the answer is, "Nothing." Almost certainly he gave you a unique sense of validation, of worth, a sense that you have value, preciousness. What did he discern in you that goes even beyond his relational gift to you? Meditating on these things, perhaps with a trusted therapist, could provide the strands of continuity—his lasting gift, your enduring value—from which you might begin to reweave the fabric of your life now.

Finally, Viktor Frankl once famously said, after surviving the Nazi concentration camps, "He who has a 'why' for living can withstand nearly any 'how.'" In other words, to the radical questions posed earlier, you might add another: "What now might be the meaning of my life, even as I work through this suffering? What purpose might I pursue, of which my husband would be proud?" This goes beyond hobbies or staying busy, as it requires listening for the clear note that resounds through the static of our grief, that calls us to what now is ours to do. Perhaps this involves relational gifts of your own, like those your husband gave you, whether these would be conferred on a child, a grandchild or someone in need who you have not yet met. Finding this renewed or revised reason for living is the strongest bulwark against the tragedy of suicide and the inevitable scars it leaves in the hearts and minds of the living. My hope is that you will seek and find the compassionate counsel you require to do the hard work outlined earlier and win back a life of richness and joy that honors your husband's lasting contribution to your life and invites the engagement of many relevant others—children included—in the next chapter of your ongoing story.

—Dr. Neimeyer

# 11
# FATAL ACCIDENT

### Loss of a Son in a Car Accident

*Dear Dr. Neimeyer,*

A few months ago, I sadly lost my boy, 18 years old, in a car accident. I have been having bereavement counseling but struggling to build up a rapport. So a friend suggested this site. Since it happened, I have been struggling with anxiety and panic attacks, something I have never suffered with before. Is this normal, and why does it happen? Stephen wasn't just my boy; he was also my best friend. We rarely argued but when we did it was normally because I was worried about him for one reason or another. He was a hard-working boy and had many friends. He was kindhearted and loved by many. So, why can't I remember any of the good times, holidays, etc.? When I try to remember them, the bad things overshadow them, such as imagining the accident and reliving the police knocking at the door. I constantly feel on the edge of tears, and I torture myself by sitting in his bedroom and smelling his clothes. I want to know that wherever he is, he is happy and understands what's happened.

I know no one can probably answer any of my questions but I would really like to hear how people have coped in similar situations. I'm a paramedic and the thought of going back to work and having to deal with similar jobs fills me with dread. I know Stephen wouldn't want me to leave my job, and I hope in time I will be in a better position and the thought of going back to work won't scare me quite so much. I look forward to hearing from you.

**Ellen**

*Dear Ellen,*

First and foremost, being only a few months beyond the death of your son, much of your anguish and anxiety is easily understandable, and altogether normal. Your world has been ripped apart by a tragic loss, and your heart with it. In the wake of such an experience, it is important to be patient with yourself and also with others who are touched in their own ways by Stephen's death; no one—least of all yourself—should expect you to have put back together the pieces of your old world, something an eternity will not do. But here, let me offer a few answers to your questions in the form of principles that could serve you as you gradually find a way to move toward an entirely different future than the one you had imagined.

1. *Find the right guide.* If you are still "struggling to find rapport" with your grief counselor after a couple of sessions, you are seeing the wrong person. Just as each of us gravitates toward different people for friends or mates, so too we need to find the right match with our therapist. I commonly tell people who consult me that they will know by the end of a single session if the connection *won't* work and they will know within three if it *will*. If after a few sessions you still don't feel understood or helped, simply decline to reschedule and look for another therapist for a single session of "consultation." If that goes well, schedule a few more.
2. *Accept the anxiety.* You are now living in a world made alien by loss, and a certain level of anxiety is an appropriate response. Moreover, we have evolved as a species to form natural bonds of caregiving to our children, and when we are separated from them, we experience an internal sense of alarm that cues us to restore the bond. Grief is in large part separation anxiety and given the impossibility of saving your son from his fate, it calls for reestablishing a new kind of bond that is feasible now, as noted next.
3. *Cultivate friendship.* We all need support in our grief and in our changed lives. Your need for friendship did not end with your son's life. Cultivate connections with caring others, even as you also honor your son's memory and impact on the world. Opening your heart to others does not mean closing it to him.
4. *Integrate the trauma.* When someone we love dies suddenly and violently, we often relive images of the death, even when we were not there to witness it. Trauma therapists can help us safely revisit, take in and make sense of the story of the dying, which if not integrated in this way can continually intrude into and eclipse memories of a more restorative, positive kind. Note that many grief counselors will not have been trained to provide this sort of intervention, which goes beyond emotional support for grieving, per se. When seeking a therapist, look for one specializing in trauma, ideally with expertise in grieving as well.
5. *Rebuild the bond.* The image of you sitting in the bedroom smelling his clothes speaks powerfully to your maternal urge to reconnect with your son. Slowly his smell will fade, but your need to build a bridge to him

will not. So, don't limit it to the small space of his bedroom; carry this intention into the bigger world. Find the people and places that will let you speak his name, share his stories, keep his memory alive. Some of these may be with family, some with friends, some in internet support groups for bereaved parents. Still more, seek dedicated actions that you can engage to honor his kind heart—perhaps carrying forward some purpose or interest you shared with him or performing acts of kindness or altruistic social action in his name. By living your life well, you can carry his forward in good ways. Grief therapists can also help you have healing symbolic conversations with your son as you speak the words in your heart and then pause to sense how he would answer.

6. *Return to work, one step at a time.* Especially given your work as a paramedic, you face the same sort of trauma triggers that a returning police officer would after being shot in the line of duty or a soldier in combat would face going back on patrol. So get the trauma-informed care that can help you step gradually back into this important but challenging work, usually by prolonged exposure in imagination or virtual reality to the sights, sounds and smells of accident sites and then a partial return to the workplace, collaborating with your supervisor to visit the hospital, then sit in the ambulance, then accompany colleagues on a call, etc., as you learn to breathe through the fear at each step. Simply returning to work without this preparation can be retraumatizing, but attempting to avoid all of the triggers could not only cost you your career but also require a claustrophobic seclusion to avoid exposure to driving, TV shows and movies and the myriad other reminders that life is fragile and of the great loss you have suffered. Think "approach" rather than "avoid," and with patience you can re-enter life with less fear.

—Dr. Neimeyer

## A Case of PTSD?

*Dear Dr. Neimeyer,*

I have a question, please. I lost my 16-year-old son in an accident only 15 months ago. I can hardly walk through this house of memories, so I stay isolated in one room. I do not want to be bothered. My mom lives here and has taken over for a bit. I have two other children (adopted niece and nephew) ages 14 and 11. I feel terrible I can't give them quality time; I just can't right now. I remember very little of the last three months, but during the last two weeks I've been getting horrible flashbacks of the night my son died. I know it's real, but it feels like a dream. My heart won't accept it. He was my son and best friend. I'm lost, broken, yet I cannot break down! Why? God and

Jesus give me strength and are the only reason I'm still here. Why do I want to be isolated? Could it be PTSD [posttraumatic stress disorder]? Sorry for so many questions.

Thank you & God bless!

**Andrea**

*Dear Andrea,*

As I read the text of your question, I can't help but imagine the many painful dimensions of this loss for you, some of which focus on the suddenness and circumstances of the death and some of which center on the irreplaceable relationship you had with your son. Just as you suspect, grief can indeed come bundled together with PTSD when we are flooded by intrusive memories and images of the death scene, whether we personally witnessed it or imagine it vividly in our minds or dreams. At the same time, in losing the child who was your "best friend," you lost a key person who would otherwise have supported you through other life crises and transitions. All of this suggests that your grief is doubly complicated and calls for attention to both the "event story" of the loss and the "back story" of your relationship with your son.

Regarding the traumatic story of the death, you might find it helpful to consult with a therapist who specializes in the treatment of PTSD, who can help you bravely review and process the troubling images and associated emotions of fear, horror and helplessness that are linked to the tragic accident. This in-therapy work would best be linked with in-home work on your own or with the support of family to help you push back against the urge to self-isolate and, in small steps taken 30 minutes at a time, begin to re-enter the other parts of your home and confront the memories they hold. Although painful, this effort to reclaim your world is essential to your effort to move forward in your life and reengage those you love, including your living children. In contrast, it is well established that avoidance of reminders of the loss tends to prolong intense grief, preventing us from "relearning the world" in the wake of deeply unwelcome change.

The second dimension of your grief—the unique loss of a special relationship with your son—also calls for attention. If you are reading online resources like AfterTalk, you have already taken the first steps toward acknowledging your grief and reaching toward the sort of changed connection to your son that is still possible now. From the way you describe your unique bond, it is clear that your son continues to live in your heart, and cultivating a meaningful connection to what he means to you is just what AfterTalk is designed to help you do. A further step, then, might be to write a letter to him, describing how you have felt and functioned after his death and asking for his counsel in what you might now do to make it better. What would he tell you about what still has value in your life? About how you can find the courage to step over the threshold of your grief into a world that also contains hope and love? About what you still have to offer to your living children? How might he use your shared spirituality to offer you consolation or support? By imagining and writing a response from him to you, you can draw on his wisdom, love and compassion in finding steps forward in the difficult terrain of your bereavement.

Dr. Neimeyer

## Deadly Car Accident Takes Two Daughters

*Dear Dr. Neimeyer,*

I was recently in a deadly car accident that took the lives of my two beautiful, funny and loving baby girls, ages six and eight. The accident also resulted in my surviving teenage daughter being a paraplegic and my husband having a TBI [traumatic brain injury] and several fractures in his face, arm, leg and hip. He's non-weight bearing on three limbs and is also wheelchair bound. I was the least injured with a broken leg and arm and am no longer using any assistive devices.

Nighttime is the worst for me. I have PTSD from the accident and relive it almost every night. I'm back in the car, looking around, telling my teenager that everything will be okay and that the ambulance is on the way. I look to see my unresponsive husband face down on the steering wheel, but snore-breathing. I hear my youngest crying, telling her teenage sister to "get off" of her but my teenager could not move, I just continued to tell them that it will be okay and help is on the way. I saw a pedestrian with my eight-year-old, lying on the ground outside of the car after other pedestrians took all of my kids out. When the ambulance finally arrived and put my oldest daughter on a stretcher, I saw her pale blue arm fall to the side as she looked asleep. I had no idea that my kids were that bad off. I just yelled to the paramedics "please hurry, she's turning blue!" I had all the faith that in their care, my kids would be fine.

I was the last to be taken, and due to my small collapsing veins, no meds were given to me. The 40-min ride to the hospital was torture as I had an open tib/fib fracture and broken arm/wrist. While in the ER, a nice man introduced himself as a chaplain to tell me that my eight-year-old did not survive. I just cried and could not believe or comprehend what was going on. A while later, two men came to me, one on either side, introducing themselves as chaplains. I just yelled "No!" As he then began to tell me that my six-year-old did not make it. These memories are so vivid, and although my husband has lost over two months of memories at the time of the accident, I wish it were me who did not have the memories sometimes. However, I'm sure that if I did not remember, I'd wish I had . . . I just want to be able to lie down at night, say my prayers, get comfy in bed and fall asleep without reliving that night over and over again. I've been told that medications can help, but I'm hesitant to try them, as I really don't like to take meds. Is there a moment where one decides that NOW is the time to start a medication regimen?

Some days I feel so depressed, angry and cheated. Even while helping my daughter shower, change her clothes or her ostomy bag or even helping her catheterize herself, I feel like my attitude stinks, and she can see it. I fear she thinks I'm angry with her, when I'm really angry at this whole situation. I find that I feel guilty when doing things that bring me joy, and I worry that my responsibilities to help my husband and daughter will prevent me from grieving appropriately, finding meaning or even finding a new hobby (as taking care of my family kept me pretty busy). I mostly worry about allowing my anger build to create relational problems with my husband and daughter.

I'd really like to find a group of grieving mothers to join and a group for my whole family to join (or for my husband and daughter to join individually).

I am a Mental Health Therapist, myself, and am less than a year away from my licensure, but since this accident, everything has been out on hold.

I'm not sure exactly what I'm asking you here, but maybe just some guidance and/or some validation? Thank you for your time.

**Margie**

*Dear Margie,*

I am sure that every reader who absorbs your story with an open heart will feel some version of the great sadness that wells up in me as I read your words; one would be hard put to imagine a loss scenario more graphic, traumatic and heartbreaking than the one you and your family have suffered. In a single horrific accident two precious lives were ended, along with the life the survivors had known to that point, and that lifetime will not return. Any thoughts I offer here presuppose this hard reality: there is no simple fix for a life story so tragically broken as the one you describe. But with effort and support, I am hopeful that a life worth living, and less anguishing, might be reconstructed in its wake.

You ask directly, "Is there a moment where one decides that NOW is the time to start a medication regimen?" Yes, there is, and that time could be now. Antidepressants are at best a partial answer to the many questions posed by your compound loss, as they don't resolve the heavy traumatic overlay of your bereavement or the acute separation distress you must feel in relation to the death of two of your children. But when the right medication and dosage are found—and this may take a few trials with a responsive psychiatrist—it can help establish a stronger emotional foundation under you on which to build. Beware reliance on fast-acting but addictive antianxiety drugs but do consider speaking with a patient and wise physician about antidepressants that can help stabilize your mood over time.

Second, as you are clearly aware, the nightmares of the horrific accident represent the tip of an emotional iceberg that calls for a trauma-informed approach to therapy. Eye movement desensitization and reprocessing (EMDR) and other prolonged exposure therapies, which require you, with therapeutic support, to reengage the hardest details of the accident story, would likely be a core part of such treatment. This requires careful management by a therapist specializing in trauma and its treatment, rather than a generalist counselor or therapist. Ask around, and for a single session, consult with any therapist you consider seeing without commitment to go further. In that session, describe the general details of your experience as you have here, and ask for his or her approach to treatment. Make sure, with his or her response, that two key conditions are met: (1) that you feel safe and understood and (2) that the therapist can offer specific, trauma-focused processing of your horrific experience. Slow-motion review of the imagery and feelings associated with the accident would be key to this, though the specific procedures (prolonged exposure, restorative retelling, EMDR) will vary. If either of these conditions is not met, thank the person for the session, ask to think about it and go elsewhere. More than general support or even grief therapy is needed in the face of losses like yours.

Third, despite the emphasis on the trauma symptoms that therapy might need to tackle first, recognize that profound grief is also central to the suffering you are enduring. Unfortunately, many trauma therapists are unfamiliar with this dimension of therapy, which may entail a close review of your distinctive grief responses for each of your little girls and the reconstruction of a nonphysical bond with them of a psychological and perhaps spiritual kind. This may therefore call for distinctive grief work with a therapist who specializes in this. Inquire widely and consider this as a third step on your road to rebuilding.

Fourth, as you recognize every minute of every day, your grief is about more than even the tragic death of your two youngest daughters: the "living losses" suffered by your daughter and husband greatly compound your bereavement. When the losses keep going and going, with no end in sight, survivors often experience a kind of "chronic sorrow" that defies the usual expectations for grief "recovery" (if indeed one can ever truly use that word when losses are profound). Different from both major depression and angry resignation, chronic sorrow can entail a sense of disillusionment in life, a recognition of our collective vulnerability and an impatience with the petty preoccupations of many in the social world. Integrated in an adaptive way, it can in time become a source of depth and wisdom—though the price paid for this, with no prospect of a refund, continues to feel disproportionate. You might find reading about this and also engagement in some form of caregiver support group helpful in this regard.

And finally, as the months make tragically clear that your old life will never return, strive to hold firm to the knowledge that many people bravely find a way forward through very great adversity to lives that are worth living. Finding support for the caregiving your loved ones will continue to require in a way that permits you to pursue your own career as a mental health counselor (as well as simply find some respite to recharge your badly depleted batteries) will probably need to be a part of this. You cannot tend to your loved ones' lives if you neglect your own. Compassion is the fuel you will need to care for them in the years to come, and self-compassion needs to be the additive required to do so.

—Dr. Neimeyer

## A Teenage Son Is Electrocuted

*Dear Dr. Neimeyer,*

My teenage son was electrocuted at home accidentally almost 20 years ago. My counselor is not happy with my saying he was killed. I know the difference because about three decades ago, another toddler son died from a cerebral aneurysm, so in my eyes one died and one was killed. So to me there are three ways of dying: (1) from old age where the body wears out, (2) from a defective body part or disease and (3) from trauma from an accident, murder, war or suicide. My counselor won't accept my analogy; she prefers that they both just died. Am I wrong in feeling the way that I do and saying it as I see it? I see things as black or white and have trouble seeing gray. I am religious and righteous in my outlook. If I get into heaven, I will be having strong words with our maker, as I hate seeing the young and innocent being struck down, whilst the nasty and wicked are allowed to survive and multiply! I know that I am carrying suppressed anger and I have the ability to forgive myself and others, but I cannot forget.

**Fred**

*Dear Fred,*

The data, as the social scientists say, are on your side. Many studies of the impact of death by various causes document essentially the distinctions you make, as traumatic or violent death losses such as suicide, homicide and fatal accident tend to lead to more severe and enduring forms of grief than do those resulting from natural death. Of course, it is important to recognize that there are many exceptions: the death of a child to any cause is tragic in many senses, and some intentional deaths (as through self-chosen euthanasia) are viewed as peaceful and welcome by many. But in general, "unnatural" losses like those of your adolescent son share many features that increase their traumatic impact, including their suddenness, their violence (even if unintended), the guilt and anger they can engender and complicating issues of human intention or inattention. If we might well say, "My son was killed in a car accident," why wouldn't we use a similar phrasing for an electrical accident?

Of course, as you point out, this is much more than a simple matter of wording; it is a matter of *meaning*. Implied in the idea of traumatic death is that it is radically at odds with our expectation of what a "just" death should be—it shatters our belief in justice, even of a divine sort, and makes a mockery of our usual belief that we can control events and protect those we love from injury. One outcome for many religious people is what we have termed "complicated spiritual grief," which implies that we have suffered not only terrible distress over the death of our loved one but also collateral damage to our belief that God is loving, fair or omnipotent. Instead, we may begin to entertain quite the opposite beliefs—that God is negligent, unpredictable or impotent. Struggling with such questions across many years can certainly compound our suffering, though it might also lead to a deepening of our belief through the revision of our spirituality along new lines. Works by authors such as Harold Kushner, C.S. Lewis and Pema Chodron, each anchored in a different spiritual tradition, are found by many to be helpful companions in this ongoing journey.

—Dr. Neimeyer

## Mother Died in Car Accident While Son Was Driving

*Dear Dr. Neimeyer,*

Thirteen years ago, I experienced a seizure while driving. My mother was killed in the accident. I had an extremely close relationship with my mother. I continue to feel guilty and struggle to make sense of this tragedy.

**Phil**

*Dear Phil,*

Your tragic story, summarized vividly in so few words, conveys the catastrophic convergence of the two roads that often merge to lead toward complicated grief: traumatic loss and broken attachment. In a single violent moment, a once-secure world was shattered for you and seemingly lost along with your mother's life. And no explanation or justification can be found to bandage the wound.

Sometimes we can't "make sense" of a senseless loss, beyond the obvious causal explanation (you had a random seizure at a vulnerable moment and lost consciousness or control, leading to an accident and death). But we can still seek meaning in how we relate to this tragedy. What meaning do you want the accident to have in your life? Will you accept the default conclusion that your life effectively ended with your mother's? Are there vital life lessons to learn from this about the fragility of life and the durability of love? Perhaps more relevantly, what meaning do you want your mother's *life* to have, a life woven so closely together with your own? Does her death cancel out the beauty of that bond, nullify all that she taught, all that she valued, all the good she strived to do during the years she had? If not, how might you review and recover the lessons of that life and give them fuller expression now? Might your doing so, as an expression of her lasting legacy, honor her more than decades of remorse and guilt? Faced with these options, which road would she advise you to take going forward—the one that opens onto new horizons or the current dead end? You have begun this inquiry by writing *me*, but a next step might be writing *her* and having a hard but honest conversation with her about your struggle to seek significance in the wake of her death. As you do so, listen closely to the voice of the mother who still lives in her son for her guidance about the route going forward.

—Dr. Neimeyer

## Advice for a Daughter Who Lost Her Soldier Husband

*Dear Dr. Neimeyer,*

My 23-year-old daughter lost her husband two years ago. He was a soldier and her high school sweetheart. He was killed in a car accident on a military base. She is so lost and devastated. She feels like she has lost her identity and has questioned everything in life now. She has started to self-medicate and is so angry at everyone. I love her [so] much and want to help. What do I do? How can I help her? Feel like I'm walking on eggshells. Any advice or resources would be appreciated.

**Donna**

*Dear Donna—*

Thanks for reaching out on behalf of a daughter whose sudden and traumatic loss clearly turned her world upside down and who apparently has been struggling to find her orientation ever since. Military losses can have many distinctive features in common, whatever the cause of death, as they are nearly always premature, without warning, violent and distant, denying family an opportunity to play the caring role that is possible, for example, with deaths from progressive illness that take place in our presence. Moreover, because the military is a special community whose families are joined in a common lifestyle, and often one of high purpose and meaning, the loss of a loved one is all the more jarring when that entire community is lost along with the service member. Just as your daughter says, such loss entails not only the death of a beloved partner but also the death of one's own identity linked to participation in a network of other military families. The loss of these connections, understandable as this may be, can greatly compound the sense of isolation and anger in one's bereavement.

So, what might your daughter do? Here are three general suggestions:

1. *Reach in.* First, she might reach deeply into herself, taking the "Who Am I?" test. That is, she could find it valuable to begin by writing down four responses to the question: "Who was I before my husband died?" The answers might focus on her beliefs, values, characteristics, things she did or people who were important to her. For example, she might say she believed in working hard to get ahead, valued caring for others, was a runner and regularly spent time with family and friends. Then repeat the exercise focusing on the questions "Who am I now?" and "Who do I want to be in the future?" This can help us reconnect with core, enduring purposes in our lives, to find strands of consistency and also consider what needs to receive more attention for us to find a way back to a life and identity that have meaning for us.
2. *Reach out.* Because military loss is unique, it can help to tap into the special services that are available for those who suffer it. To explore this, check out TAPS—the Tragedy Assistance Program for Survivors [www.taps.org] for military families, which offers a variety of services, from grief counseling, to help with benefits, to a national helpline, to access to care and support groups. Moreover, TAPS offers many ways to connect with others, whether in a one-on-one, community-based, online or peer mentor fashion. Survivor resource kits and a library of materials are likewise available. Connecting with this community of others whose losses share many features with her own could represent a big step forward.
3. *Reach beyond.* Finally, you might suggest to your daughter that she explore the resources also offered by the AfterTalk website. Writing to her husband, and perhaps writing a letter back from him to affirm what he found special about her and to clarify and support how she might

now live in a changed future in a way he would fully support, might be as relevant as the care and encouragement she receives from living people in her life. Tragic as her husband's dying was, it need not end your daughter's life as well.

—Dr. Neimeyer

## Unanswered Questions After the Death of a Husband

*Dear Dr. Neimeyer,*

I lost my husband in an accident over 25 years ago while we were getting ready for his grandmother's funeral. There were so many unanswered questions, as our daughter was only a year old, and she is now nearing 30. But my question is why I still have my moments of tears and sadness. I can talk about it, and I will tear up as if it just happened. I still function, but I feel like I'm not where I ought to be in life. Can you help me understand?

**Connie**

*Dear Connie,*

As you have found, with the death of a loved one, life changes in an instant, but the repercussions can be felt for an eternity. Even though many survivors of sudden loss continue to function, as you have, many also feel vulnerable to a welling up of grief for years or decades when thoughts, conversations or circumstances call our loved one to mind. More seriously, just as you have described, we may also accommodate the loss with a long-term sense of resignation, accompanied by a kind of bleaching out of emotion and meaning, even if we continue to work and provide for our families. This state, sometimes termed "chronic sorrow," can contribute to a sense of not quite fitting in with the broader social world as we fluctuate between avoiding the painful recollection of the death and occasional rumination on it. The result is often a sense of surviving, but not genuinely thriving, in a world made poorer and more tragic by the trauma.

One key to understanding this is provided by my colleague, Therese Rando, who speaks of the "secondary losses" that surround the central and obvious one of our loved one's life. The other losses, implied but unrecognized by many, can haunt us for a lifetime, without the clarity or validation of the central loss itself, which is universally recognized through rituals of commemoration of the dead such as funerals and memorial services and short-term rituals of support for the survivors. In contrast, secondary losses can be nearly invisible yet pervasive: the forever-empty chair at the family table, the gaze of photographs that yellow with time. More painful still than these continuous daily reminders of loss are the periodic vivid reminders that arise when a daughter's graduation, wedding or birth of a grandchild goes unwitnessed by her father, or we anticipate a retirement alone. Finding words for these losses, and an audience with whom to share them, can therefore be a first step toward acknowledging them and finding a way to reinvest in life.

Finally, it can be helpful to recognize that the secondary losses that attend a traumatic death like that of your husband in an automobile accident in which you were present can also include the loss of basic world assumptions, such as the innocent belief that life is just, that the universe is safe and that we have the ability to control events and protect those we love. All too often, these beliefs are lost along with the life of our loved one, and speaking with a counselor who is willing to join us in reviewing and revising our worldview can begin to reopen doors long closed, allowing us to step more fully into an imperfect world that has not lost all its beauty.

—Dr. Neimeyer

## Daughter Accidentally Killed a Young Man

*Dear Dr. Neimeyer,*

My daughter killed a young man when her car ran into his motorcycle. It was determined that the accident was not her fault. Nevertheless, she was so bereaved that we had to take her to a critical care facility. How does someone grieve for someone they don't know? How does someone recover from being responsible for killing someone, not intentionally?

**Lynn**

*Dear Lynn,*

Unfortunately, as your description of your daughter's reaction to this tragedy illustrates, being faultless does not protect us from the traumatic effects of horrific death, particularly when, even through no fault of our own, we were implicated in it. Nor are fatal accidents of the kind you describe the only instance of this anguishing reality, as guilt and trauma commonly attend other violent deaths as well, such as those resulting from suicide. There as well, innocence in a legal sense rarely shields survivors from the punishing emotional consequences that can follow.

However, it is important not to mistake your daughter's response for bereavement, per se, as grief, in the sense of yearning for or experiencing deep loneliness for another, is far less likely to feature in her emotional reaction to the accident than other equally profound responses, such as corrosive self-blame; persistent rumination about the accident punctuated by attempts to avoid reminders of it; and visual, auditory and perhaps somatic flashbacks to the accident, in which she relives it in uninvited intrusive memories or is frequented by related images and emotions in nightmares and night terrors. No amount of well-intentioned rational counterargument is likely to dislodge such symptoms, nor are attempts to suppress them likely to be successful; research indicates that such attempts can actually have a "boomerang" effect and lead to their coming back all the more forcefully. This toxic blend of what is now understood as "moral injury" (witnessing or participating in an act, like killing, that assaults our sense of core values) and trauma (struggling with images, anxiety and hypervigilance associated with the scene of the death) requires different, and stronger, "medicine."

What form would this take? Likely it would require a trauma-informed approach to therapy, in which a specialized therapist would safely walk your daughter through a prolonged recounting of the trauma narrative, either in an extended slow-motion retelling or in multiple briefer ones. The goal of this would be to develop more emotional mastery of the tragic circumstances in all their troubling detail, mindfully reviewing the experience scene by scene with the therapist's support for staying with and gradually modulating spikes of negative emotion (meaning to hold the image until the feeling begins to dial down). There are many different procedures for accomplishing this, some of which use specific breathing methods, self-instructions, therapist stimulation or prompts for making meaning of the chaos of imagery and emotion, but all involve drawing close to the troubling experience under conditions of safety. Sometimes these can be followed by healing actions (in the form of making amends in some fashion with survivors of the deceased) or rituals (such as seeking forgiveness from oneself, from another or from God). The important point is that the specific symptoms or emotions experienced by your daughter will help an expert therapist determine what she most needs as she strives to move through this awful accident, learn from it what she can and attempt to live fully and compassionately in an imperfect world in which we have less control over outcomes than we often wish.

—Dr. Neimeyer

# 12

# SUICIDE AND OVERDOSE

### Survivor Guilt Following a Wife's Suicide

*Dear Dr. Neimeyer,*

My wife took her own life a few months ago, and it has busted me wide open. I'm better than where I was but far from being better. I wrestle with the *coulda, shoulda, woulda* of survivor guilt and anger. I miss her terribly, and now have somewhat come to terms that this will be a lifelong endeavor of trying to heal. We had a bad fight the prior night, and I believe that was the trigger—that and she was messing with her meds. She was a beautiful, vibrant woman of 60, with her whole life ahead of her. I'm in counseling, on meds and in a support group, and they definitely help, but at times I feel so all alone in this wilderness and am weary of this fight.

**Gill**

*Dear Gill,*

When a loved one ends her life in an act of suicide, it leaves us drowning in a sea of questions: Why did this happen? Why did she do this to herself? To other family? To me? What was my role in this tragedy, and how can I ever forgive myself? And with the unanswered and perhaps unanswerable questions come a host of anguishing emotions—shock, confusion, anger, abandonment, shame and guilt being among the most common and intense. And as research, clinical observation and personal experience all suggest, the shock waves of this form of traumatic loss typically are felt across years and decades, rather than weeks and months, and call for patience, self- and other compassion and bravery on the part of surviving family members and those who support them.

You clearly have taken the first crucial steps in responding to this crisis by reaching out not only to me but also to a trusted counselor and support group. In the case of the latter, survivors of suicide loss usually find that consulting with therapists who specialize in traumatic bereavement and participating in mutual support communities that have themselves been touched by this uniquely distressing form of bereavement is important, as they can bring to bear a level of professional expertise and personal understanding that more general forms of counseling or support groups cannot. In addition, it can be wise to consult websites like that of the American Foundation for Suicide Prevention, which offers helpful resources and advice to people who share this hard passage with you: check out https://afsp.org/find-support/ive-lost-someone/.

Above all, recognize that you are not alone: hundreds of thousands of other survivors are experiencing some version of the same feelings and questions that you are and are slowly feeling their way forward toward a life of renewed hope and resilience. The act of suicide is clearly the outcome of multiple factors, which range from the suicidal person's biological disposition toward depression and other forms of mental illness, to substance use or abuse, a troubled upbringing, contemporary stressors, the sense of being a burden to others and more. Resist the temptation to simplify this equation by assuming that the responsibility for this tragedy resides solely with you. Listen instead for the deeper understanding of this trauma that might be gleaned from the wise counsel of professionals, survivors, others who love you and your own heart. Drawing on each, you can find a light beyond this darkness, and in time even grow to be a support to others groping through a darkness of their own.

—Dr. Neimeyer

## Moving on After a Husband's Suicide

*Dear Dr. Neimeyer,*

My husband of over 30 years killed himself over two years ago. I went through survival mode the first year, and now have my life "working" in a sense, but still ruminate too much about "why" and what I could have done to change it. I want peace, to accept that this is what happened to him. But I am the one who has to suffer now, and our children and grandchildren who will never know him. How does one move on?

**Katie**

*Dear Katie,*

I suppose the answer to your final question is, "With difficulty, but with resolve." As a survivor of my own father's suicide when I was young, I became intimately aware of the devastation his death left in its wake. The impact was prolonged and life changing, and my mother's means of coping (numbing her pain with alcohol and clinging anxiously to her three children out of fear of further loss), while understandable, contributed across many years to the complicated post-loss adaptation we experienced. Your ability to get the train of your life back on the rails in a far briefer period paints a more optimistic picture of the future toward which you and your family are moving.

But of course, the corrosive and ruminative self-questioning continues. I have come to understand this not simply as a symptom of prolonged grief to be controlled or eliminated (though it can be that, too), but rather as a signal of what we need in the aftermath of suicide loss—some way to "make sense" of a seemingly senseless death and, more broadly, of the suffering that it introduces into the lives of those most intimately touched by it. In seeking this, we commonly have to do two things that are difficult given the reality of how our minds work: (1) develop radical empathy and (2) accept the limits of human knowing. Neither is easy, though both are possible. Let me therefore share a brief thought about each.

First, *radical empathy* means taking a "deep dive" into the mindset of the other, in this case that of your husband. As incomprehensible as his suicide may be from your standpoint, the challenge is to enter fearlessly into his emotional frame, which by definition made suicide the inescapable choice. However much we might disagree with the "logic" of his decision or imagine other alternatives that could have produced a different outcome, the sad reality is that in that place and moment, he could not. Thus, doing a "psychological autopsy," perhaps assisted by an experienced grief therapist, can give us a deeper, if still painful, understanding of the state of mind and heart that led to his fatal act.

Second, *acceptance of the limits of human knowing* means reconciling ourselves to the incompleteness of our understanding—even understanding what moves and motivates those closest to us. In this life we lack a "God's-eye view" and instead "see as through a glass darkly," in the words of one wisdom tradition. This implies that there are inevitably aspects of critical life events that we will never fully grasp to our satisfaction, and we can rarely discern larger purposes that would "explain" or "justify" such tragedy. Coming to accept the limits of our knowing further implies self-compassion for all we could not understand, predict or control at the time. And finally, it implies acceptance that life involves unavoidable suffering and that, as the Buddhists recognize, this is not our fault.

But this stance of humility in the face of all that is unknowable does not have to lead to despair. It can also lead to learning, as we gradually relinquish asking the unanswerable and ruminative "why" and "why us" questions and make way for other questions that can lead to life-affirming answers. What can I learn from this about what contributes to despair and to hope? What of value can I retain from my shared life story with my loved one, before the dark cloud of self-destruction began to overshadow him? What can I discover about what my children need, and I need, to go through this and emerge as wiser, more compassionate and intentional beings for having done so? And how can we affirm love despite or indeed because of this tragedy in a way that connects us more securely to one another and to the larger life purposes that will keep us going forward, even in the face of future difficulties? Seeking the right companionship in addressing these questions can reinforce and deepen your resilience and help you find meaning in the wake of this tragic loss.

—Dr. Neimeyer

## Suicide and Cancer: A Traumatic Death

*Dear Dr. Neimeyer,*

My brother died a few months ago from suicide. He shot himself in his bed after fighting cancer for two years. The last time I saw him he looked like a skeleton, and the police said he was so dehydrated that there was almost no blood on the sheets. I've been able to manage okay in my daily life, and at least I am retired so I don't have so many demands. But I can't seem to get the pictures of him out of my mind—both my last memory of him wasting away and what I imagine his deathbed scene looked like. His wife doesn't want to talk about it, so I feel so alone with this.

I've started going to a suicide loss support group, and it is good to feel understood by other people who "get it." But I am reluctant to share these troubling images with other group members out of fear of overwhelming them. As a result, I stay silent or just talk generally about how bad I feel and how I can't sleep very well. I feel almost like I am keeping a secret from them by holding back on sharing the imagery, but I tell myself it is for their own good. Some of the people seem so fragile, and others seem like they are "over it," after being in the group for a couple of years, and really [are] there just to help other people out. I trust the couple who runs the group, but don't know if I should say something to them or not.

My question is, should I say something about the pictures in my head that torment me, or will they just fade away over time?

**Carla**

*Dear Carla,*

In some ways, it seems like the circumstances of your brother's death present you with the worst of both worlds—watching helplessly as he was slowly reduced by the cancer, and then receiving the traumatic news of his self-determined death. And the images of both, unlike more typical grief-related sadness and missing of a loved one, may not simply dim with time. In fact, the attempt to suppress intrusive thoughts and images can actually prompt their unbidden return at times when your guard is down, as during sleep and dreaming. So how can you best use your suicide support group to help you through this? Here are a few ideas:

1. *Acknowledge your needs.* In some ways, intrusive thoughts can be seen as intruding for a reason—to receive the attention they require. Being able to invite them in—on your terms—represents a first step. Asking your group leaders for some time to focus on this with the group is appropriate, especially if the group members are genuinely compassionate and understanding.
2. *Ask permission.* With the help of the group leaders, ask the group for some time—perhaps 15 minutes—to share some of the more troubling aspects of your memory of your brother's death. The leaders will probably want to caution members that some of the images may be graphic and difficult and may involve not only what you saw in reality but also what you saw in your fearful reconstruction of the scene in your own mind. If the leaders are comfortable with this, one leader can accompany members who do not feel ready for this explicit discussion to another room, while remaining group members bear witness to your account, listening, asking questions and providing support.
3. *Set a timer.* In advance of the sharing, agree with the group leader on a certain amount of time to spend with this, with 20 to 30 minutes usually offering enough time to let you tell the story and receive what the group has to offer you. Note that the most helpful thing is likely to be the opportunity to speak about what had previously been a silent story, as the group guides you in just "sitting with it," rather than trying to offer simple advice on how to "solve the problem." Setting a time after which the leaders will steer the conversation to others or reconvene the whole group can help make the telling "safe enough" for both you and other members, avoiding the feared possibility of an unbounded, overwhelming traumatic account.
4. *Consider if more is needed.* If your group leaders seem uncomfortable about accommodating your request, recognize that it may say more about their lack of training for handling the retelling of traumatic stories than it does about the legitimacy of your request. If the group seems like the wrong place to address the haunting images, consider consulting a trauma-informed grief therapist, who likely will be familiar with exposure-based treatments of the kind described earlier. Whether with the support of a group or a private therapist, you can gradually come to

master the troubling imagery surrounding your brother's death, so that you can turn fuller attention to mourning a beloved sibling whose memory you want to recover from the traumatic circumstances of his death.

—Dr. Neimeyer

## Ex-Boyfriend Died by Suicide

*Dear Dr. Neimeyer,*

A little over six months ago my ex-boyfriend committed suicide. We had dated for five years and were actually trying to work things out so that we could get back together because we believed we were each other's soulmates. After he ended his life, I couldn't sleep, eat, get out of bed or do anything except [lie] there and sob uncontrollably. For a couple of months, I was doing fine. I stopped crying as much and thought I had come to a healthy spot that I could finally go back to my normal everyday life, despite thinking about him constantly. Now, ever since his birthday passed in June, I have been a train wreck. I cry almost every day over it. On the days I don't cry, it's because I can't cry for some reason. I thought I was doing so well handling the situation and now it's as if I've only gotten worse. I'm so confused and was wondering if you had any insight as to why this could be happening and what I can do to begin to move on.

Thank you,

**Ros**

*Dear Ros,*

First it is important to acknowledge the unique impact of suicide loss, which is almost inevitably complicated by our human need to understand this seemingly incomprehensible act, and to sort through the anger, guilt and blame with which we often struggle as survivors. The great majority of survivors of suicide loss describe reactions like your own, with images of and thoughts about the death being preoccupying and intrusive and the path to adaptation being long. In this respect, your report that you already have experienced a couple of months during which you began to find again your footing in the world is hopeful; you seem already to be finding a way forward, even if it has not solidified into a reliable path.

From what you describe, the major struggle you have now is figuring out what to do when the great waves of grief crash over you. Here, two things might be helpful. First, paradoxical as it seems, invite the grief, but on your own terms. By setting aside a safe time and safe place to spend some time with the pain, followed by a strategy for exiting from it (for example, by getting together with a friend, engaging in exercise or doing something else that is self-healing and involving), you essentially give yourself permission to grieve this enormous loss of a person and a dream that this tragic death took from you. For example, many people find that by setting aside and scheduling 30 minutes per day for journaling about the loss, they are better able to postpone the inevitable grief, and in this way find some measure of control over it. Importantly, making time to be with the pain also tends to give us permission to be without it at other times, as we learn to "dose" our exposure to the grief. By contrast, simply trying to suppress it indefinitely often leads to greater rumination and intrusive thoughts and feelings when they are not invited.

Second, it could be helpful to remember that suicide poses a particular threat to our system of meaning, that is, to our assumptions about the world, our loved one and our future. Strong and preoccupying feelings and thoughts can therefore be a kind of signal from ourselves, to ourselves and about ourselves, drawing attention to something that requires more processing. It might be that these feelings are pressing forward at this time precisely because you are more ready to confront them, to sort through the fragments of your assumptive world and dreams for a future with your partner or to address the "unfinished business" of a relationship that had stumbled and seemingly was trying again to move forward. In this, a compassionate counselor could be a useful ally, along with friends and perhaps members of a suicide support group in your area who are willing to stand with you in your loss. Be patient, be brave and be hopeful about a life that can find new meaning, even in the dark shadow of this loss.

—Dr. Neimeyer

## Coping With a Child's Autopsy

*Dear Dr. Neimeyer,*

My son John died just 14 months ago at 31 years of age. The coroner's findings were that he died from Mixed Drug Toxicity, Drug Induced Cardiomyopathy and Chronic on Acute Pancreatitis. John was also Hep C. His father died from a long and complicated course of illness that extended through John's childhood and early adolescence, and John developed significant learning difficulties and ADHD [attention deficit hyperactivity disorder], and I'm sure there were many other undiagnosed problems that compounded his poor self-concept/esteem. John was experimenting with various illicit substances probably as young as 12 years of age. During the course of his father's illness, John's drug taking escalated. By the time his father finally died, John was on heroin.

This may sound strange, but my instinct told me that even when John was a little boy, he had so many problems that I knew he would go down the drug path and die an early death. The years after his father's death were nightmare years, and there were times when I didn't know whether he was dead or alive. I did everything possible to keep him alive in the hope that he would eventually be able to live some sort of semi-normal life. He lived on the streets or couch-surfed. It is a long story, and one filled with many turbulent relationships and family crises. Even so, I was shocked and numbed when I got "the call" from one of his friends to say that John was dead. It was the most horrible moment of my life, after so many attempts to save him.

My main reason for writing now is that I'm starting to see John on the table at the morgue over and over again, whereas, for a long time, I couldn't bring that image up for longer than a few seconds. I'm feeling angry that no one asked permission to cut into John's body when the autopsy was performed. I thought I could handle reading the full autopsy report, but didn't realize how graphic it was, and I read it once and that's where the horror part comes in. I keep getting pictures of the entire procedure. He was my child, I carried him, I nurtured him, I tried my hardest as a mother to keep him alive.

It doesn't matter that he was an adult when he died; he was still my child and I feel he was totally violated when they sliced him open and did what they do at an autopsy. I know it doesn't happen this way, but I feel someone should have asked me if it was okay to cut him open like that. It's taken me this long to get to this point, and I'm wondering do other parents feel this way? Why didn't anyone consider a parent might feel this way on finding out their child has been cut open and then sewn back together again? It's all wrong, and I suppose some of the numbness is starting to wear off and I'm starting to feel and think more.

My question is, what can I expect will happen with this terrible imagery, and what can I do about it?

**Jeanmarie**

*Dear Jeanmarie,*

Your letter makes visible to others who read it the awful images and preoccupation associated with your son's tragic death, compounded by the coroner's investigation of its causes. Even if the latter is mandated in cases where the cause of death is ambiguous, and for good legal reasons, your horror and heartbreak are surely understandable to every bereaved parent. As a great French poet once said, "The heart has its reasons of which reason knows nothing."

But to acknowledge that your reaction is understandable is not to say that it is inevitable or one that you can sustain across a lifetime. Ideally you would have been accompanied by a compassionate and knowledgeable professional as you gradually digested the autopsy report in a way that helped you take in, one step at a time, what it had to tell you or teach you about John's death. For example, I have helped clients integrate the content of autopsy reports by silently reading a part of the document, perhaps a paragraph at a time, describing in very general terms its content and then assessing the mourner's readiness to hear more (e.g., "This section describes the scene of the death and the position of his body when he was found. Do you have any questions about that? Would you like me to summarize it or read it aloud and discuss it with you?"). Taking in the reality of the death is extremely painful under any circumstance, but doing so alone and often in an unbuffered way can make it even more surreal and clinical, rather than couched compassionately and with assistance in "dosing" the report and making sense of the hard parts.

Of course, you did not have this opportunity, and so the question is now what can be done about the imagery of the autopsy and the associated emotions it triggers. Simply suppressing them is not an option: both research and clinical experience suggest that this is not possible for long and that the unwanted images often come back with renewed force. More useful might be to accept, or even invite, the images, but under "safe" conditions of high support, perhaps with an experienced trauma and grief therapist. Slowly reviewing, talking through and making sense of the images, just a bit at a time, with ample opportunity to breathe mindfully through the related feelings as they arise and subside can be a helpful step, and one that might be repeated until you can confront them with less reactivity.

Many people also find it helpful to use expressive arts techniques to give shape to the imagery and distance from it, putting it "out there" on paper—even in simple drawings—rather than have it live only in their minds. This can also lead to the use of healing imagery, slowly, deeply and repeatedly imagining or drawing yourself caressing or healing John's broken body, perhaps even "magically," although you cannot restore it to life. These and other practices described in some of the books on grief therapy mentioned elsewhere (such as using an artist's renderings or photos of John in a healthy state to display in your home) might help a therapist guide you through these procedures toward a less horrific way of holding the imagery and gradually to overwrite it with more sustainable pictures of the John you want to remember. Along with broader therapeutic work on the other "unfinished business" of a complicated relationship, it could help restore your sense of being a mother who did all she could to care for a son whose own experience of tragic loss ultimately led him down a dark path.

—Dr. Neimeyer

SUICIDE AND OVERDOSE

## Daughter Took Her Own Life

*Dear Dr. Neimeyer,*

My only child, my 16-year-old daughter, took her own life just one month ago. She showed no signs at all. Straight A student, worked as [a] cashier part time, saving money for college. She just finished her College Boards and got an amazing score. I know this wasn't planned—she had placed orders for items on Amazon and the day she did this went and rented her Tux for Prom with her stepfather. None of this makes sense to me. I am fortunate enough to have a letter she left for me which clearly says she can't tell me why she killed herself because she doesn't know why. But she wanted me to know that it wasn't my fault and that I was the best mom anyone could have ever asked for and I'm strong and that's why she knows I will get through this. My daughter was lesbian but was definitely not bullied. We taught her to be proud of who she was and to be strong, and we supported her 100%. I am just so lost now and cannot understand why or how I was not able to stop her from doing this.

I know you don't have the answers but maybe something you can say will help me with this unbearable grief and pain I am feeling right now. My baby girl was fun, smart, and very much loved by everyone who knew her. I miss her terribly and cannot even bear to think about living the rest of my life without her by my side. I'll never see her graduate or go to college and become a wonderful author—I have been robbed of all of these things. How in the heck do I move forward?

**Melissa**

*Dear Melissa,*

Ironically, your letter reaches me as I return from the meeting of the American Association of Suicidology, a meeting attended by 1,400 professionals and lay persons, many of whom—myself included—are survivors of suicide loss. Although you are certainly right that I lack the specific answers you seek, I can assure you that hundreds of bereaved parents, children, partners and siblings in that gathering know some version of the pain you feel, the shock, the horror, the helplessness, the struggle to understand. And while many of them continue to process the raw anguish of these losses, many others have eventually found a way forward despite them, often finding some measure of meaning in their tragedy by reaching out supportively to others touched by similar tragedy. My hope for you is that you find the companionship and compassion of such fellow travelers, rather than having to walk this road alone.

Although the suicide of a loved one is frequently foreshadowed by a long struggle with depression or other emotional problems, for a surprising number of survivors, the death comes with little or no warning, seemingly in response to a dark impulse known only to the deceased. Tragically, LGBTQ+ youth are at particular risk for self-injury and suicide, largely as a response to a judgmental and rejecting culture, even when enlightened and loving parents like yourself instill pride and self-acceptance at home. Bullying does not always take overt forms, as the terrible rise in cyber bullying attests. And while many young people in gender minorities find friendship and close relationships in a community that embraces them, many more strive to live authentically in a world that subtly or unsubtly punishes their self-expression. And events like proms, with their predominance of heterosexual couples, can underscore the lack of inclusion of those who have or seek other relationships.

It would be presumptuous to link your daughter's death to her gender orientation without knowing much more about her silent struggles, which of course could be much like those of many young people, whoever they love or are attracted to. But you might find some provisional meaning and understanding in hearing the voices of other young adults who are attempt survivors and who can speak to the often-invisible despair that drove them to the edge in their own lives. The Loss conference associated with AAS could be one source of such understanding, as might a remarkable film, *The S Word*, that tells their story with insight and compassion. With your letter to me you have already taken a first step toward telling your own story, and your daughter's, for what I hope will not be the last time. In mutual support groups you can access on the internet (click Alliance of Hope for one important resource; or in face-to-face mutual support forums near you, which you can identify through the American Foundation for Suicide Prevention), you can find others contending with similar questions and working together to find the answers that will make life livable in the wake of devastating loss.

—Dr. Neimeyer

## A Friend's 16-Year-Old Daughter Died by Suicide

*Dr. Neimeyer,*

Last week, my friend's 16-year-old daughter committed suicide. As far as what is known, there is nothing that indicates the "why." As I read through your materials, I have learned that we try to bring an understanding to the un-understandable and it eats at us. He and his ex-wife divorced a couple of years ago, and they also have two younger daughters.

My question is what can we, as part [of] our friend's support group, do for him? We are encouraging counseling for him, as well as his younger girls. But are there things we should (or should not) be doing?

**Jack**

## SUICIDE AND OVERDOSE

*Dear Jack,*

Your description of the quest for meaning in a seemingly meaningless loss is as pointed as any I have heard: "We try to bring an understanding to the un-understandable and it eats at us." As my friend and colleague, Diana Sands, says, we attempt to "walk in the shoes" of a loved one who dies of suicide following this tragic form of bereavement, as we strive to step into the mindset of the deceased to grasp the thoughts and feelings that led to that traumatic conclusion. Your letter suggests that you are seeking a way to help your friend as he undertakes such a quest and merely survive day to day.

And so let me offer a few suggestions, for the near term and the long term, as this wounded friend and the family to which he remains connected try to regroup and move forward:

1. *Make an offer.* Reach out to your friend with small, concrete acts of kindness. Drop off a complete dinner for him or for him and his children when they visit or if they live with him. Ask them over to your home, offering a specific choice of dates. Help with transportation of the two younger girls to school or soccer or suggest a sleepover or joint family outing if the girls are friends of your own children. The key is to avoid generic offers ("If there is anything you need, don't hesitate to call"), which rarely are accepted. Just act, doing what you think best. If you know them well and put yourself in their place, you can probably think of a dozen things. Such actions speak louder than words.

2. *Speak her name.* Counter the shroud of silence that tends to descend over those who die this potentially stigmatizing death. Voice his daughter's name aloud: "How are you doing today, a month after _____'s death?" "What would _____ want for her little sisters?" You get the idea. As your friend's bereavement moves forward, speaking about his daughter will eventually become easier, and he may have a need to tell the story of her life, and perhaps her death, many times, to make it more real. Eventually, speaking her name with love and appreciation may be more possible for everyone in the family, as they attempt to revive comforting memories of her life that are not overwritten by her death. This is a long process for most of those who have known such loss, but it is a great resource to have others who can participate in both the hurtful and healing conversations.

3. *Advocate for support.* Both peer-led bereavement support groups by trained facilitators and professional help from specialists in grief therapy can provide critical opportunities to work on the loss with people who have walked the walk and who can offer specific advice and understanding that is otherwise scarce in the social or even professional mental health communities. Begin by exploring and referring your friend to

the American Foundation for Suicide Prevention site (http://afsp.org), and also make some inquiries in your own geographic region; a group for men, or even bereaved fathers, may also be available, including at survivors' conferences held each year. Suicide bereavement is an isolating experience, and breaking down the walls that separate your friend and others in the family from a world of caring others can go a great distance toward helping them find a way forward. In all of this, also take care of yourselves, as you likely also knew his daughter and are touched in your own way by this terrible loss.

—Dr. Neimeyer

## Complete Shock After Son Took His Life

*Dear Dr. Neimeyer,*

My son took his life several months ago. He was in his 30s and had three children in their teens from a previous marriage. He was totally devastated over finding his wife of a few months was trading sex for drugs. He talked to a few friends the evening he found out, when one of the men sent him pictures of them having sex. He found out she was married and thought he was doing the right thing letting my son know.

My son didn't try to talk to any of his family. I guess he didn't want us to talk him out of it. It was a complete shock as he was a silly, fun-loving, happy guy. He was a very sweet man, and we all miss him horribly. I feel like I'm sleepwalking, and I wish I was dead. How can I help his children when I can't deal with it?

**Anna**

*Dear Anna,*

A suicide death raises many troubling questions for survivors, questions about the deceased person's state of mind behind the fatal decision, about our inability to intervene and about the nature of the universe that permits such tragic outcomes and its impact on those left behind. Afterward, the stigma and avoidance that typically surround this form of loss further complicate adapting to life after loss for survivors, who can feel utterly alone and isolated in their grief. For all those who love your son, this must be an excruciating period.

Your description of your son as "silly, fun-loving and happy" conjures a sense of innocence that contrasts with his wife's dark secret, whose discovery must have been devastating for him. Tragically, death may have seemed like the one sure way to "turn off" the pain, shame and hurt of her betrayal, although his seemingly spur-of-the-moment decision to end his life, perhaps by violent means, left all of you with overwhelming pain of your own.

You ask how you can help his children when you can't deal with this traumatic reality yourself. Ironically, acknowledging your own struggle and letting them see some of your own distress may actually be one way to help them, as it could give them permission to acknowledge and display their own feelings of hurt, abandonment and anger—directed, perhaps, at both of their parents. Of course, such feelings can be greatly complicated if they remain in their stepmother's care, given the role that drug use and random sexual encounters seem to have played in leading to your son's despair and which suggest a very poor environment for continuing to raise the children and support them in their grief. Given this, your own involvement in their lives as a more stable figure ultimately can be crucial in helping them process this trauma, rebuild a sense of secure attachment to a stable and loving adult and continue to move into a young adulthood marked by hope and possibility. For each of you, participation in a suicide bereavement support group can provide a healing context for sharing with others who have suffered this terrible form of loss and overcoming the silence and stigma that can surround it. Moreover, especially if their biological mother is not engaged with them as a functional parent to help the children cope with the loss and rebuild their lives, I would recommend professional family therapy with someone accustomed to working with family systems and bereavement. One of the clearest ways you can help is by securing the professional guidance and support that both you and the children need to come to terms with this heartbreaking loss and to reaffirm the value of your own lives as individuals and as a family.

—Dr. Neimeyer

## Suicide of a Grieving Son

*Dear Dr. Neimeyer,*

I lost my son Charles a few months ago to suicide. Charles lost both his babies four years ago. Their first baby was a miscarriage and the second was born with a rare cancer and only survived two and a half months but lost his battle and passed on. This broke my son, and the four years after losing his babies was a roller coaster ride for him. He became suicidal and tried everything to get rid of himself. This included overdosing on drugs, hanging himself on a tree in our garden, cutting himself to inflict pain on himself and the list goes on. I saw a young man full of life with a vision and a dream, and part of his dream was to be a dad and have his own family. This, however, never happened for him. We went through so much as a family and lost our home twice because of my son's unstable lifestyle and behavior after using drugs. Unfortunately, nothing we tried to do was ever enough to save him.

I am taking it one day at a time, as each day comes with its own set of challenges trying to deal with the loss of my son.

My question is that throughout Charles's life I always connected with him on a spiritual level and could feel when something [was] wrong or when he was in trouble, but for the life of me, I didn't feel any connection the night he passed on. This has left me angry, and I sometimes feel robbed. My life revolved around my boys, and I vowed to take care of them and be there for them whenever they needed me. I feel like I have failed him. He used to tell me how lost and alone he felt and that he was empty after losing his children. I beat myself up thinking that I heard what he said but I didn't listen to his cry. I see the sadness in his eyes every time I think of him. The other thing that haunts me is that I found him in his place hanging and when I close my eyes, this is the last picture I see of him. How can I get through this?

He promised me that he would never try to hurt himself again but yet he left me. Is God punishing me for not hearing the cry of my son? Will I ever forgive myself for not being able to save him? How do I move on if I wake up with thoughts of him and go to sleep with thoughts of him? I know that he knew that I loved him and prayed for him more than I did for myself, yet still I feel I could have or should have done more. Why am I unable to connect with him in my dreams like I [used] to?

**Loretta**

*Dear Loretta,*

Yours is indeed a complex loss, in which the death of a child before that of the parent is compounded across two generations. In the years following the death of your grandchildren you helplessly observed your son's complicated grief and his tragic attempts to mitigate it through the use of drugs, and now following his completed suicide you struggle with a complex grief of your own. And surely every parent who reads of your anguish in not being able to love him through these losses can identify with that painful sense of insufficiency, which leaves you, like him, on the brink of despair: neither of you could save your own children from a tragic death. The critical difference is that, however great the pain you describe, you are reaching out earnestly for more adaptive ways to cope with this trauma. To the limited extent I can in a brief reply, I want to join you in that reaching.

The urgent questions embedded in your letter deserve my best attempts at answers, so let me offer a response to each:

1. *"The thing that haunts me is that I found him in his place hanging and when I close my eyes this is the last picture I see of him. How can I get through this?"*

Horrific events like discovering the body of your dear son leave indelible and intrusive memories in their wake, and this is one of the hallmarks of posttraumatic stress disorder (PTSD). Recognizing this, it is important to understand your reaction as involving not only profound and pervasive grief but also classic symptoms of traumatic stress. Indeed, witnessing the violent death of a loved one has been established by research to be the single strongest predictor of PTSD. And this means that you, like countless others before you, are likely to benefit from trauma-informed treatments that feature compassionate support as you slowly review or revisit the terrible scene and gradually accommodate the hard emotional reality, probably across multiple sessions of treatment. Evidence from many different therapies that share this feature of "prolonged exposure" to the scene (such as eye movement desensitization and reprocessing [EMDR], Prolonged Grief Disorder Treatment, Restorative Retelling and various cognitive-behavioral protocols) suggest that this "strong medicine" can make a huge difference in reducing the power of such images to ambush you and eclipse your memories of Charles's life with this single brutal scene of his death. Look for a specialist in trauma therapy or, better still, trauma-informed grief therapy, to take the first steps toward liberation from this repeated nightmare.

2. *"Is God punishing me for not hearing the cry of my son?"* The most deeply religious people often share your sense of spiritual struggle in the aftermath of tragic loss, questioning God's intentions, power or love. Indeed, our research and my clinical experience suggest that this sense of rupture in relation to the divine is strongly associated with complicated grief, as a once firm and meaningful faith is shaken or shattered by traumatic loss. While it is tempting to offer simple reassurance that God can provide a sense of refuge even in the context of great suffering, ultimately the answers that will matter will be those that come from your own best attempts—on your own and with trusted members of relevant faith communities—to reconcile the reality of human tragedy and brokenness with a robust or revised spiritual framework that nonetheless provides orientation and support. Spiritual journaling, in which you meditate deeply on how your beliefs can serve as resources in this troubled time, and how they are changed by it in turn, can be one way to engage such questions. Another is to write a "letter to God" expressing all of your feelings and questions, then pause for a day or two, return to the letter, read it aloud and write a response, attempting to sense God's reply. Some people also find honest discussions with trusted clergy helpful, while others explore alternative spiritual traditions that make more sense to them in the wake of their experience.

3. *"Will I ever forgive myself for not being able to save him?"* When we are unable to protect the lives of those we love most—and perhaps our children most of all—we can easily fall into a pattern of self-blame that at least answers the agonizing question, "Why did this happen?" by responding that, at some level, it was because of us. But of course, this is an answer that also seems to call for unending punishment for our sin or crime, and that compounds the problem by leaving us unable to provide the genuine care and love to our remaining children and others who deserve our care. "Loving kindness" meditation can be an alternative, helping us cultivate an attitude of compassion for ourselves and others. Another would be writing a letter to Charles presenting your struggle for self-forgiveness, then pause a day or two, as with the "letter to God" mentioned earlier, and respond as he might, imagining him fully healed of his emotional and physical pain and fully able to engage your letter. Grief therapists who practice "chair work" can also provide strong support and direction for such imaginal dialogues, which typically are very healing.

4. *"How do I move on if I wake up with thoughts of him and go to sleep with thoughts of him? And why am I unable to connect with him in my dreams like I [used] to?"* You can't banish the thoughts, however hard you try; research indicates that thought suppression simply leads them to come back all the more forcefully. But you have some choice over the kind of thoughts you invite. If his image materializes for you with sad and tearful eyes, vividly imagine yourself drying them, soothing him and loving him through it. If you visualize him after he died, conjure a competing image of your lovingly tending to his body, much as most of humanity has done for deceased family members throughout history. In other words, look for ways to engage the image in a healing fashion, speaking the words that you had no chance to speak, providing the care that his private act denied you. Again, therapists acquainted with trauma-informed grief therapy can assist with this, and in so doing help you gradually reopen the door to dreams of better times that are currently eclipsed by the traumatic and intrusive thoughts and images.

Finally, bear in mind that your loss, though uniquely your own, is shared in other variations by hundreds of thousands of others who have also survived the suicide of a loved one. Websites sponsored by the American Foundation for Suicide Prevention and the Alliance of Hope offer bridges into these support communities, both online and face to face. Consider taking steps toward others who share this walk, combining principles of self-care with engagement with a community of others seeking similar paths through and beyond a most difficult loss.

—Dr. Neimeyer

## Traumatic Death by Shotgun

*Dear Dr. Neimeyer,*

My 17-year-old son took his own life not even a month ago. I find I can't even type the details. He used a shotgun in our basement. Our whole family found him shortly afterwards.

I recently read about "atypical depression," which very well described Edward's condition. He was doing well. He was brilliant, funny, caring, compassionate and had good friends. He had the support and respect of his college-aged gaming community. He was seeing a therapist. He had plans for the future. He knew he was well loved. He was successful in school and in the activities he loved best. He certainly had moments of great joy.

However, he also was occasionally moody and had bouts of depression from which he seemed to bounce back. In his final note he said he didn't believe he could change, that it wasn't in his DNA or character. He reiterated how vehemently he was opposed to medication because it would change who he was. He hoped we understood that he was going to be honest and true to himself to the very end.

He and I were very, very close. We talked about everything. I gave him all the time he needed and unconditional love beyond measure. He promised me he would always talk to me when he was down. And he did. Many times.

I'm now inconsolable. Did I miss a clue? Why didn't he talk to me? I've spent my entire life devoted to being the best Mom to all of my sons. How could I have been so blind to Edward's last despair? I've been so in tune with him for so long. His therapist told me she didn't see ANYTHING to be concerned about. She called him "The Great Pretender."

The very night before his suicide, I asked him how he was doing. He said, "I'm fine, Mom," and hugged me. It was kind of a joke between us, and I asked, "No, really, how are you doing, son?" He looked me right in the eye and said, "Really, Mom. I'm fine." We hugged again, and I told him I loved him.

I'm a wreck. We all are. We started individual and family therapy. I journal. I draw. I've written his friends to share memories and many have.

Even though he wrote to me in his note that he knew how much I loved him, thanked me for my support and always standing up for him, he also said he imagined my face when I saw him dead and it made him sad. Then he said he loved me and that he would continue to love me even after his heart stopped beating. I'm not feeling comforted.

I cry and cry and cry and cry. I'm not sleeping or eating and am deeply depressed. (I started an antidepressant a week ago.) I cannot imagine a life without Edward. He was my heart. I have frequent panic attacks and have to take an antianxiety medication because I am hysterical.

My main question is: Is it common with atypical depression to miss signs?

What else can I do to help my family now? I'm so useless. I'm not functioning. I can't cook. I can't do much of anything except cry, write and draw. Not much of that either because I can't focus.

Help, please!

**Nancy**

*Dear Nancy,*

Tragically, many survivors of suicide would no doubt identify with your sense of shock, horror and self-reproach in the aftermath of a family member's suicide, which evidence suggests hits mothers especially hard. Especially when one has strived for a lifetime to "be in tune" with a deeply loved child, through triumphs and tribulations of all kinds, it can seem impossible that one "missed the signs" of imminent self-destruction. And yet, especially when our loved one masked an underlying hopelessness, sense of alienation or perceived burdensomeness with a sense of equanimity and reassurance—especially, as is often the case, once a highly lethal suicide plan has already been decided on—the cues are often few and faint and hard to distinguish from other troubled times from which he or she had "bounced back" before. Ironically, the same brilliance and compassion that Edward evidently displayed in abundance could also be drawn upon to conceal his fatalism and "protect" you from his growing depression or despair. As a result, you, like far too many suicide survivors, are left replaying the tragedy without answers to your anguished questions and blaming yourself for failing to discern his secret intents and avert the trauma of his dying.

What then can you do to help yourself and your family now? One answer would be to be compassionate to yourself. You are unlikely to be cruelly accusing other family members of inattention to Edward's pain, so try to treat yourself with the same understanding. Recognize that the terrible isolation of suicide loss might call not only for the professional therapy that you have sought but also for the community of others who have known some version of the same pain. Mutual support groups for suicide survivors online, like *Alliance of Hope,* or optimally in person through the *American Foundation for Suicide Prevention* support groups can help restore a sense of connection in the face of stigmatizing loss, just as internet resources like the thoughtful *Grief After Suicide* blog can help provide provisional answers to the many questions that arise in the wake of such loss.

And finally, recognize that finding one's footing in the world again after suicide bereavement is a longer-term proposition, not something that can be measured in a few weeks or months. My advice in this regard is to start small and stay connected. Collaborate with your family to prepare a meal together.

Go for a walk with your husband daily. Make an effort to stay involved in the lives of your other sons, and open to their grief about your common loss. Share your art and journaling with responsive others, both professional and in your world of family and friends when it feels appropriate to do so. It is clear that, despite his pain, Edward loved you greatly, and adopting a loving attitude toward yourself even in your grief can meaningfully extend a positive legacy of his life and help recapture it from the overshadowing circumstance of his tragic death.

—Dr. Neimeyer

## Suicide Avoided by Friends

*Dear Dr. Neimeyer,*

I lost my oldest son nearly eight years ago to suicide at the age of 24. He shot himself in our home. Friends and people from church were very kind to us after it happened. We have three other sons. They are all grown now, but one has had a drug problem and is currently incarcerated. We have stayed in our home, as it was my husband's childhood home and he didn't want to leave. Anyway, now it seems as though friends and family avoid us, and I'm wondering if it would have been better if we had moved? My husband and I are raising a granddaughter, but outside of that, we don't connect either. I feel very isolated and misunderstood. Any advice would be helpful.

**Joanne**

*Dear Joanne,*

Your direct and honest account presents such a litany of loss, from the vivid and traumatic death of one son in your home, through the heartbreak of another's drug abuse and incarceration, to the seemingly unexplained thinning of relations with friends, family and even your spouse. As much joy and meaning as raising your granddaughter might bring, I can well imagine the sense of aloneness that otherwise pervades the house, which seems in too many ways emptied of the life and love it must once have held.

No "quick fix" can make this sad scenario instantly better, so I won't insult you by offering you one. But I am moved to offer at least a few principles that might help as you navigate this sea of losses and try to find your way back to safe harbor and human companionship. Think of them as possible responses to the sometimes stark and sometimes subtle grief you encounter and consider whether one or more of them feels like a step that you are ready to take.

1. *Acknowledge the stigma and push back against it.* Suicide loss in particular tends to be heavily stigmatized and "disenfranchised," in the sense of

being uncomfortably ignored or invalidated by much of the social world. In your case, you were fortunate to receive a much kinder and more compassionate response from your church and community after your son's death, but it is often the case that the outpouring of support that survivors receive in the immediate aftermath of tragic death evaporates after a few weeks, leaving mourners with a "silent story" of suffering that cannot easily be shared. It is for this reason that *Survivors of Suicide* groups can offer uniquely valuable mutual support for people in your position who might well be troubled by this traumatic event even many years later. Trauma-informed therapies can address residual images and feelings, and resources like those offered by the *American Foundation of Suicide Prevention* to long-term survivors can often pick up where local and limited support leaves off.

2. *Voice the unspoken losses and find an audience for them.* Your other son's incarceration, and very likely a turbulent history of drug use that preceded it, must have introduced their own losses, perhaps in the form of a loss of control over the situation, the loss of trust in your son and perhaps even the loss of hope for a meaningful life you must have harbored for him in more innocent years. In facing such ambiguous losses, it is often helpful to "name them and claim them," putting yourself in a quiet, reflective frame of mind during a period of privacy, with your phone turned off, as you ask yourself repeatedly and honestly, "What have I lost?" Then pause and patiently let the answer come to you, writing it down in a word or phrase. Then repeat the question, and wait for the next answer, recording it, too, when it comes. Do this 10 times. Then survey your list and ask, "What do I most need in relation to each of these losses? And what would be the first step I could take toward getting this?" Take action on three of these steps, and in the loss journal that you have begun, record the results of your efforts. Where you see some signs of success, do more of that, or ask yourself, "What's the next step here?" Where you are disappointed by the results, learn from them, and ask, "What step might I try instead?"

3. *Reweave the ties that bind.* There was a time that you were held in loving arms, in a tender gaze, in the caring concern of a faith community and friendship circle. Spend some time reflecting on what happened, without resorting to the morally satisfying but ultimately futile tactic of merely blaming the loss of this connection on the failings of others . . . true though this may often be. Instead, try to understand the thinning or sundering of these ties usefully—what do they teach you about what is required to keep a relationship in good repair? Consider how you might restore, renew or replace strained or broken connections by reaching

out to others in their own pain or grief—which inhabits every life, to a degree large or small. Or is a bolder step needed, in the form of joining a new congregation, or simply engaging a community of people who share an interest (perhaps in the arts, cooking, a book club or civic organization) you once indulged but in your years of suffering have allowed to atrophy? And perhaps most centrally, take the risk of speaking frankly to your husband about both your appreciation for his coparenting and the lonely part of you that misses the intimacy and closeness you once shared. Whether with the help of a couples therapist or through creative reengagement and the cultivation of shared interests, strive to recover some of what you have lost, so that the rest does not have to be borne alone.

—Dr. Neimeyer

## Suicide of a Son: Wanting to Join Him

*Dear Dr. Neimeyer,*

I lost my son to suicide, and I am struggling with the urge to join him. I try to stay here for my beautiful granddaughter that he left for me to enjoy. There are days that it is almost like living that day over again and that is when I struggle the hardest. There is loss, and then there is this terrible feeling of loss that goes beyond words. I think about how I was able to prevent a total stranger from committing suicide some years ago but could not help or stop my son. Where is the justice in that? It will be two years soon, and I hurt so badly thinking of him and what he brought to my life. How could I not see how much pain he was going thru?

Thanks for listening. I have faced adversity in my life, but never anything like this.

**Jacqueline**

*Dear Jacqueline,*

Just as you imply, there is no justice in suicide, any more than in cancer or a random automobile accident, and too often, our ability to avert each of these deaths is tragically limited. However, weighing the immense pain you bear following his suicide, I hope you will do all in your power to keep from visiting similar pain on others you love, continuing a chain reaction of explosive impacts that only deepen the devastation. Sadly, many survivors of suicide loss contemplate dying themselves as a way of relieving their anguish, and too many act on that impulse. Please take the actions necessary to avoid being one of them.

Begin by constructing a safety plan. If you are contemplating a particular means of ending your life, take steps to mitigate the risk: give the gun to a relative, flush the pills down the toilet. Then make an appointment with a skilled therapist, and ideally a psychiatrist as well. You will likely benefit from trauma-informed grief therapy as well as medication, both being delivered by someone who is aware of your level of distress and risk.

Become informed about the specialized services for and issues faced by those who have lost loved ones to suicide. In one respect, at least, your reaching out with this question is well timed, as we are now entering Mental Health Month, and the *American Foundation for Suicide Prevention* has just responded by extending its range of resources to assist people in understanding and responding to this tragically common psychological problem. Check them out for full information about suicide, surviving suicide loss and support groups that can give you a safe place to share your feelings about the loss and to learn from others who are contending with grievous losses of their own.

Most assuredly, your son did not intend to take your life when he ended his. Allow yourself to receive his gift of life and seek healthy ways to move through this dark and difficult transition to a life that retains or regains meaning even in the shadow of this profound loss. In doing so, you may ultimately find that you have much to give, not only to your granddaughter but also to others struggling with suicide and its aftermath.

—Dr. Neimeyer

## A Son's Suicide and the Holiday Season

*Dear Dr. Neimeyer,*

My 18-year-old son hanged himself in a tree last June. Since that day, my life is full of guilt and heartache. I've seen multiple counselors, and many of them have been great, and they all tell me the same thing: it's not my fault. But I cannot forgive myself for not getting him help sooner, for not seeing the signs, for not saving my son. It is my job as a mother to keep her child safe and I didn't. Every day I put a mask on and pretend I'm okay but I'm not. I hide from the world for the most part. I cancel plans. I don't date. I've gained weight and I drink too much to numb the pain. I don't know how to move forward with this guilt. I know somehow I need to for my daughter and most importantly for my health.

As a little background, my first husband attempted suicide when we were married and many years later completed suicide. My nephew hanged himself in our garage when we were on our honeymoon. I should have seen the signs! I should have been more vigilant. If you can give me any advice or any books to read I would appreciate it. I've read so many books but nothing has helped. I love my son and I miss him so much. This time of year is particularly difficult. Christmas was always so special for us and his birthday is January 1. Thank you for taking the time to read this.

**Hannah**

*Dear Hannah,*

As this holiday season begins, I cannot imagine a more tragic contrast between the meaningful and joyous family times you once knew and the achingly broken mask of holiday cheer you have tried to wear in the months since your son's suicide. In the silence beneath that mask so many tormenting questions live on, compounding the loneliness and incomprehension with self-accusation. Like so many of us who have lost a loved one to suicide, you find little consolation or reprieve in the reassurances of well-meaning others, even the otherwise thoughtful and empathic counselors you've consulted. And so now you bravely bring your urgent questions to this forum seeking some kind of answer that can restore hope, ameliorate the corrosive guilt and allow you to begin to reclaim at least one life that is teetering on the edge of being unlivable—your own. With a full recognition that the deep anguish and questioning you feel will not easily be erased by my response, let me offer at least a few thoughts that might suggest some way forward.

First, recognize that nearly every survivor of suicide struggles with seemingly unanswerable questions about why their loved ones ended their lives and how they failed at the critical moment to recognize the risk and take action to avert their dying. And sadly, the fact that nearly 50,000 people die by suicide annually in the United States alone underscores how very difficult it is to read the warning signs and take effective precautions. In fact, with the widespread availability of firearms and lethal drugs, the National Center for Health Statistics confirms that suicide has increased by nearly 25% over the last two decades. So there are literally hundreds of thousands of other families struggling to make sense of similarly horrific losses, with no easy answers at hand.

Our best understandings of the dynamics of suicide, however, clearly suggest how complex and multidimensional the factors are that lead to its pervasive presence in our lives. Biological factors such as a disposition to depression and other serious mood disorders, interpersonal circumstances such as losses of or alienation from crucial relationships, perceived burden on others and personal factors such as substance use and hopelessness all play a part. In the case of your son, the heavy presence of suicide in the family across generations strongly suggests a genetic disposition to depression and despair, at a level that even medical experts do not fully understand. In the face of such complexity, it is understandable that we strive to find simpler answers, even if they take the form of the "if only" thinking that places the blame for the tragedy at our own doorstep. But we pay a terrible price for this illusion of control—the idea that had we acted differently in a critical moment, it would all have worked out differently. Certainly, suicide awareness and prevention are laudable goals, but retrospective self-blame ignores the harsh reality that often is greatly more complex than our feeble efforts to control the course of events arising from a convergence of factors to which we at best make a modest contribution.

So what might you do now to move through this grievous loss and begin healing your heart and your family? One step would be to seek the mutual support and understanding that can be offered by others who know their own losses to suicide, as through onsite and online groups organized by the American Association of Suicidology, the American Foundation for Suicide Prevention or the Alliance of Hope. In the community of concern each offers, you may begin to find genuine comprehension of your pain and inspiration for living despite the shadow of this heavy loss.

A further step would be to seek truly specialist professional care. Many features of suicide and violent death loss require specialized interventions in which the average counselor or therapist simply has no training. These could include practices such as a slow-motion "restorative retelling" of your experience of the loss, accompanied by a therapist who can help you compassionately acknowledge the feelings that arise and make greater sense of the experience, or use of well-developed protocols for working with images and associated emotions connected to the loss in a way that lets you bring healing resources to bear on them. Facilitated symbolic "conversations" with your son can also be a powerful vehicle for addressing your pain and perplexity, moving toward a restoration of a loving bond with your son that was cruelly broken by his death. Organizations such as the Violent Death Bereavement Society, the EMDR Institute, and the Gestalt Therapy Institutes that operate in many large American cities can point you in hopeful directions.

In closing, it is understandable that this most tragic of losses has stirred deep anguish, incomprehension, guilt and self-neglect, but these responses need not be lifelong companions. I encourage you to continue your quest to seek fuller understanding of both your son's circumstances and your own and to reach out for a level of mutual support and professional assistance that the world is prepared to give. These might prove to be the most precious gifts of the holiday season for your daughter, yourself and all those who love you.

—Dr. Neimeyer

# 13
# HOMICIDE AND MASS TRAGEDIES

### Violent Death of a Son

*Dear Dr. Neimeyer,*

My son was stabbed this spring and lost his life two days later, and they let the guy walk free. I continue fighting for justice for my son, but I am so lost without him. I am literally going crazy. I can't sleep, I don't eat properly, and I have lost 25 pounds since May. I am truly devastated. I used to be the happiest fun-loving person and always smiled but that is no longer true. How do I recover?

**Briana**

*Dear Briana,*

The short answer to your question is undoubtedly "gradually." With your son's sudden and violent death, your world has been shattered, and it will take some considerable time to put it back together. Even when you do, it will have a big piece missing, which time alone will not replace. And yet, as far too many tragically bereaved parents might tell you, there can be life after loss, and perhaps even a sense of renewed purpose, which emerges slowly from the fragments of the life that was. Here are a few steps to consider as you do so.

1. *Begin with self-care.* There can be no prospect for a meaningful life if it is founded on self-neglect. If your profound sleeplessness and weight loss reflect your despair, seek treatment for your depression. Grounding your actions in self-compassion, ask yourself what would help, even a little, to restore some sense of equilibrium. Seek a healthy routine of awakening and going to bed at the same hour, eating regular meals and watching coffee and alcohol consumption. Give yourself the gift of a routine you can depend on, especially if others in your family also depend on you.

2. *Make connections.* Homicide can destroy more than one life, as it can isolate and stigmatize survivors, leaving others in the social world too often in the role of horrified onlookers who withdraw out of a sense of helplessness or—still more hurtfully—intruding with morbid curiosity or even blame regarding the circumstances of the death. To counter these wounding dynamics, actively reach out to others who you believe will understand, whether to trusted friends and family, to others who have known tragic losses of their own in a support group environment or to professionals who should be able to hear what others will not and be willing to sift through the anguishing experience alongside you as you attempt to relearn life in the wake of this trauma. Your writing to me is already a first step.

3. *Revise and restore your "world assumptions."* Among the invisible losses that often accompany the visible one following homicide are the "deaths" of many taken-for-granted core beliefs: beliefs that the world is just, that people can be trusted, that we have the power to protect those we love and that our future is in some important measure predictable. But the murder, suicide or sudden accident that takes the life of our loved one challenges all of these beliefs in an instant, and it can be a hard and deliberate process learning to live on the basis of very different assumptions. We may, for example, need to come to terms with the reality that justice is uncertain and that seeking it for ourselves and others is a lifelong quest, that trust is rebuilt in one intimate relationship at a time, that we can comfort and honor loved ones even if we can't protect them and that the future can and must be reinvented when the old story lines of our lives are shattered by unforeseen events. This can be long and hard work and require patience and courage in the face of great pain.

4. *Turn tragedy into tribute.* Finally, consider the examples of those mothers who, faced with their own devastating losses, sought justice for others in founding or joining Mothers Against Drunk Driving, advocacy groups for the treatment of depression, support groups for suicide survivors or organizations to assist Parents of Murdered Children. In these and countless other examples, mourners have found meaning and purpose in pursuing noble missions as tributes to those they have loved and lost, during which they again found value in their lives, connections with others and a path toward a changed, but deeply significant assumptive world. Your passion, combined with your pain, can become a powerful force for good, in a broken world that badly needs it.

—Dr. Neimeyer

## Accidental Death of a Mother at Another's Hand

*Dear Dr. Neimeyer,*

My therapist showed me your website, and I'm grateful for her suggestion to join and get involved here. My mother was killed eight years ago, and I'm still struggling very much with what I'm told is called complicated grief. I was very, very close to my mum, who was my best friend, my nurse and my boss at work. And yet I became her caregiver in a lot of ways too due to her mental and physical health problems.

About five years ago she was hospitalized for a suicide attempt and was released within a year with another patient she had befriended with complex mental health issues. This lady moved in with my mother and accidentally set the house on fire with candles. She managed to get out with assistance from a neighbor, but my mother did not. There was no goodbye, no justice served at her death being as a result of another's hand, no funeral for a month while they attempted to find a way to identify my mother's remains and then I was given a full postmortem and all witnesses statements to read alone in my home. As a result, there's grief, but there's also guilt for not being able to stop this happening to my beautiful mum, and boiling rage in my veins at the woman who did this, and the injustice of no one caring or doing anything. They never did identify her body, and it was closed at that.

I guess I don't see an end to this and I'm struggling to let go of the rage at this woman who killed my mum. Do you have any suggestions for someone in a situation like this?

**Charlene**

*Dear Charlene,*

It is easy to imagine why you are experiencing prolonged and preoccupying grief in the aftermath of this tragic loss, complicated as it is by the traumatic circumstances of the death, the issue of blame and responsibility and perhaps also by the complex relationship you had with your mother across a period of many years, in which her caregiving for you alternated with your necessary caregiving for her. Integrating this sad loss in an adaptive way therefore likely will require assistance in processing the "event story" of the death itself, as well as the "back story" of your relationship to her as you now face a future in her physical absence. Let me offer a few thoughts on some potentially useful steps in both directions:

1. *Ground yourself in what was good.* Though it can be painful to do so, look for opportunities with your therapist, in a conversation with friends

and family or in an AfterTalk letter to reminisce about your relationship with your mother during a good time—perhaps before the gathering storm of her own psychological problems emerged on the horizon, in those days when her friendship, her nurturance and her direction were strong and reliable contributions to your life. Flesh this out with specific memories—maybe "illustrated" in family photographs of the period—that convey the loving and reliable contributions she made to her daughter's life. Doing so is one step in useful "grief work" in itself, as well as providing a secure anchor point for other steps to come.

2. *Revisit the loss event to gain more mastery of the trauma.* Research demonstrates that traumatic events retain their power when we attempt to avoid them, as well as—paradoxically—when we replay them in a ruminative fashion without finding new meaning and new ways forward through the experience. Revisiting or retelling the event in slow-motion detail with a trained trauma therapist who can help regulate the emotions that rise up for you is a "third way" to engage these painful memories, staying with them long enough to take them in, identify and manage the difficult feelings they trigger and address the troubling questions that come with them. Doing so in the safety of a trusted relationship with an experienced therapist can contribute to the security you need to "sit with" the reality of the death, drawing on any of several well-developed procedures for confronting the imagery, thoughts and emotions the revisiting engenders. Doing this review patiently, bravely and often on more than one occasion has been found to leave people feeling that they have more control over the memory, rather than the memory having control over them. However, I do not advise you to tackle this step alone, as your aloneness in the experience is itself one contributor to your suffering, and we naturally benefit from an ally in confronting the scenes that violent dying can conjure in our mind.

3. *Draw on the healing power of imagination.* As strange as it may seem, it then can be helpful to conjure vividly and lovingly how you would have worked to ease your mother's passing had you been able to do so, the factual impossibility of your having this opportunity notwithstanding. That is, one of the cruel injustices of violent death is that we are denied the opportunity to care for our loved one as we would have been inclined to do had the death been natural and anticipated. By imagining into being how we would have comforted and caressed our loved one, speaking caring or forgiving words to her, we help vivify a story of love that was equally real and validate a dimension of our relationship that was eclipsed by the death. Reclaim that loving intention, recognizing what you would have given if you could, and consider how you can continue to care for your mother's memory now.

4. *Consider giving a "moral gift" of forgiveness.* Finally, your words make clear the strong and understandable rage you feel about the carelessness on the part of your mother's friend that resulted in this traumatic loss for you both. Nothing compels you to excuse her action or inaction, and you have no obligation to find her innocent of wrongdoing. However, just as your mother's own struggles with mental health seem to have complicated her life and likely affected her judgment, it seems probable that her friend's history also did so for her . . . with tragic consequences, perhaps across a lifetime. Compassionately piecing together what you can, or can imagine, of this woman's history could provide some context for understanding this terrible event as one chapter in a longer story of struggle against her own demons and circumstances and perhaps allow you to release some of the anger that holds you, and holds you back now. If you find yourself strongly resisting this idea, remember you are under no compulsion to forgive, but at least reflect with a therapist on the question, *What would be there if the anger wasn't?* Sometimes we unconsciously harbor one kind of suffering because it seems to protect us from another that seems still worse, and an emotion-focused therapist who is used to helping people sort through different layers of emotion in response to the same event can help us negotiate these complicated currents.

—Dr. Neimeyer

## Choosing to Forgive

*Dear Dr. Neimeyer,*

How do I forgive the person who dumped my first-born son unconscious out of his car and left him to die? I lost my son almost three years ago; someone left him unconscious and he died in an empty parking lot alone. He was an organ donor and saved five different lives.

And to this day, we don't know what happened to him. His criminal case has been closed. We are devastated, our family is broken and everyone seems to be moving on, except for me. Each day I miss him more and more! I am angry and sad, and I don't think I will ever be able to move on. Do you think there will ever be healing and recovery from this tragic loss?

**Miriam**

*Dear Miriam,*

As I read your brief questions, I sense they carry with them many unspoken challenges and implications that stem from the unthinkable circumstances that led to your son's tragic and unnecessary death—your rage at the abandonment of your son at a moment at which medical attention might have saved his life, the horror of his dying alone, your own helplessness to prevent what came to pass. And along with all of these is a silent assumption—that you should forgive the perpetrator or negligent driver who left your son to his fate. We are taught that forgiveness is a virtue, or even that it is necessary in order to move to a place of "acceptance" regarding a traumatic loss like the one your family has suffered. Both, however, are at best half-truths.

In fact, forgiveness is a *choice*. We might well choose *not* to pardon someone who has done us and our loved one irreparable harm; we can continue to hold them accountable for their actions and inactions. Whether or not the justice system doles out appropriate punishment, it is our option to continue to find them guilty of serious wrongdoing. And taking this stance does not necessarily lead to simmering, impotent rage of a kind that undermines one's life—indeed, it can give rise to meaningful social action to stiffer sentences for impaired drivers, as in the efforts of Mothers Against Drunk Driving (MADD), or to curb gun violence, as through the advocacy work of Parents of Murdered Children. Finding a constructive outlet for legitimate anger can in this sense make the world a safer and more just place, perhaps by joining campaigns to educate young people on the risks of substance abuse, if this was involved in your son's dying. Finding purpose in the pain can be one way of seeking meaning in a meaningless loss. Perhaps you have already taken steps in this direction by your decision to allow your son to give the gift of life to five people who greatly needed it.

On the other hand, you can also choose *to* forgive, though not to condone. This path meets with its own challenges, one of which is our understandably righteous resistance to really step into the mindset, emotions and circumstances of the guilty party. How much experience did he or she have with such an emergency? What role might substance use have played in blurring his or her judgment? What powerful emotions—of fear, anger or personal liability—might have led to an impulsive and tragic decision? None of these questions exonerates this person's actions, but especially if he or she was young and overwhelmed, they might call up an attitude that contains elements of compassion as well as rage.

Finally, it is worth asking oneself honestly: *What would be more vivid for me if the anger I feel were reduced or released?* Sometimes anger can be adaptive in the sense that it protects us from a deeper hurt, such as powerlessness, abject grief or self-blame. Being ready to deal with these primary feelings may be a necessary part of considering forgiveness as an option.

—Dr. Neimeyer

# HOMICIDE AND MASS TRAGEDIES

## Daughter Murdered by the Father of Her Children

*Dear Dr. Neimeyer,*

My daughter was murdered by the father of her children. Her children at the time were a toddler and an infant. It's now seven years later. My daughter was just 21 years old. I had to get my granddaughter's things out of the apartment she was murdered in, so it was very traumatic to see. I have PTSD [posttraumatic stress disorder] because of it. I didn't cry or break down at her funeral because of the children. I can't sleep because I think about her so much. I'm very dedicated to trying to get better gun laws and advocate for domestic violence. I think those help some. But I need help for myself. Where do I turn?

**Miriam**

*Dear Miriam,*

Even in the brief and unelaborated form in which you have summarized this horrific story, it is hard to read—and all the more so for those readers who themselves have suffered the loss of someone to homicide or other forms of violent death. As you imply, there are many factors that make the already searing pain of losing a child that much more anguishing, including the following:

1. *Suddenness of the loss.* With no time to prepare, you were blindsided by death, denied any possibility of providing protection or comfort to your daughter or even the opportunity to say goodbye.
2. *Violence of dying.* Especially having seen the apartment in which your daughter was murdered, presumably by gunshot, you were immersed in indelible images that likely return unbidden, and very likely a vicarious sense of what you fear she may have suffered in that terrible final confrontation.
3. *Complicated issues of human intention.* Unlike accidental deaths, even those that are horrific, your daughter's death was the result of the decision of a specific human being to end her life. This commonly triggers rage as well as grief, which, in combination with the PTSD you understandably suffer, can greatly disrupt your ability to mourn your daughter and process the meaning of your physical separation from her.
4. *Questions of justice and the legal system.* Homicide loss shares with suicide and other tragic deaths the tendency to shatter our assumptions of security and ability to protect those we love, and sometimes even undermines our trust in a divine order or caring God. Compounding this in the case of murder, an imperfect and protracted legal system can keep the trauma

activated for many months or years, while rarely delivering a verdict that feels just to survivors. Moreover, most legal proceedings even deny public voice to survivors, compounding their sense of marginalization.

5. *Family systems complications.* In your case, two small children effectively lost both parents, and the older of them might actually have been aware of the killing. However well you or other loving family members step into the void, it may always feel like a family with a hole in the middle, one joined by shared grief as well as shared love.

In our studies of homicide survivors, we've observed several common struggles. These include a high percentage who qualify for complicated, intense and prolonged grief responses and clinically significant depression and a smaller, but substantial, number who meet criteria for PTSD. We also observe a large proportion of those who are religiously inclined having severe struggles with their faith, as reflected in an anger at God, an estrangement from the faith community and the loss of ability to find solace in spiritual practices and rituals. And finally, we encounter many survivors who suffer from a shrinking social world that pulls back from them in horror or helplessness—or worse, steps in intrusively out of morbid curiosity or with subtle or overt blame for the victim or the family as a whole. The result is an anguishing fog of grief and other intense emotions; a common feeling of distrust, isolation and betrayal by society or specific others or groups; and a sense of helplessness, fear and uncertainty about how to move through the horror.

And so, you ask, where can you turn for help and toward a healthy way forward through the tragedy? Here are a few recommendations:

1. *Seek others who have been there.* Both face-to-face and online support is available from groups that share some or all of the dimensions of your loss: The Compassionate Friends, Parents of Murdered Children and faith-based groups like Victims to Victory. Some of these groups are national or international, and others are local, but an internet search will usually help you find support services accessible to you.
2. *Know when to seek professional care.* Even the best peer support may not be able to provide the sort of specific trauma interventions, family therapy or therapy for prolonged grief that a growing number of professionals can offer. Note, however, that these skills do not necessarily come with a PhD, PsyD, LCSW or LPC credential or license. Before setting up an appointment with a provider for services, explain your experience succinctly as you did in this letter and ask this person if they can offer trauma- and grief-specific interventions or whether you might be served better by someone with specialized credentials. Most professionals will

respond candidly and are usually well positioned to help steer you to someone who can offer the relevant help.
3. *Look for empowerment and purpose beyond the trauma.* Functioning as a surrogate parent for children who lost their own mother can be a gift beyond measure, just as true engagement in challenging and changing the social conditions that give rise to an epidemic of deadly violence can add meaning to life through altruistic social action. Acts of meaning cannot erase the needless pain engendered by senseless violence, but it can help transmute it into something noble in the wake of great tragedy.

—Dr. Neimeyer

## A Relational Rupture Before the Murder

*Dear Dr. Neimeyer,*

My daughter was murdered a year ago. She was upset with me before it happened. I saw her the morning it happened, and we only waved at each other. Later, I saw her body lying on the floor in her house, and I can't get that image out of my head. I live it every moment of the day. I feel I'm a bad mother because I didn't turn around and make her talk to me. I never thought that would be the last time I saw her. I can't get past it either. I saw a doctor who told me I had posttraumatic stress syndrome. He wanted to give me drugs because I don't sleep much, but drugs are not for me. I have cried so much there are no more tears. She has never come to me in a dream. Every day it gets harder for me. All I see is my baby lying on the floor with a bullet in her chest. She left two boys and a husband. No word from law enforcement on where the case is either.

**Anabel**

*Dear Anabel,*

Surely your experience is every parent's nightmare: the violent death of a beloved child, complicated by traumatic imagery, guilt and the sense of irresolution resulting from the tension in your relationship when you last saw her and from the failure of justice to be served in apprehending and punishing her murderer. Little wonder, then, that as you begin a second year of bereavement, you find yourself struggling with preoccupying grief, sleeplessness and posttraumatic stress. I am gratified that you are reaching out for help, to your doctor, to me and perhaps to others. You and other members of your family—most especially your son-in-law and grandchildren—could benefit from a supportive community of concern, with the handful of ideas I will share here representing just one modest contribution to that.

First, recognize that the bullet that took your daughter's life wounded you as well. Though your injury was not physical, it is no less real, and you need care in order to begin healing. Among other things, this might take the form of active self-care practices, such as ensuring that you do what you can to restore normal daily rhythms of sleeping, eating and exercise. Though these routine means of nurturing your physical wellness are not a simple cure-all, they can provide a crucial hedge against depression, rumination and the descending spiral of self-neglect that deepens your suffering and saps the energies needed to engage life and the people and projects that comprise it. In other answers throughout this book, I offer numerous suggestions for how these self-care strategies can be cultivated.

Second, seek treatment for the trauma. Nearly every community offers specialized services by professionals who are trained to treat the troubling images and preoccupying thoughts that you describe, using not merely medication but also well-studied methods for helping you process these horrific experiences so that they have less power to disrupt your daytime thoughts and nighttime dreams. Look for psychologists, counselors and social workers who specifically use exposure strategies, which go beyond general talk about the trauma of your daughter's death to include close, step-by-step review and visualization of her dying, while containing these distressing images in the context of a trusting relationship that can help you integrate the experience emotionally. Among other strategies, clinicians who are trained in EMDR and "restorative retelling" may be especially helpful in this regard.

Third, consider "reopening the conversation" with your daughter that was closed prematurely and tragically by her death. In keeping with the emphasis of AfterTalk, you might write your daughter a letter to express your regret about the circumstances of your leave-taking, just as if you had had a conflict in the course of everyday life that led each of you to distance angrily from the other for a time. What might you say to her to mend fences, to make an apology, to ask for her forgiveness, to invite her back into contact with you? What kind of dreams would you like to have in which she might feel at home? If you welcome her back into contact with you in some sense, what would you like to do with her, and what kind of home would you like her to come to visit? How might you serve as the vehicle by which her love is now extended to her children? Beyond the words, take steps to make it so, by planning outings to places you and she might have once enjoyed, where you can sense her presence again, perhaps having inner conversations with her, or including stories of her special moments or qualities in conversations with others, and your grandchildren especially. As you gradually take better care of yourself, of your traumatic symptoms and of your ongoing relationship with her and those you both love, you can begin to heal some of the wounds that currently fester so painfully and embrace once more a life of which she can be proud.

—Dr. Neimeyer

## War and Terrorism

*Dear Dr. Neimeyer,*

This might seem like a strange letter, because I'm not writing about my own losses or even those of my immediate family. I'm writing about the losses of the world and of people who live in places I've never even been. I guess I'm just overwhelmed by the horrible scenes I witness every day on television and news feeds of the terrorist violence that involves people being tortured, raped, abducted and executed, and equally horribly, having their cities bombed and reduced to rubble, often losing dozens of members of their extended family crushed and left in the ruins.

I am grieving about the lives lost and the lives changed. The grief I feel about this is that it is not the first time, and won't be the last, whether in the Middle East, in Ukraine or in seemingly safe Western nations that are targeted by political groups for their own dark motives.

How do I insulate myself and move on from these feelings, knowing terror and war are the trigger for my grief and sadness, and knowing that they most certainly will continue?

**Lisa**

*Dear Lisa,*

I am sure you speak for many who have been shocked, sickened and saddened by the tragic terrorism we have all too recently and frequently witnessed in the news, the shock waves of which have rippled around the planet. Such events and the festering wars to which they both give rise and to which they are a response remind us of our collective vulnerability to violence in a world in which political, economic and ideological agendas can fuse into an unholy, lethal and unpredictable form of aggression. With a world awash in weapons, the ideal of full security is illusory, and we come to recognize that at best we can merely mitigate, not fully prevent, such trauma.

How might we respond to this brutal and increasingly universal phenomenon, while still retaining our humanity? Unfortunately, insulation has its limits, as no one is truly safe from the random or systematic violence that can end a life. Insulating ourselves psychologically from the victims by emphasizing our difference or distance from them might bolster a shaky sense of security for a time, but as the foreign and homegrown terrorism on our own shores, or the homicides and mass shootings in our own cities, make clear, such security is a fragile defense, and one easily undermined by harsh realities.

So what can we do beyond putting our heads in the sand? One answer is not to avert our gaze from scenes of trauma and devastation, but instead to acknowledge them in our thoughts, our emotions and our actions. If we accept the reality of widespread trauma, violence and death that touch countless lives and recognize the universality of suffering in all communities, we also are given the option to respond thoughtfully and empathically with compassionate actions in our own sphere of influence. What might we do to promote understanding and peace across frontiers of difference between people? How can we practice and promote nonviolent conflict resolution and social justice in our own families, communities and the larger world? How might our dream of peace inform our choice of candidates in coming national elections? Can we even draw upon our grief for a wounded world as a source of inspiration or motivation to mitigate its pain, on whatever scale our particular lives make possible? Perhaps your taking the time to write this letter or read this response already is a step in this direction.

Peace,

—Dr. Neimeyer

# Part 4

# FURTHER QUESTIONS

Not all questions relevant to loss and grief arise from the broken hearts of mourners, even if those that do are especially painful and poignant. Some have general relevance to bereavement, focusing on self-care or the role of medication, or even an earnest attempt to understand the nuances of grief beyond the conceptual simplifications of older models. Still others are voiced by the helping professionals who strive to accompany the bereaved, providing compassion, companionship and consultation as they search for a way of integrating the loss while reaffirming life. And some cut to the heart of the matter, bearing on the nature of life itself, in all of its troubling imperfection. This final part of the book addresses these questions and points both grievers and professionals toward further perspectives for seeking meaning in mourning.

Readers interested in further web-based resources relative to personal or professional engagement with grief are encouraged to explore the list provided by AfterTalk at the following link: https://www.aftertalk.com/grief_organizations.

# 14
# PRACTICAL AND PHILOSOPHIC QUESTIONS

### Getting Through Grief Without Antidepressants

*Dear Dr. Neimeyer,*

Is the best and probably only way to get through complicated grief through the use of antidepressants?

**Demi**

*Dear Demi,*

Both clinical experience and clinical research suggest that antidepressant medication is a mixed blessing in the context of bereavement, for several reasons. In fact, for many years psychiatrists agreed that depression could not be diagnosed in the early months following the death of a loved one because profound sadness and its disruptive effects on the survivor's life could be understood as essentially normal, rather than a "mental disorder" that required medical intervention. However, this has recently changed, as bereavement is no longer excluded from the diagnosis of a depressive disorder, opening the door to more widespread use of drugs as a treatment option from the early weeks following loss. However, evidence suggests caution in following this path.

One reason for caution is that reaching for a solution to a profound and very real existential challenge in the form of medication could lead professionals, potential social support figures and the bereaved themselves to neglect other forms of support and coping that have been shown to be at least as effective as medication in addressing depression. For example, closely retelling and reviewing the circumstances of the loss, processing the meaning of the loss for our lives via journaling, prompting ourselves to actively re-engage the world and circumstances we have avoided since the loss and seeking the practical and emotional support of others in our lives have all been found to improve adjustment to bereavement in general, and depressive reactions in particular. Sometimes medication can help people find the energy to engage in these other forms of self-help, but it does not in itself accomplish the many psychological, social and family changes that bereavement requires.

A related reason that antidepressants rarely "fill the bill" as an adequate treatment for bereavement is that grief and depression are substantially different things. Granted, sadness, lack of energy and withdrawal may be common to both, but the key symptoms of prolonged grief (profound separation distress, preoccupation with the death, feeling that our future is without meaning in the absence of the loved one) cannot be found in any list of symptoms of depression, and in fact have more in common with anxiety states than with depression, per se. Accordingly, multiple studies have shown that these core features of separation distress simply are not helped greatly by antidepressants, even if medication does improve symptoms of depression (inability to experience pleasure, loss of energy, disrupted sleep, etc.) more narrowly defined.

So, what might the appropriate role for antidepressants be in treating prolonged and complicated grief? Perhaps the most enlightened view would be that they can play a useful role in addressing depression triggered by the loss, though not separation distress, when both conditions co-occur for several months following a loved one's death (as one study suggests might be the case for approximately 25% of survivors of a loved one's violent death, for example). In other words, antidepressant medication is rarely, if ever, a sufficient treatment for bereavement distress, though it can contribute to survivors' adaptation when depressive symptoms compound complicated or prolonged grief. Used alongside social support, personal efforts to process the loss and re-engage life and professional counseling or psychotherapy, it can sometimes provide a partial answer to the many biopsychosocial challenges of loss, though not a comprehensive one.

—Dr. Neimeyer

## Grieving and Exercise

*Dear Dr. Neimeyer,*

I've heard that exercise can make a big difference for people who are suffering grief after a loved one dies. Is that really true? I know exercise is good for you in general, but how does it help when you are broken-hearted after the death of someone who meant the world to you? If it really does work, what kind of exercise would you recommend?

**Brittany**

*Dear Brittany,*

Exercise is not a panacea for the many ways in which loss erodes the quality of our lives, nor does it answer all the hard questions that can be opened up by a death of a loved one, from the question of how we will embrace a changed future, to concerns about our loved one's intentions in ending his or her life in the case of suicide. But it can indeed help us in adapting to bereavement, in several respects, both for the direct benefits it confers in terms of our mood and health and in terms of its indirect benefits of a social kind. Here I'll comment on several payoffs to giving your body the attention it needs, even—or especially—when contending with grief:

1. *Exercise is one of the best antidepressants.* Many studies have demonstrated the effectiveness of exercise regimens, especially of an aerobic type, in improving mood for people who are moderately depressed, effects that are observed within a few weeks of beginning a fitness program. Although walking and/or running are the best documented forms of exercise, even anaerobic exercise such as weight training shows a good deal of promise, suggesting that the benefits of exercise are not limited to activities that yield cardiovascular benefits primarily. Instead, factors having to do with mastery (setting progressive, achievable goals and accomplishing them) may be at work here, countering the sense of helplessness and hopelessness that is at the heart of depression.
2. *Getting up and getting going counteracts rumination.* In the wake of loss, we can easily be pulled into the quicksand of rumination—going over and over the events leading to the death or forlornly cycling endlessly through the memories of what we will never have again. In addition to contributing to depressive lassitude, this vicious cycle of corrosive self-questioning or focusing on a frightening future alone can feed into our self-blame and anxiety. By launching ourselves out of self-imposed isolation and into the world, we work against this tendency.
3. *Action precedes motivation.* Psychologists use the concept of "behavioral activation" to refer to our follow-through on our action plans—including engagement in an exercise program. As we do so, we may naturally connect with others who share our interests, as with joining a cycling meet-up or senior swimming group or arranging to take a regular afternoon walk with a neighbor, in a way that also invites natural conversation. In other words, one positive behavior tends to lead to others, building our motivation as we go along. In contrast, "waiting until we feel like it" is a recipe for disaster, as inactivity feeds upon itself, generating more of the same.
4. *Fitness pushes back against the health risks of bereavement.* Research suggests that having a regular exercise regimen helps introduce a healthy structure

into life, making mealtimes and bedtimes more regular and contributing to better nutrition and sleep patterns. In this way exercise promotes positive health outcomes directly, as well as indirectly, mitigating the negative impact of eating poorly and relying on caffeine, cigarettes or alcohol to perk us up or calm us down, often creating two problems in the place of one.

5. *Some forms of exercise can promote mindful stress reduction.* Yoga, for example, shows promise in reducing our reactivity to catastrophic thinking or avoidance-based coping in bereavement, as we breathe through feeling states that rise up and fall away, or focus on the demands of a challenging position rather than a preoccupying image or thought. The key to this is a kind of nonattachment to a particular impression, emotion or cognition, just observing it with an attitude of, "Oh yes, there's that fear again. That's interesting." Viewed dispassionately with no intention to elaborate on or resist the thought or feeling ultimately reminds us that these are simply subjective states that rise and fall, like the waves of the sea. Watching them as if from the beach, we can come to recognize that we need not wade in and drown in them.

And so, what are a few useful tips for pursuing exercise as a constructive dimension of your self-care in bereavement? Here are some practical ideas:

1. *Start small.* Walk a block. Set your step counter or exercise watch for 3,000 steps a day. Meet your goal and then increase gradually as you become more active.
2. *Meet the need.* Do you need help getting moving? Start walking or commit to 20 minutes in the gym. Do you need help slowing down and making peace with silence? Take a yoga class. Craft a routine that works for you.
3. *Double the payoff.* Walk to the store on an errand, killing two birds with one stone. Or take a hike with a friend, building social support and fitness at the same time.
4. *Add meaning to your moving.* Work up to a road race for charity in honor of your loved one. Imagine him or her walking or talking with you as you stroll through the park.
5. *Practice self-compassion.* If you miss a day or fall short of a goal, cut yourself some slack, but give yourself encouragement to return to the program the next day. Consider what advice your loved one might have for you in that circumstance.

In sum, working (out) through grief doesn't solve all the challenges we face in bereavement, but it can provide a key platform in our self-care plan that can connect us to others, as it also improves our emotional and physical wellness. Consider how you can best make exercise work for you and take a step in that direction today.

—Dr. Neimeyer

## Unpredictability of Grief: A Letter to Sofia

*Dear Dr. Neimeyer,*

I'm a writer for my high school's award-winning newspaper, and I'm writing an article about the unpredictability of grief. I would love if you could answer some of my questions regarding the subject, because a lot of the students at school have lost people recently. Here are my questions.

**Sofia**

*1. Does the way someone grieves vary from person to person?*
There are both universal and highly individual expressions of grief. Of course, we usually feel profound sadness when we lose someone or something we greatly love, and we tend to draw into ourselves and away from others at such times. But how we grieve is a function of who we are, how we cope, who we have lost and how we have lost them. When we have plenty of personal resources for managing difficult changes, when we show resilience in the face of adversity, when those we have lost have not been the most central people in our lives and when the deaths are expected, as in later life through advanced illness, we tend to move through grief with less distress and extended anguish. But when we ourselves are anxious about our connections with people; have struggles coping in other areas of our lives; lose people who are very central to our life stories; and lose them tragically, prematurely and suddenly, then our course of grief can be far more difficult.

*2. Are there benefits from learning about death earlier on in our lives, as children, or should we "shield" children from death?*
We should not try to shield children from death and hide them from the reality of loss, but we should be loving companions to them as they experience the natural losses of people, pets and possessions in the course of their young lives. Small losses can provide teachable moments for mastering later and larger ones.

*3. Are there clear-cut stages of grief, such as in the Kübler-Ross model?*
The popularity of stage theory aside, there is little evidence for it. Instead, there are many differences in how we grieve, as a function of gender, culture

and the sorts of factors I have mentioned earlier. Sometimes our psychological models are much simpler than our emotional realities.

4. *Does grief ever end? Why do we grieve even years after the death of a loved one? How does grief in the long run look different from grief right after a loss?*

In a sense, grief does not end, but it can and usually does change. A heavy sense of despair and depression in the early weeks or months of grief may mellow into a sweet nostalgia or feeling of gratitude as months turn into years. Grief is how we love someone after they die, but it does not have to be anguishing and life limiting.

5. *Is there an "acceptable" or expected grieving period in society? How does the process of grief look when someone begins grieving later than the expected grieving period?*

There are widely different norms in different cultures and subcultures about how long visible grief is expected or tolerated, but a general principle would be that our private grief typically lasts longer than the social role of being a mourner. There's not really much evidence for the concept of delayed grief, but of course a mourner can tend to avoid and minimize the impact of a loss early on, usually with an evident form of anxious inhibition or running away from the associated feelings. Of course, there are also many losses that simply do not touch us deeply, and so our grief may be minimal.

6. *Even though you mentioned that there aren't necessarily clear-cut stages of grief, is denial a common reaction someone might experience after, or even during, the death of a loved one? What might denial look like?*

Outright denial that a loved one has died is rare when the evidence of death is clear, although a subtle psychological denial of the implications of the death may persist. For example, a spouse who loses a partner could avoid some of the difficult decisions that will follow from this, such as whether to remain in the home they previously shared or to give away the loved one's possessions. But when the death is ambiguous, as when a loved one simply disappears through abduction or an airline accident, denial of the reality of the death is more common.

7. *Does time heal?*

In our research we find that time does little to heal the wounds of grieving. Instead, it is a question of what people do with the time that matters.

8. *Is it important to not only accept the death of a loved one but also the grief that comes with it?*

Self-acceptance and self-compassion are always good qualities to cultivate in ourselves and others. We cannot hope to change that which we refuse to even recognize, and this applies to our grief as well.

## PRACTICAL AND PHILOSOPHIC QUESTIONS

9. *Is it better to give yourself time to be sad or to keep yourself busy after the death of a loved one?*

The answer to your question is *yes!* That is, it is best to do both. Make a date with your grief as frequently as you need to, whether that takes the form of 30 minutes of reflection, journaling or listening to music that reminds you of your loved one, perhaps daily or at least a few times a week. However, also give yourself permission to have fun, hang out with friends, engage in a creative project or give time to your studies or work. Don't simply flee into "keeping busy," but instead choose people and projects that have real meaning for you. This will help you grow through grief, rather than simply run from it.

10. *What are some things that can help someone who is grieving?*

People are not things, but they can be very helpful when we are grieving! We also do well to exercise, eat well, allow time for reflection, try new things and perhaps things that are even a little weird, like writing letters of love or appreciation to the person we have lost in our journal or on their memorial Facebook page. We can even imagine their advice for us as we move forward with our lives, and it can be an interesting process to write that down to, in the form of a letter from them to us. Be creative and attempt to maintain a healthy bond with those you have loved. And a healthy bond of any kind does not mean that we spend all our time or energy only with one person. A healthy relationship—whether with the living or the dead—is a safe harbor to return to to feel cared for and a launch pad to take off from to explore other worlds. Coming and going and then coming again, easily and without drama, is optimal in both cases.

11. *How can someone support a friend or family member who's grieving?*

We can be helpful to a mourner in lots of ways. By listening more deeply than others do and withholding simple advice or the temptation to just cheer them up. By offering practical help with schoolwork or other tasks of living. And by simply giving them a chance to have some fun and take a break from their grief for a while. But we don't help much when we offer them drugs or alcohol as a temporary and potentially addictive way of dealing with feelings without really understanding them.

12. *What's the difference between mourning and grieving? What might the two processes look like?*

People use these terms in different ways, but the most general understanding of them would be that grieving represents the personal and psychological process of moving through a loss, whereas mourning represents the public and ritualistic ways in which we do so.

13. *What are some ways that grief can shape someone's outlook on life?*

Managed poorly, grief can leave us feeling embittered, distrustful, angry and alone. But managed well grief can make us wiser, calmer, more compassionate and more connected. We rarely choose to lose someone through death, but we certainly can make choices in bereavement that shape how we grieve and who we become.

—Dr. Neimeyer

## Dealing With Insensitive Consolations

*Dear Dr. Neimeyer,*

My husband has been gone less than a year, and I can't believe the stupid things people say to me, trying to make me "feel better." "Time heals all wounds," "You just need to stay busy," "You've got to look on the bright side," "At least you had him all these years" and "God never gives us more than we can bear" are just a few. Sometimes I feel that these clumsy consolations are more than I can bear! It makes me just want to avoid everyone; nobody seems to "get it."

What can I do when people approach me with this sort of advice or comment? It feels like they are minimizing the importance of his death or just trying to push me in a direction I don't feel ready to go. Should I just try to steer clear of social situations and go it on my own?

**Helen**

*Dear Helen,*

It is ironic, but when we are approached with the wrong kind of "consolation," our grief can be compounded by anger and a deep sense of isolation, even in the midst of a social gathering. What our hearts generally crave in bereavement is compassionate understanding, patience and sometimes genuine partnership in stepping back into life, rather than to be offered Hallmark card platitudes or prescriptions that seem poorly attuned to where we are. But the reality is that not everyone will have the empathy and ability to meet us in the difficult emotional space in which we find ourselves and offer the sort of social support we really need.

So, what can we do, you ask, when we are blindsided by these unhelpful comments? Here are three suggestions that might help:

1. *Recognize the intent behind the words.* Often the people making the blunder genuinely want to be helpful or express that they care, but they simply don't know, or in an anxious moment can't find, the words that

adequately convey that. In such cases, especially if you know the person to be caring and supportive in other contexts, try listening beneath the language to the feeling that is finding only very awkward expression. Practice responses that you can draw on in such situations, such as, "I appreciate your understanding at this hard time," or simply, "Thanks. I hope that is true, too." Just as we can continue to love a child without accepting his or her behavior, it is often possible to embrace the intent even if not its awkward expression.

2. *Set your boundaries.* Some advice is welcome, especially when we seek it from trusted sources. But unsolicited advice is often misdirected. Like a "postage due" letter delivered to you by the mail carrier, you have the option whether to accept it at a price or simply decline it. Affirming your boundaries in this way need not take the form of a hostile or angry response; it could be as simple as saying, "Thanks for your suggestion, but I just can't do that right now," or "I'm not ready for that yet, but I'll keep that in mind for the future." If you share a religious faith with someone who is being a bit pushy about offering spiritual consolation, you might respond simply, "Thanks. Keep me in your prayers." In other words, with a bit of forethought, you can often acknowledge the advice or consolation without taking delivery of it, but also without rejecting the person who clumsily offers it.

3. *Look elsewhere.* Most of us have some reliable people in our lives who can provide genuine support of a tangible or emotional kind and who are better at listening than speaking when what we really want is an audience rather than an authority. Seek out contact with these special people who can hear what others cannot and try to balance your need to express your grief with reports of your genuine efforts to embrace life once more. The deepened discussions and friendships that follow can do much to alleviate your isolation and provide true companionship on the path going forward.

—Dr. Neimeyer

## On the COVID-19 Pandemic

*Dear Dr. Neimeyer,*

I am sure that I am not alone in saying that the COVID-19 crisis really rocked my world. Even though the worst of it clearly is over, people are still dying from this disease, and we never know when the next pandemic will break out or how long it will take to get on top of it. Of course, like most people I followed the advice of medical authorities regarding hand washing, social distancing, curtailing unnecessary travel and the rest. But for a couple of years it just felt like the world was falling apart, from our usual household routines to our school systems, businesses, healthcare and even our global financial system. And then there was the real and terrifying threat of severe illness and death of our loved ones or ourselves. I just felt so helpless and anxious, and so did most of my friends and family. Is there anything you can tell us that would help us in future versions of this awful nightmare, whether or not we experience the death of our loved ones to some awful global virus?

**Shirley**

*Dear Shirley,*

We are wired for attachment in a world of impermanence. As much as we yearn for stability, predictability and control of our lives, we often find these taken from us. Sometimes this occurs with the news of our own serious illness or that of someone we love; sometimes it comes with the loss of a relationship or a valued role; sometimes it comes in the form of apocalyptic firestorms and floods; and sometimes it happens with the devastating suddenness of the recent pandemic that swept away 7 million lives throughout the world. In one form or another we then learn the lessons of loss: that life is change, predictability is fleeting and our customary sense of control is an illusion. How then can we live in a world transformed by frightening and traumatic loss, of people, places, projects and protections that we once naively took for granted? Here are a few ideas, but the most genuine answers arise in our own hearts and in deep conversation with those we trust and who are asking similar questions of their own.

*First, find respite from the storm.* Allow yourself, where possible, to take momentary refuge from the whirlwind of circumstances that bring you grief. Perhaps this will take the form of a simple ritual, such as having a quiet tea in your garden surrounded by the signs of spring or in a moment of mindful meditation during a difficult day. "Dose" yourself with the hard reality of the situation, knowing that it demands attention, but not constant attention. Find ways of growing still, cultivating inner peace. Explore moments of solitude, rather than running from them toward electronic distractions. Center down. Seek beauty and refuge where they can be found.

*Second, take action.* Perhaps there is something, however small, that you can do to solve the problems brought by the mounting losses that crisis brings in its train. This might be for yourself and your immediate family, as you seek to restore some sense of security in an insecure world. Or this might be for another—even a stranger—who has also suffered, in a random act of unexpected kindness that helps them understand that the world still contains love. Reach out, if not with your hands, then with your heart. Make virtual contact with someone dear at a distance. Engage in a creative or artistic project. Play a board game with your child. You will both win.

*Third, express gratitude.* Search for the blessings, the silver lining in the dark clouds of fear and tragedy. Has someone extended to you an act of kindness in your suffering, and if so, how might you acknowledge it? Who matters to you, and how can you thank them—perhaps in a text note, a call or a small symbolic gift—for touching your life? Disciplining ourselves to do this three times per week reminds us that goodness exists in us and in all around us, even in hard times. Seek out stories of everyday heroism and compassion. And be inspired by them.

*Fourth, seek meaning.* What personal life philosophies or spiritual perspectives help you understand and adapt to life's many losses, and how have these core beliefs been tested and deepened by what you have suffered? What affirmative meaning could emerge from your present pain, at the level of your own life, that of your family or the larger community? Seeking some way to make sense of the threat of a terrible pandemic or other large-scale catastrophe can help us bear it with grace. Might it even sharpen our appreciation of who and what truly matter?

*And fifth, embrace unwelcome change as a teacher in times of transition.* What do such unexpected transitions teach us about the nature of human life? And how can we learn to live with impermanence without cynicism or bitterness or greed, embracing the people, places, projects and possessions we now have for this short time? In learning the lessons of loss in a constructive way, we move closer to wisdom.

—Dr. Neimeyer

## The Meaning of Life

*Dear Dr. Neimeyer,*

I have just one question, but it is a big one. In your opinion, what is the meaning of life?

**Nicolae**

*Dear Nicolae,*

I'm a practicing psychologist who works alongside people who are struggling with deeply unwelcome changes in their lives—the breakdown of intimate relationships, the loss of career or meaningful work, the onset of life-threatening illness and especially the death of loved ones, often in tragic circumstances. As a scholar and researcher, I also study how people meet, and typically surmount, such adversity. Decades of doing this work have shaped my understanding of the meaning of life, and specifically how people rebuild or reconstruct life's meaning when it is devastated by events beyond their control. Here I'll reflect briefly on these "lessons of loss," viewing them through a narrative lens that has proven helpful in our research, as well as to the people who consult me in my practice.

First, it strikes me that we generally only reflect on the meaning of life when it is called into question. Mostly, meditations on life's significance do not arise spontaneously when we are brewing a cup of coffee for breakfast, singing "Happy Birthday" to a child, dining with friends or working on an art or carpentry project. At all of these moments, whether social or solitary, living is simply taking place as a verb, rather than inviting reflective consideration as a noun or object of contemplation. Another way of saying this is that the meaning of our life story is implicit in our practical activities, alone or with others; it just "makes sense" in an uncontested, taken-for-granted way. Simply stated, it just "is."

But there are times—many of them—when this familiar life world skips a beat, is rendered strange or even alien, when our implicit expectations are challenged and sometimes decimated by events we had not foreseen and in the face of which we are powerless. We or a loved one could receive a diagnosis of cancer. Our life partner succumbs to a heart attack. Our child dies of an overdose. A parent dies by suicide. In all of these cases and a hundred other life-altering transitions, life's familiar meanings are "up for grabs," as we try to process the "event story" of the death itself and its implications for our lives now, as well as to access the "back story" of our loved one's life, braided together with our own, in order to rework rather than relinquish our attachment to them. Another way of saying this is that grieving entails reaffirming or rebuilding a world of meaning that has been challenged by loss.

Just how people do this is as varied as the people who consult me in the wake of personal tragedy. A young widow now stands at the grill once manned by her husband as she wears his oversize apron and continues the annual ritual of a neighborhood Memorial Day cookout. A retired engineer who lost his son and grandson in a boating accident launches a multistate safety program at numerous state parks, offering free loans of life vests on signs displaying their image under the slogan, "Kids Don't Float." A bereaved mother gradually morphs visits from consoling friends on the monthly "anniversary" of her son's death into a monthly meditation and shared meal for 12 to 24 other bereaved parents and supporters, who find sacred sanctuary in this non-denominational gathering with those living with analogous pain. Many others draw upon their spiritual and philosophic resources to survive such tragedy, and more than a few question, deepen, redefine or abandon these same beliefs to seek others more adequate to the contours of the new worlds in which they find themselves. But all are in a sense reviewing, revising or rewriting their life stories, in deeds, in works and in relationships, in the wake of loss.

Witnessing and sometimes facilitating this reconstruction of meaning have deepened my respect for the everyday nobility of people seeking to rebuild a sustainable life from the ashes of the old. Doing so is rarely easy when the loss is profound, and as the complicated and sometimes life-threatening outcomes of bereavement demonstrate, resilience is far from certain. But whatever the outcome of this process, in the short or long term, it is commonly the case that it is the lessons of loss that shape and reshape our lives and its meanings going forward.

—Dr. Neimeyer

# 15

# QUESTIONS FROM PROFESSIONALS

### A New Grief Therapist Asks if Being Empathic Is a Liability

*Dear Dr. Neimeyer,*

I am a new therapist who is just beginning to work with grieving people but wonder if I've chosen the right career. I've always known I was an empathic person, someone who could feel genuinely for others who were hurting, and this made me a good listener for friends when I was growing up. But now that I am working with clients, I worry that my empathy could be a liability to me personally, and even contribute to my eventual burnout or compassion fatigue. Do I just need to get used to it, harden my heart, or just better balance my empathy with objectivity, or something else? In your answers to clients, it is clear that you too are very empathic, and you've found a way of retaining this for your whole career. Can you help me understand this issue so that I can try to do the same?

**Megan T., LCSW**

*Dear Megan,*

Your comments about the downside of therapeutic empathy prompted me to think more about this conundrum: if empathy is crucial for therapy, and especially grief therapy, is it also inherently painful or punishing for the therapist? Certainly, if we are sensitive people, we can feel another's hurt, and even cry responsive tears—I do it all the time, in and out of therapy! But this in itself is not a liability—if we do not cry longer or louder than our clients, this sort of responsiveness is typically validating and helps us feel "what it is like to be them," which can be a kind of precondition to understanding what they need to really be of help. The problem arises when the emotion stays with us and carries throughout our day or evening . . . or career.

In this case I think something more is going on. Perhaps we have an unfounded presumption that we can "solve" another's problems, maybe because we were cast early into the role of problem solver or caretaker in our families of origin and have not yet learned the lesson that companioning or consulting in someone's life is not the same as living it. Perhaps we were ourselves wounded in some of the ways our clients were and have not given sufficient attention to our own healing, so our personal pain is activated by theirs. Or perhaps our earlier experiences of helplessness, as in the face of a family member's inconsolable grief, leaves us alert to and fearful of similar emotion in our client's lives, so expressions of this stick with us like tar and become the focus of ruminative concern.

There is actually an easy test for whether our empathy is responsive and adaptive or personal and problematic, in the sense of pointing to something unresolved in our own lives: if we carry just certain feelings of the other forward beyond our immediate interaction with them (e.g., grief, hopelessness, anxiety) but not others (e.g., anger, joy, guilt), then this might tell us that it is not our empathy, or capacity to "indwell" another's feelings, that is the issue—it is our vulnerability to just *certain* emotions that could be problems for us, in some way or another. Of course, this insight is itself useful, as it suggests parts of our experience that need more attention in order to heal.

But in considering your own sensed obstacles to becoming or remaining a therapist, also consider that obstacles of some kind are universal in this career we pursue. That is, working as a therapist will always require work on ourselves, and this is always a work in progress. Certainly, the contrast to the empathic response you describe is no solution to the struggle; unless the therapist merely becomes a psychoeducational robot offering generic advice from a distance, we will always resonate with our clients' suffering (and success). But this does not mean that we are condemned to hear endless echoes of their distress or have it drown out the music of our own lives. Attending to those lives, and the implicit needs still to be found and met within them, will leave us optimally positioned to similarly hear and engage the needs of another.

—Bob Neimeyer

## Prolonged Grief Disorder in the ICD-11 and DSM 5-TR

*Dear Dr. Neimeyer,*

For years now there has been a lot of controversy about whether grief can be considered a mental disorder, especially since the diagnosis of Prolonged

Grief has been included in the DSM 5-TR [*Diagnostic and Statistical Manual of Mental Disorders, Fifth Edition, Text Revision*]. I confess that I as a practicing grief therapist am ambivalent about this development, because severe grief seems like a normal human reaction after a major loss. Bereaved people have enough to deal with, without being labeled or pathologized. But I also recognize that some forms of grief can go on and on and take a great toll on survivors individually and as families. What is your take on this issue of diagnosis, as a clinician and a scientist?

**Luis M., PhD**

*Dear Luis,*

Just as you say, official announcement of the inclusion of Prolonged Grief Disorder (PGD) in the DSM 5-TR revived the simmering controversy over whether any form of grief should be considered a "mental disorder," alongside life-limiting forms of anxiety, depression, eating disorder, substance abuse and the myriad other conditions given attention and definition as diagnoses within this psychiatric compendium of human distress. Here I'll offer just a few thoughts about this important development in the hope of contributing clarity to the ongoing conversation.

First, it merits emphasizing that grief per se is an entirely normal response to the loss of someone (and, in a broader definition, *something*) to whom (or which) we are greatly attached. In the context of bereavement, grief has been described aptly as the price we pay for love and is of course nearly as universal as death itself. Moreover, the ability to mourn our losses can promote adaptation to a world changed crucially and irreversibly by the death of another, as we characteristically navigate a sea of shifting emotion, realign our attachment to the deceased without relinquishing it and subtly or substantially revise our own sense of purpose and identity as we make meaning of the loss and our own lives in its wake. Nothing in this is inherently disordered even if it is disorderly; it is simply the normative way we reconstruct our worlds in the aftermath of bereavement.

Except when we don't. A large and scientifically impressive body of research across cultures documents that for a small subset of the bereaved—perhaps 5% to 10%—very little reconstruction ensues in the months and sometimes years following the death of a loved one. Instead, the bereaved may find themselves adrift in a seemingly boundless sea of despair, preoccupied with the circumstances of a traumatic death or corrosive and unresolved relationship issues with the deceased. They may report drowning in anguish, being lost in unfulfilled yearning or consumed by guilt, anger or hopelessness—little of which attenuates as months meld into years. And the real effects of this suffering are obvious enough to those close to them, as they find themselves struggling interminably to show up for their partners, parent their children, maintain friendships or perform adequately in the workplace—all to an extent and duration that greatly exceeds their community's cultural norms following loss. When these conditions persist nearly unchanging a year or more following the loss, posing documented risk of suicide, substance abuse and serious illness, both the American Psychiatric Association and the World Health Organization concur that a diagnosis of PGD may be indicated.

Note, however, that genuine grief may persist long beyond a one-year criterion—indeed, we may continue to experience periodic waves of significant sadness and missing mingled with nostalgia and gratitude for the loved one's ongoing contribution to our lives for the rest of our days. However, the constructive *integration* of grief into life deepens rather than cheapens it, and we may even live our lives with greater purpose and intention, and greater compassion for self and others, as a result. Such a pattern of growing through grief does not deny its painfulness, but instead takes it as a prompt to review and revise one's values and choices and affirm a life that still has significance and even beauty. This image of life changed by loss is a very different trajectory than the one captured in the DSM 5-TR.

But crucially, PGD is only one formulation of this painful and protracted form of distress. Like all diagnoses—and all other abstractions that we use to orient to life and its challenges, such as *justice, human rights, crime, chance* and *freedom*—*prolonged grief disorder* is a social construction, no more or less "real" than any other. Granted, there is ample evidence that the relatively few bereaved people who it describes suffer grave consequences, but this condition could in other contexts be formulated in other terms, perhaps as a *crisis of meaning, a dark night of the soul, a rupture in the network of social relations* or a *neurological process*. Each such construction would carry its own implications for understanding and supporting the bereaved, and none could claim absolute "validity" in a sense that invalidated the others. Stated differently, all social constructions, diagnoses included, are useful for some purposes and not others and should be judged on the grounds of their pragmatic *viability* rather than their epistemological *validity*, per se. The relevant questions therefore include: *In what ways might a PGD diagnosis be helpful and harmful* (as all social constructions will serve some purposes and not others) and *Who benefits and who suffers if this social construction is adopted?* These are complex issues that merit serious attention, and they do not admit of simple answers.

In the case of PGD, a diagnosis could have pragmatic benefits in opening the door to relevant professional care in many cultural and economic contexts, without requiring the rationalization of misdiagnoses (such as generic depression or anxiety states, for example) to do so. More specifically, a PGD conceptualization of a mourner's distress could highlight some of what is *distinctive* in incapacitating grief, focusing attention usefully on the disruption of an attachment bond and a world of meaning unique to the precipitating loss. But it is also likely to have a downside, including empowering professional healers (and especially physicians) at the possible expense of informal caregivers and supporters, and perhaps contribute to a broader Western trend to construe distress in merely pharmacological terms rather than intrinsically existential ones. All of this suggests that responsible and critical analysis of the impact of such discourses for good as well as ill is called for in the years to come.

Of course, none of this resolves the very real suffering entailed by many forms of loss or the intense and life-limiting forms of suffering in which bereaved people occasionally become stuck—sometimes for the rest of their lives. With or without a diagnostic label to describe this predicament, these extreme and intractable states of suffering call for humane and informed attention from all compassionate persons, professional or nonprofessional, who respect both the legitimacy of grief and the human capacity for resilience even in the wake of tragic loss.

—Bob Neimeyer

### Risk Factors for Prolonged Grief

I am a hospice social worker with a large bereavement center that offers community support services for grieving people of all kinds, not only surviving family members after a loved one dies in our home care or residential facility. But recently we've been stretched thin in our outreach and response services and are trying to make evidence-informed decisions about therapeutic triage—who to provide simply educational information (such as through brochures or our website), who might benefit from an invitation to one of our ongoing support groups and who might need assessment for grief therapy of a more professional or individualized kind, which might require referral to a specialist beyond the services we ourselves can offer. So our question as a team is whether there are any evidence-based risk factors for who among the bereaved are likely to experience complicated or prolonged grief and call for a closer assessment of their needs. We've found some existing scales or criteria, but mostly these just seem to categorize people based on [the] nurse's impressions rather than actual data on who suffers the greatest risk of complication. Can you point us in a helpful direction?

**Elaine W., MCSW**

*Dear Elaine,*

One of the hazards of compassionate care is that it can be extended so widely that the safety net it provides grows thin and insubstantial, so that those whose grief is heaviest may not receive the support they need, while mourners who are likely to adapt well on their own receive attention they may not even want. But evidence suggests that some grievers are at greater risk of intense and prolonged grief than others, although more research needs to be done to clarify exactly what factors in what combination are most worrisome—a task that several collaborating colleagues in our research network are undertaking even as we write. So while a strong evidence-based checklist of risk factors is still on the horizon, it is possible to scan for the following factors that dozens of recent studies individually suggest pose the prospect of poor outcomes following loss.

For the sake of clarity, let me divide these factors into those that focus on (1) the circumstances of the death, (2) the background of the bereaved, (3) their relationship to the deceased, (4) their styles of coping with the loss and (5) the broader social and institutional systems in which they are engaged.

### Circumstances of the Death

- *Cause of death:* In general, violent death losses—through suicide, overdose, homicide, disaster and fatal accident—provoke more complicated grief than death through natural causes.
- *Peri-event variables:* Finding the body of a loved one, especially after violent death, as well as witnessing a loved one's great suffering at the end of life, tend to intensify grief responses.
- *Lack of care at the end of life:* Especially in the COVID-19 era, studies demonstrated that inability to "be there" for a loved one at the end of life as a function of necessary safety protocols, concerns about the patient being left to die alone, dissatisfaction with the absent or scaled-down funeral and other factors are associated with prolonged and functionally impairing grief on the part of survivors.

### Background of the Bereaved

- *Gender:* Other things being equal, women appear more susceptible to prolonged grief than men, perhaps as a function of their deeper attachments.
- *Demographic disadvantage:* Poverty and lower levels of education increase the risk of bereavement complication, as mourners may have fewer tangible resources and perhaps less medical literacy to negotiate the illness and loss of a member of the family.

### Relationship to the Deceased

- *Kinship:* Other factors being equal, closer kinship to the deceased places people at greater risk of complication, although psychological closeness is a better predictor of this than degree of legal or biological kinship per se.

- *Marital dependency:* Concentrating one's emotional, financial and practical dependency on a partner places the surviving spouse at risk for feelings of decimation when widowhood occurs.
- *Caregiver burden:* Especially in the context of progressive illness, family caregivers can become exhausted and isolated, while also experiencing a thinning of their social network, all of which can worsen eventual bereavement.

### Coping Style

- *Attachment style:* People who are chronically anxious about abandonment by others and fearful of rejection may be deeply threatened by the loss of a loved one to death and feel too vulnerable to reach out to others afterward.
- *Meaning-making:* Mourners who struggle to make sense of the death or their lives in its aftermath suffer more intense and protracted grief.

### Social Systemic and Institutional Factors

- *Social support:* Survivors with the least practical and emotional support from others are vulnerable to worse bereavement outcomes.
- *Institutional responses:* Disengagement by (often overworked) healthcare professionals can deprive families of the informational support and joint decision making that they require, thereby predisposing them to a sense of disempowerment and self-doubt following the death.

No single factor is likely to be definitive, but the presence of any of these factors, and particularly the co-occurrence of multiple factors, suggests that closer assessment and monitoring of survivors are indicated, coupled by referral to higher levels of care as problems emerge.

—Bob Neimeyer

### When Does Grief Require a Clinical Intervention?

*Dear Dr. Neimeyer,*

I am a nurse who works in a palliative care unit of a major metropolitan hospital, where I specialize in bereavement care. Although the work is very satisfying, it is also frustrating, as I seem to be flooded with referrals for grief therapy from several hospital units when a patient dies and the family responds with what I would regard as appropriate displays of emotion. Although many are understandably immersed in grief, few really seem to need treatment, and their referral simply increases my administrative demands to a point that it is hard to meet the needs of those who really do need care.

So, my question is, how can I get staff to stop referring inappropriate cases to me so that I can do a better job with those in genuine need?

**Maria Teresa S., MSN**

*Dear Maria Teresa,*

I hear your frustration, which seems to be born of both the compassionate intention to provide care to mourning families genuinely struggling with their loss and the humble recognition that most people do not require grief therapists to respond adaptively to the sad transition that the loss of a family member represents. Distinguishing these sometimes-ambiguous groups would be one useful step toward clarifying who needs professional help versus peer or family support in their grieving. Let me offer three ideas that might be helpful in addressing your concerns.

First, a good deal of evidence now exists to help professionals distinguish between normal, adaptive grieving on the one hand and complicated or protracted grief courses on the other. In fact, based on hundreds of studies, Prolonged Grief Disorder, with its focus on anguished preoccupation with the loss or yearning for the deceased; high levels of distress, anger or guilt regarding the death; and significant disruption of one's work, family and social life, has now been recognized in both the World Health Organization's International Classification of Diseases (ICD-11) and the American Psychiatric Association's *Diagnostic and Statistical Manual of Mental Disorders, Fifth Edition* (DSM 5-TR). However, it is important to note that the 10% of the bereaved who are likely to qualify for this diagnosis must have struggled with such symptoms for a year or more, meaning that a diagnosis of prolonged grief by definition cannot be made in the near aftermath of the death. Thus, a longer-term follow-up would be required, perhaps with screening calls at 6 and 12 months after the loss, to identify those survivors requiring preventive interventions or ongoing therapy. Few institutions, however, currently meet this standard of care, at least outside hospice settings.

Second, and as a related point, consider what can nonetheless be accomplished in a single screening consultation. For example, research has established that women who lose a husband may be 10 times more likely to die by suicide in the early weeks of bereavement than married women and that men who lose their wives may be at over 60 times the risk of killing themselves in the same period. This might not be diagnosable as complicated grief, but many other conditions ranging from severe neglect of self or others through depression to various forms of family conflict can all be observed in the near aftermath of loss, warranting professional screening when warning signs are observed. However, this is likely to apply to a very small percentage of the bereaved overall, the great majority of whom might benefit from practical and emotional support of a nonprofessional type (such as offering a list of mutual support groups in the community) and especially when meaningful relationships have developed with staff over the course of months, appropriate professional expression of compassion, as through participation in memorial services or acknowledgment of the loss through correspondence and other forms of contact.

Finally, your question suggests the relevance of offering continuing education on the diagnosis of prolonged grief and other complications for medical, nursing, chaplaincy and psychosocial staff at your hospital. The goal of this training or grand rounds would be to share some of the recent developments in bereavement research, help your colleagues understand what does and does not require referral, encourage the development of appropriate supportive protocols for normal, adaptive grievers and to "put a face" on the distinctions between these and more complicated cases through offering prototypical case studies. With a clearer sense of who needs professional grief therapy, who needs screening and who simply needs routine nonprofessional support, your colleagues are likely to make fewer and more informed referrals, leaving you more time to serve those who require your care.

—Bob Neimeyer

## Reaching Out to Hospice Families to Offer Bereavement Support

*Dear Dr. Neimeyer,*

My question is related to the bulk of my role as a hospice bereavement coordinator, which is to reach out via telephone to identified bereaved family members of our hospice patients after the patient has passed. The bereavement model employed is a "clean break" model, meaning the team that cared for the family prior to the death is not part of the aftercare. That is where I come into play. I send a pamphlet, *You're Not Alone*, within a few days of the death. In the opening page it states someone will be calling to offer support in the coming weeks. I try to contact the identified person within two to three weeks following the death. My calls are usually met with expressions of appreciation for the call and the care demonstrated to their loved one while in hospice care. When asked about how they are doing since the death, the majority of people state that they are doing well, they were expecting it, it was a relief, they had time to prepare, etc. Almost half refuse the offer of additional reading material, further calls and support group resources.

Granted, I am a stranger (to them), calling out of the blue and interrupting their day to ask them a rather personal question about something that people are usually reluctant to talk about in the best of circumstances!

I am left wondering if there is a better way of initiating the conversation and getting to some depth? Is it even ethical to do so—open someone up to potential pain against their desire/or seeking it out? I would be most interested in any insight or thoughts you might have on this.

**Holly P., LCSW**

*Dear Holly,*

Regarding your question, I imagine that the appreciative but "no, thanks" response that you receive from the great majority of families to whom you reach out after the death of a loved one in hospice care is one part reflection of the families' resilience—as 90% of responses to bereavement tend to be adaptive under such circumstances—and one part reflection on the "clean break" model you describe. Not surprisingly, perhaps, families are likely to be more disclosing and receptive to further services when a "continuity of care" model is adopted by the hospice, palliative care or other institutional setting involved in end-of-life care. Not only do families come to know and trust the staff involved in bereavement care during the time their patient is receiving treatment, but staff can also develop a clearer idea of which families are struggling and are likely to merit close aftercare follow-up. Often it is quite clear which families also need care even in the end-of-life period, when individual or family counseling can be extended to those who display particularly anguished anticipatory grief reactions.

But on the presumption that you cannot singlehandedly change institutional policies, what can you do to help ensure that a higher percentage of those who merit post-loss support actually receive it? Here are a few ideas to consider:

1. *Touch base during the pre-loss period.* If the policy of your hospice is to offer support to all families after the death, whether or not they accept it, then might you make your preliminary contact with them during the period of hospice care, rather than after? A face-to-face meeting at that time to express concern and interest in how they are doing can do much to consolidate a relationship, as you can then let them know that you will check back with them in the future. The later call is then more likely to be received with greater openness and receptivity to more contact.
2. *Evaluate known risk factors for complicated grief.* In our research, such factors as lower levels of education and economic constraints are associated with more anguishing anticipatory grief during the end-of-life period,

and emotional or practical dependency on the patient, anxiety proneness, spiritual struggle during the end-stage illness and difficulty making sense of the pending death and its implications for survivors' lives all predict higher levels of complication during palliative care as well as in the months following the death. As valid measures exist for all of these factors and others that forecast poor bereavement outcome (e.g., death of a spouse or child, violent death loss), monitoring these circumstances during hospice care could help determine the minority of families that are likely to benefit from more support or therapy following the loss. Where this is not possible, identifying these in case conferences that pool professional evaluations may prove a feasible alternative. For such families, an in-home visit might go further toward opening the door than a simple phone call would.

3. *Target your inquiry to those who are most vulnerable.* Very likely you will speak to a single family member in your follow-up call and not necessarily the one most in need of help. Inquiring into who in the family seems to be coping best with the loss and who seems to be having a harder time could open some doors to further contact or conversation with the most relevant person(s). For example, in the case of the death of a young or middle-aged parent, the surviving spouse might decline offers of support but welcome attention for the children, and adult children who do not themselves feel the need for further care or counseling might welcome it for a surviving parent who is grieving deeply following the loss of a partner. Expressing an interest in working with the recipient of the call to address these needs ("Yes, that does sound like he/she is having a hard time. Do you think it would be better for me to check in by phone with \_\_\_\_ directly or find a time to stop by?") might help you reach those most in need, rather than attempting to throw a lifeline randomly to whoever answers the phone.

—Bob Neimeyer

## Dealing With Patient Loss on an Oncology Unit

*Dear Dr. Neimeyer,*

I work on an oncology unit in a large metropolitan hospital as a senior nurse, supervising several RNs and nursing assistants who care for many seriously ill patients. Although most of the care we provide supports their recovery, we also lose many patients each week, some of whom are offered palliative care services on the unit. Even though the typical stay is brief, readmissions are common, and we get to know many patients and their families well across a period of months and years. This makes it hard when patients die, as many inevitably do, and I fear that many of my staff are experiencing an accumulation of grief, stress and burnout, which seems to be contributing to several staff members missing work or leaving for other units with less mortality risk or quitting the profession altogether. I have to confess that I myself have sometimes felt a wave of emotion and had to suppress tears when I learned of the death of some patients I have grown fond of or when I encountered the weeping family afterward—especially when they included children.

My question is: Is this normal? And is there anything we can do about it, aside from just try to deal with it and move on? The hospital is a demanding environment, and I understand the limits of time for self-care, but I sense that there must be a better way to deal with patient loss than we have at present.

**Joyce T., MSN**

*Dear Joyce,*

First, I have to say that I applaud your candor, as well as your sensitivity to the impact of patient death on the nurses serving under and around you. The stress associated with multiple patient losses is a common issue in oncology and other healthcare settings with high risk of mortality, but the pace and demands of the hospital typically leave no time and no venue for self-care, and even less for mutual support in the face of this major contributor to burnout and compassion fatigue, as well as absenteeism. Symptoms of burnout can be physical (feeling tired and drained at work), cognitive (being too exhausted to think clearly or finding it hard to concentrate) or emotional (being unable to be sensitive or responsive to the psychological needs of patients and their families). Nearly half of all oncology nurses have been found to report burnout in these terms.

What can be done about this common and serious problem? Some factors that we have found in our research to protect against burnout in palliative and bereavement care are personal, such as more frequent daily spiritual experiences (feeling connected to the divine or being thankful for one's blessings), whereas others are both personal and institutional (such as the amount of training one has had in psychosocial dimensions of end-of-life and bereavement care). Interestingly, whereas both spirituality and training seem to buffer against physical and cognitive burnout, only spiritual experiences appear to protect professionals from its emotional aspects.

But as important as these background factors are, the question remains of what can be done on the unit to mitigate the grief-rated distress of staff. Here, it is encouraging that some practices are gaining wider implementation in a great range of hospital settings, especially in the United States and UK. One such is the weekly Schwarz Round, a multidisciplinary gathering of physicians, nurses, psychologists and allied health professionals involved in patient care in critical settings, especially those characterized by frequent patient death. In a minimally structured environment, professionals meet on a "level playing field" to discuss their ethical dilemmas, questions and feelings regarding the treatment of patients with serious illness or injury, especially in the wake of their death. Although learning certainly occurs in the open discussion than ensues, the central goal is expression of personal reactions to the work that otherwise have no institutional outlet, in the presence of mutual support and compassion on the part of professional peers.

A second creative response to the cumulative grief of professional caregivers in general and nurses in particular was formulated by Popkin and her associates, who designed a music therapy–centered grief intervention for staff working in cancer settings much like your own. Stemming from the collaboration of expressive arts, clinical and pastoral care professionals, the intervention took the form of a weekly ritual in which 10 or more members of the patient care team would convene in a circle in the unit conference room, as senior nurses arranged for their coverage for the 45 minutes assigned to the activity. The time was divided into the following segments, as described more fully in their report of the work in the journal *Music and Medicine*:

1. Improvised music on harp and guitar by two music therapists, establishing a reflective, contemplative tone (5 minutes).
2. Welcome, explanation of the aims of the ceremony and brief introduction of participants by name and role (3 minutes).
3. Reading of an inspirational piece that acknowledges loss but also gain (2 minutes).
4. Reminiscence on the part of participants about patients who have died recently under their care, perhaps using a structure like, "I would like to remember _____. She was important to me because _____." These can be sad, humorous or uplifting, as the speaker prefers (25 minutes in total).
5. Second reading of a piece that suggests hope or rededication to caregiving (5 minutes).
6. "Blessing of the Hands" ceremony that validates the work and healing of each participant's hands, as a member of the chaplaincy pours scented water over them in a basin and dries each with a fresh towel, while they invoke a nondenominational blessing, softly spoken: "May your hands be blessed in what they hold and what they let go. May the work of your hands be blessed in gentleness and strength. May your work be blessed with care and love. Thank you so much for all the work and care you give." Accompanied by improvised music on harp and guitar (5 minutes).

As implied by the inclusion of the music, readings and blessing, the ritual has a spiritual aspect, though this does not invoke any deity or any particular faith or tradition. The ceremony requires careful time management, as most staff must return immediately to work afterward, and the time-limited structure supports this goal. Impressively, preliminary research on staff reactions to the ritual suggests that it is highly effective, especially in the reminiscence and blessing components, in giving staff an opportunity to honor their losses, express their grief and feel validated in their role as care providers. While Schwartz Rounds and Popkin's work represent merely two of a potentially large range of creative responses, they illustrate how multidisciplinary collaboration in the construction of practices and rituals could go a long way toward reducing the risk of burnout in critical care settings.

—Bob Neimeyer

## A Therapist's Grief and Questions About Leaving Her Career

*Dear Dr. Neimeyer,*

Following a succession of family deaths over an 18-month period, compounded by a difficult move to another part of the country for my husband's work, I find myself struggling emotionally with my career as a psychologist. Feeling overwhelmed, I took time off from my practice and now have to start again in another region. I don't know if I am capable of continuing my practice until such a time that I feel confident in my abilities. A recent indication that I wasn't there yet came when I tried to attend a training workshop on grief. My response to the conference content took me by surprise; I felt panic and dread and tolerated the topic until lunch time and then fled.

I have made limited progress in getting back into my practice, and my feelings about this vacillate from guilt, to enthusiasm, to absolute dread. I have no idea where I'm heading, where my passion lies or what capabilities I have left. I am terrified and ashamed of myself. Are these feelings reasonable, or am I just avoiding "getting back on the horse after a fall"? I want to be enthusiastic, productive and compassionate in life, but the truth is that I am not.

I'm happy for this to be shared with others who may be struggling with grief. My hope is that by revealing, with humility, that even those of us who have spent many years learning, advising and suggesting how to cope with life's adversities will let others know that we can be equally lost, confused and vulnerable at times in our lives.

**Briana C., PsyD**

*Dear Briana,*

First, thanks on behalf of all readers for the gift of your humility and transparency. Certainly, it is true, as you imply, that we stand on the same level playing field as our clients when our own lives are torn apart by heavy losses, and particularly when those losses are multiple and closely clustered. [Elsewhere in this volume I offer some concrete ideas on disentangling multiple loss.] Here are some ideas about your conundrum as a "wounded caregiver" who is trying to figure out how to address your own preoccupying and sometimes surprisingly disruptive pain, while also contemplating how to return to a professional career that has long been a source of meaning to you.

You ask whether your feelings are reasonable or whether you are avoiding getting back in the saddle. My initial sense is that the answer to both parts of this question is "yes." That is, it is entirely understandable that we are vulnerable to the same disorienting and disruptive grief that our clients can suffer and equally understandable that a wise part of us lets us know that we are not yet ready to resume life as usual—especially when that life centrally involved listening, without distraction or personal "triggering," to the suffering of others.

What then is needed to manage these tumultuous and self-critical feelings, so as to gradually embrace once again a meaningful career? A critical step could be cultivating self-compassion alongside other-compassion, as in *metta* meditation in which one focuses on a repeated mantra after calming and clearing a space through focused and deep breathing, in the course of which one directs "loving kindness" to oneself, beloved others and benefactors, casual acquaintances and even problematic or difficult people. As a professional caregiver, you might also extend this list to include a "difficult client." Numerous internet sites and books can offer instructions for this practice, which helps to both soothe painful emotion and direct compassionate attention to those who need it—oneself included—without the immediate pressure to engage the distress of others in a face-to-face way.

A second step is to take an honest inventory of your own needs. Who in your own life displays willingness to listen with a compassionate heart and be a gentle companion in a time of despair? This could be a friend, family member or another caring professional who is not currently burdened by the same or comparable losses. Perhaps your grief needs as its most essential audience you yourself, bidding you to give it the time it deserves through journaling, expressive arts or body work. In other words, if you deeply ask, *What do I need in my grief, and what steps am I ready to take to secure it?* you may find that the way forward begins to open.

Finally, as you make progress in self-soothing, cultivating loving kindness toward self and others and identifying and acting on your own loss-related needs, you will begin to naturally make room in your heart, mind and conversations to again hold the suffering of others. Very likely this will first become evident in the form of greater patience with the distress of friends and acquaintances and then begin to generalize to people you don't know personally but who you encounter in informal ways. When you can sit with their distress without it triggering your own, with no attempt to push them toward some answer for which they are unready or to push them away altogether, you will know that you are again ready to begin seeing clients. Though doing so should be undertaken slowly, just beginning with a few sessions per week, even this will require bravery—exactly like getting back in the saddle after a bruising fall from a horse. No one requires that you immediately enter a rodeo or lead a cattle drive, but merely stay on the horse and find a path forward together for the hour of a conventional session. With steps like these, reengagement with your career as well as your grief can again come to feel natural.

—Bob Neimeyer

## Integrating AfterTalk Letters to the Deceased Into Grief Therapy

*Dear. Dr. Neimeyer—*

I'm a grief therapist who works frequently with clients who have had difficult losses—sometimes of life partners, sometimes of parents, sometimes of children. And I've been fascinated by AfterTalk ever since I encountered it, as many of my clients are eager to restore a sense of connection and communication with those they have loved and lost. The *Therapist Portal* on the site sounds like a great way to facilitate this, simply by encouraging my clients to include me as a recipient of an email whenever they post a "shared conversation" on which they'd like my comments. One big advantage of this is that it provides a secure way to have exchanges between scheduled counseling sessions, allowing me to provide more support while helping my client practice positive coping and meaning-making about the loss and strengthening their continuing bond with their loved one.

But in using this convenient tool in therapy, do you have any tips or cautions I should observe? I've asked people to write letters to their loved ones before, but usually in their journal. I don't know if there are any special considerations that come to mind for you as you do this, but I have a couple of clients in mind who I think could really benefit.

**Bryan W., PhD**

*Dear Bryan,*

I agree with you that "saying hello again," as our colleague Michael White once put it, can be a healing practice in grief therapy, encouraging clients to restore a conversation with a loved one that was interrupted by death. As you likely have discovered as well, it is equally helpful when there is "unfinished business" in the form of unresolved relational issues with the deceased that call for postmortem negotiation or forgiveness. And just as you state, AfterTalk can provide a convenient and contemporary forum for doing so, one that grants total control to the bereaved to decide who, if anyone, can view an otherwise "private conversation" with the deceased. In this respect, it strikes me, as it does you, as the optimal tool for grief therapy.

And yet, like other components of therapy, it pays to approach the integration of AfterTalk or other forms of letter-writing to the deceased with thoughtfulness to maximize its benefit. Here are a handful of suggestions for doing so:

1. *Assess the client's need and readiness.* Not all bereaved clients need primary attention to restoration of the relationship: Some may need to build basic "self-capacities" for emotion regulation, self-care and ability to voice personal experiences, and others may feel greater need to process the "event story" of the dying before turning attention to the relationship to the deceased. Approaching clients with an open query along the lines of, *What do you sense you need now to help you cope with this loss?* can help you get a sense of this and whether relational work of corresponding with the deceased is the highest priority or if something else is higher on the client's emotional agenda.

2. *Negotiate a specific focus.* Talking a bit about what the client might like to say or hear in an "exchange" of correspondence with the deceased can help give direction for the task, without becoming overly prescriptive. Depending on the issues that are surfacing in the therapy, you might suggest one or two "conversation starters" like, *You always supported me when . . ., The biggest gift you gave me was . . .* or *What you never understood was . . . .* But use a light touch: most clients can find their growing edge without a great deal of therapist priming.

3. *Establish conditions of safety.* People who write an AfterTalk letter on their own probably have an intuitive sense of when and how to do so. But when we as therapists suggest the idea, it helps to talk through briefly such issues as *where* they would write (in privacy or with a trusted friend or family member nearby; at home or in nature), *when* they would do so (to avoid interruption and to offer a transitional period before work, social or family demands) and *whether* they would find a preparatory period useful to put them in the right mood for the writing (such as meditation or listening to a particular kind of music). Helping clients think through these issues of context greatly improves "compliance" with the assignment and leads to deeper engagement with the task and the deceased.

4. *Plan an exit strategy.* For most people, writing a letter to the deceased (or from the deceased to them) is an emotional experience, especially when undertaken for the first time. So, plan with the client what he or she might do to shift from the writing back into life. For example, my clients have used some of the same things on the back end that they use on the front end, such as listening to soothing or inspirational music or meditating for 20 minutes. But others prefer something more active, like planning to have a coffee with a trusted friend with whom they can process the experience or exercising. As the Dual Process Model reminds us, grieving commonly involves alternating between reflecting on the loss or the loved one on one hand and reengaging life on the other. Helping clients segue from one to the other is therefore a useful service.
5. *Integrate the writing into therapy.* Consider with clients whether they would prefer that you respond in an email to the letter or that you bring a copy of the letter to the session to process further face to face. In the latter instance, I typically invite clients to read it aloud slowly, which commonly brings the relevant emotions, questions and issues into the room for further discussion, or alternatively ask if they would prefer that I read it aloud as they listen. The latter "self-distancing" perspective tends to promote more client perspective-taking, almost like examining oneself in a mirror. Each therefore has its advantages, and I occasionally do both, beginning with the client's reading, followed by my own, cuing the client to reflect on whether hearing the letter in the two modes led to any different observations or insights.
6. *Consider circulating the letter to a community of concern.* Talk with the client about whether there are others, such as trusted friends and family, who might benefit from sharing access to the letter or whether it is really something simply for an audience of one. Appreciative letters that express gratitude for the past, present and future role of the deceased in the client's life may be especially heartening to circulate through AfterTalk's sharing function, soliciting others' support of the client and celebration of the deceased. This helps overcome some of the isolation of grieving, making it clear that the client is still a vital member of a community that holds them and their loved one. For more about this, click the AfterTalk link: Friends and Family and Therapist.
7. *Build a bridge to action.* The cathartic and reflective functions of letter-writing are most meaningful when they open naturally onto constructive action. Thus, we might encourage clients to identify some concrete step that would follow from their letter, one that is in keeping with its central theme or message. For example, the client might be moved to write a letter of gratitude to friends who were especially generous in their support or undertake a "random act of kindness" in the deceased

person's honor, perhaps of a kind that he or she might have done in life. This underscores how the goal of grieving is not merely to manage turbulent emotions in the privacy of our hearts and minds, but ultimately to draw on the relationship with our loved one to reengage life with renewed vitality and compassion.

—Bob Neimeyer

## A Widow's Complicated Grief Rituals

*Dear Dr. Neimeyer,*

I am a therapist who is seeing a woman who lives alone and without children for prolonged grief, and one of the people for whom she is grieving is her husband. They were married 4 years before he died 19 years ago. Every year on their anniversary, she has a very complicated ritual to celebrate, which includes certain flowers, candles, music, his ashes, champagne and pictures. It takes her a week to prepare for this. She says this doesn't hurt anyone and she sees no reason to stop it. She has been doing this longer than they were married. I'm wondering how she can move past this need and would appreciate any suggestions to help her. By the way, she has been successful in moving through her grief for several other family members since working with me and doesn't have such angst over their deaths, which were decades ago.

**Marie B., LCSW**

*Dear Marie,*

Yours is a good question and one that likely arises in some form for many therapists who are confronted with long-term expressions of grief that persist years, or in this case, decades, following the death. Especially in modern Western cultures that place a premium on efficiently "moving on" and reconnecting with life, such behavior can seem puzzling at best and pathological at worst. So, let me share a few thoughts that I hope will be helpful.

First, it can be useful to recognize that on the scale of world history and across contemporary cultures, our normative Western response to death is among the least ritualized and extended. Much more typically, people in many times and cultures maintain, rather than relinquish, sentimental and ritualistic bonds with the dead, whether through annual prayers and rites associated with various world religions or through folk practices like the Mexican *Día de los Muertos*, Japanese *Obon* festivals or Chinese *Qingming* celebrations, all of which symbolically conjure connections or conversations with the deceased or honor their role as ancestors. Although the United

States has its own Memorial Day, this is far less associated with family rituals commemorating the dead and more a public acknowledgement of those who died in the armed forces. For most Americans over the past century, therefore, regular rituals to honor or remember the dead have eroded or been tacitly discouraged.

But it was not always so, and in fact until the advent of World War I, whose enormous losses overwhelmed Europe's capacity to recognize individual deaths, a broadly Victorian sentiment of maintaining ritual bonds with the deceased was the norm in the Western world rather than an aberration. Viewed through this lens, it may be our contemporary Western and especially American customs that are out of sync with a natural human impulse to periodically revisit the dead, honor them and reaffirm our sense of attachment and appreciation over time . . . perhaps a lifetime, or in Asian variations, across successive generations.

While this does not resolve the question of whether your client's behaviors are deleterious to her adaptation to her husband's death or not, this does suggest that such rituals of reconnection are not necessarily unhealthy, and indeed may be an adaptive and appreciative expression of love. The crucial question would be whether your client wears her grief in a way that hampers her functioning in practical ways, as in being unable to maintain her home or her health, or that erodes the quality of her work or relationships to others. Is it associated with a morose, ruminative preoccupation with the death and a sense that life is devoid of purpose or meaning in her husband's absence? Or is she managing pretty well for her age, maintaining friendships and home in a way that permits her to experience pleasure or even joy to balance life's inherent disappointments? Answers to questions like these would help determine whether her grief rituals are serving her well or poorly and whether they are something to preserve or transform.

If indeed your client seems to be living a tragically constricted life characterized by substantial deterioration in social, occupational or relational functioning, and if this seems to be worsened by her elaborate rituals of remembrance, then it can be both wiser and more feasible to extend those rituals in healing directions than to abandon them altogether. The two of you might consider how she could tip a celebratory glass to their loving past but also look to carry her husband in some fashion into a fulfilling future. What kind of life would he want to accompany her on in spirit? What would be one or two actions he would be proud to see her take or goals to which he would be proud to see her devote herself? Is there a way that she can extend his legacy in some fashion into the future, rather than only burying it in the past? Like an earnest New Year's resolution made as the calendar page turns to a fresh one, how might she take inspiration from the past to embrace life anew, as a dedicated act that honors, rather than abandons, the man she loves? In this way, perhaps the lighting of the candles will also light the way to rituals of renewal, as well as those of remembrance.

—Bob Neimeyer

## Unfinished Business: Adult Children and Parents

*Dear Dr. Neimeyer,*

I'm a clinical psychologist. I work with many adults who have very difficult relationships with their parents. Some say they anticipate they will feel relief when their parents die. Then they feel guilty for feeling that way. Do you have any advice/thought for people whose grief or anticipated grief is complicated in this way? These adults also say they feel isolated because these feelings are not socially acceptable, so they can't share them with others.

**Sonya K., PsyD**

*Dear Sonya,*

Yes, our research on unfinished business in bereavement confirms what our clinical experience has long suggested: that those clients who have unresolved relational issues with family members and intimate others do indeed tend to experience more struggles with complicated and protracted grief. What may be more surprising is that over 40% of bereaved adults acknowledge some form of unfinished business, especially in their closest family relationships, and their distress about this is a significant predictor of complications following the death of the relevant person, and very probably of complex anticipatory grief as well. Other studies we've done have reported even higher rates of unfinished business following sudden, violent death, as in the case of suicide, or when parents contend with the death of a child, even from progressive disease following the best available treatment. And most recently, we have found in large samples of people bereaved in the pandemic that *literally 100%* of them reported corrosive guilt, regret, shame or unfinished business following deaths of loved ones to COVID-19, which prevented them from "being there" for their loved ones at the end of life or having opportunities to validate the relationship or resolve complicated histories. In summary, study after study underscores the complicating role that unfinished business can play in bereavement of many kinds, especially those that are likely to find their way into our offices or online practice.

In developing the first valid measure of this construct, the *Unfinished Business in Bereavement Scale*, or UBBS, our research group, spearheaded by Jason Holland, has determined that this form of complication can be conceptualized and assessed as two distinct dimensions. On the one hand, many people struggle with *Unfulfilled Wishes*, in the form of not having expressed their love for the other, not having had a chance to say goodbye, having had too little time together and anticipating the person's absence in significant future events. On the other hand, people can be tormented by *Unresolved Conflict* in the form of abiding disappointments, guilt, deep and corrosive anger, troubling secrets, relational breaches and lack of forgiveness over some form of wrong committed by one or both parties. Across different samples of bereaved adults, unfinished business is associated with more intense symptoms of prolonged grief disorder, greater attachment insecurity and less meaning made of the loss. In fact, the potency of this effect is clear when one considers that just two factors— unfinished business and meaning made of the loss—together account for 50% to 60% of symptom severity of prolonged grief, a debilitating response to bereavement now recognized in the *Diagnostic and Statistical Manual of Mental Disorders, Fifth Edition* (DSM 5-TR). Our further research in the pandemic context documents that 40% of functionally impairing grief symptoms can be accounted for by *Unresolved Conflict* alone—clearly a clinically compelling problem that deserves the attention of any therapist who encounters it.

So, what might be done clinically when we find ourselves working with adults who have very difficult relations with their parents, as you describe? Here are a few ideas:

1. *Don't leave the business unfinished.* If issues can be addressed when both parties are living, they needn't weigh as heavily with the survivor when the other party dies. In some sense, this is the fundamental premise of family therapy: that imperfect, disappointing or even conflicted relationships can be reviewed and repaired when the relevant parties come to recognize that it is in their mutual interest to do so. Of course, this often requires skillful facilitation by a therapist who resists triangulation and alignment with one party against the other and who is capable of "joining" with each empathically to elicit the vulnerability, fear or defensiveness that led to their suboptimal treatment of the other to begin with. For example, in the presence of such conflict I will often request the permission of the conflicted parties to have a deep-going one-on-one conversation with me in the presence of the other, who I request to remain silent and attentive until we have finished a 10- to 15-minute interview. In that interview—say, with an angry or hurt adult child—I will try to empathically delve beneath the anger or distancing to the source of the pain, often experienced initially early in life, or at a point of earlier loss (as in the unavailability of a parent or being caught in the middle of a parental divorce). As we deepen into this, tears often flow, the empathy of the witnessing other is engaged and genuine dialogue

becomes more possible. I then solicit the reactions of the witnesses and invite them into a similar dialogue in the presence of the adult child. This commonly opens doors to rapprochement.

2. *Talk to the absent other.* When in the context of parent/adult child conflict the parent is geographically absent, ill, suffering dementia or simply unwilling to participate in therapy, invite them anyway . . . symbolically. Ask the client to imagine them present, healed psychologically and physically from whatever they had suffered in life and accepting the invitation to meet with their child for a heart-to-heart conversation. Develop this in a sensory way for a few minutes, as the client closes his or her eyes: *How would your father be dressed? How would he be seated in the chair opposite you? What expression would you see in his eyes as he prepares himself to hear the truth about your relation to him? What might he be feeling as he did so?* Then, instruct the client to open her eyes and state how she is feeling at this point in their relationship, as the parent's life grows short or after it has ended. Reflecting and deepening the client's disclosures (*Tell him more about that. What more can you say about what you feel?*), work toward what the client needs from the parent and would like to see happen. How would he like to feel five years from now about their relationship? Keep all of this in direct *I-you* language, not in the form of third-person commentary—have the client speak it while looking directly to the chair, to the parent. Then, at a moment that calls for a response, ask the client to rise, take the chair of the parent, "channel" his or her voice and respond from the heart to what the child has just said. Again, deepen this toward emotional truth with brief restatement and empathic reflection. Rotate the client to the alternate chair as needed to allow the dialogue to move toward greater resolution. Then de-role from what is commonly an emotionally evocative encounter, take a few deep breaths together to clear the screen and reflect on what the client learned and observed, considering what action steps might now be taken to move the process forward. This might well lead to real-world conversations with living parents or relevant others, such as siblings, that nurture transformation.

3. *When in doubt, write it out.* Some clients might decline the chair work format of dialogue with a problematic parent and might feel "safer" writing their feelings and responses to the parent than speaking them. This can be done in the form of an "unsent letter" that cuts to the source of the hurt, the goal of which is to be vulnerable and truthful about the suffering of the child, rather than merely judgmental and accusatory toward the parent. Sometimes the therapist might offer sentence stems to "jump-start" this process (*What you never understood was . . . What I need you to know is . . . The one question I have wanted to ask*

you was . . . *I feel ready to change our relationship by* . . .). AfterTalk's convenient format for writing, archiving and sharing such letters with the therapist can facilitate this work. Then, after a session talking through and perhaps reading aloud the letter, consider asking the clients to write a letter back to themselves, as if from the standpoint of the parent. As with the spoken dialogue, this written dialogue often opens the doorway to change.

4. *Rebalance the power.* In some parent-child relations, great damage has been done—perhaps a father physically or sexually abused a child, or a mother tormented or abandoned a son or daughter. When the offense feels beyond forgiveness or redress, much can still be accomplished using the previous techniques—but without allowing the powerful and injurious parent to "speak" or "write" back. Instead, like someone accused of a high crime, the parent is called into court as required to sit silently as the "witness" or "plaintiff" speaks to the wrong that has been committed, in effect giving the client a voice and authority he or she previously lacked. However, I find that this one-way interaction is required in no more than 5% to 10% of difficult cases, as much can often be done in a more dialogical format . . . ideally, when the significant other is still living.

—Bob Neimeyer

## A Symbiotic Relationship and a Tragic Loss

*Dear Dr. Neimeyer,*

I have been working intermittently for many years with a woman named Pam who was divorced when her adult children were adolescents as a result of the father's unpredictable and violent behavior and alcoholism. Likewise, two of her four children have had long histories of drug and alcohol use, despite her funding their efforts at recovery in several treatment programs. Pam herself reports drinking a "glass or two" of wine each evening, but this seems not to have interfered with either her work as a manager or her volunteer activities in helping disadvantaged children from chaotic homes, an activity that seems to have special meaning for her because of the chaos of her marriage.

Two months ago, however, tragedy struck, when her oldest daughter, Lucy, died from apparent kidney failure as a result of her long history of anorexia and a bout of heavy drinking when she was attending a friend's wedding in another state. Unsurprisingly, Pam plunged into a guilty and abject grief, which I believe is complicated by her codependent, symbiotic relationship with her daughter for a lifetime. Pam believes her daughter's death was an accident, but Lucy also had made a serious suicide attempt some years before, and at this point the family is awaiting the autopsy report.

Here is my question. Although I am accompanying her as I would another bereaved parent, aware that the process of reconstructing her life will be a slow and arduous one, it seems that there may be other considerations of which I should be aware due to the elements of addiction and the extreme degree of symbiosis that characterized the relationship. Do you have some thoughts I might consider as I accompany her?

A few final comments: I have worked closely with her psychiatrist, and we have connected her with other bereaved parents whose children have similarly died. She is open to the suggestion of creating some structure to "contain her grief," which she has found helpful . . . but has some days filled only with tears, which is understandable. She returned to work for a few days this week and found that helpful. And she is going to volunteer to work with some young girls in a local school with her expressed hope that this would give her a sense of purpose. As I write this, Bob, I'm aware there may be little else to do other than accompany her in these ways, but I have continued to feel uncertain, that I may need to understand better the huge significance of her loss through a different lens. But then again, she has never been open to my invitations to differentiate from her children, so maybe she will move through her grief just as she has moved through her life, as so many do. So, supporting her is all I may be able to do.

**Lisa B., LCSW**

*Dear Lisa,*

First, thanks for relating Pam's history, loss and current conundrum with such care. Just as you imply, complicated histories can predispose people toward complicated grief, except when they don't. That is, it is often helpful to entertain two possibilities in relation to our most complex clients, two hypotheses that are (intentionally) in some contradiction to one another. The first might be that who people are will shape how they grieve, with the corollary that who they are is a function of the relational patterns they have lived out across a lifetime. Clearly, this would lead us to be concerned with Pam's likelihood that she will struggle with a symbiotic relationship with Lucy in death as she did in life, marked by long-term guilt, inability to "move on," preoccupation with the unfinished business of their relationship and the circumstances of her daughter's life, etc. This is the classic territory of prolonged grief, with the bond made more sticky by the long previous history they had as mother and daughter, with the death of the latter serving as the final proof of the mother's "failure." Of course, a fair amount of this would be expected in this case in any circumstance, but the question would be whether you would observe any movement across the months toward lightening of this load, the establishment of self-compassion and so on. An essentially unchanging pattern or worsening one across time would reinforce this concern.

The second hypothesis might be that Pam's grieving for her daughter, while painful, might actually turn out to be adaptive and the one thing she could do "successfully" for her daughter, without the daughter's own addiction undoing it. In this possible scenario Pam might be able to mourn, memorialize and metabolize the loss, meaning to integrate it in an adaptive way. This might look across the months like a capacity to experience brief but gradually lengthening periods of purpose or even pleasure, to remember her daughter fondly without falling into rage or guilt, etc. Of course, this would not likely emerge quickly, but the trend line should become apparent over time.

But what to do clinically? Basically, I would do just what you are doing, providing support for appropriate expressions of loss to others (including to you as a therapist) but also help her "make sense" of her life with Lucy and its implications in some adaptive way. For example, the latter might entail serious periodic engagement with questions like, *What lessons might be found in your life with Lucy for how you might adaptively mourn her now? What might be the patterns to watch out for? What were Lucy's brightest moments, and how can you help keep memories of these times alive? When did you feel most loving and effective with her as a mother, and how might you extend these forms of relating to her in life to how you might relate to her memory in death? What of a constructive sort did the complicated history with Lucy teach you about how to help other struggling young people now and in the future?* In other words, winnowing some lessons from this life and loss and implementing them concretely as she moves forward might make a critical contribution to the goal of helping Pam consolidate the second of the possible futures outlined earlier rather than the first. There are numerous specific tools that could assist with this, many of which are described and illustrated in the *Techniques of Grief Therapy* volumes [referenced in the following chapter], which are perhaps already on your bookshelves or in your own clinical toolbox.

I hope these thoughts are helpful, Lisa, as you continue this important work.

—Bob Neimeyer

## Traumatic Images of a Loved One's Dying

*Dear Dr. Neimeyer,*

As a therapist I often work with people who suffer from traumatic images of their loved one's dying, even when these result from a difficult death in the hospital. Can you comment on how to help the bereaved who are struggling with difficult images and memories? How does one work through traumatic images in therapy?

**Kerry L., LPC**

*Dear Kerry,*

Just as you say, troubling or haunting visual memories of the deceased are not limited to circumstances of violent death bereavement, although evidence suggests that the latter are especially likely to lead to prolonged and complicated grief reactions, and seeing the loved one's body at the scene of the suicide, homicide or accident has been found to predict more intense struggles in bereavement. Whatever the source of the imagery, it can have remarkable staying power, lingering and intruding into the survivor's consciousness (and nightmares) for years beyond the death, commonly bringing with it waves of anguish, horror and helplessness.

In recognition of this common clinical concern, creative clinicians like Laurie Perlman, Ted Rynearson and their colleagues have developed specialized procedures for working with troubling imagery in grief therapy using a trauma-informed approach. Rynearson's group, for example, practices "restorative retelling," a slow-motion review of the narrative of traumatic death, typically beginning when the client first discovers or is informed of the dying and moving forward through one or more "chapters" of the story through the client's visual recollection or reconstruction of the scene of the dying, whether witnessed or imagined. Stretching over one or more sessions of therapy, in my own adaptation of the method, such retelling tacks from the *external* story of what the client saw, heard and smelled to the *internal* story of what she or he felt at emotional and embodied levels as the therapist provides emotion regulation and support for the exposure to these hard realities. The result of one or more such sessions tends to be more mastery of the trauma story and its associated imagery, desensitization to its triggering aspects and greater meaning-making about the event story of the death and its role in the client's life.

Supplementing this retelling, Rynearson and his colleague, Fanny Correa, advocate the use of drawings of the scene of dying, both as an aid to reviewing the story and as a means of externalizing the story and giving it a more public audience with the therapist or support group with whom it is shared. In shifting the scene from private preoccupation with it in their own minds and dreams to a shared processing of it in therapy, many clients report relief and greater capacity to distance from the troubling visual components of the scene. A further step can be taken by asking clients to draw themselves into the scene, not in a way that can reverse the reality of the dying, but in a way that would let them provide some measure of comfort or care for the loved one as it occurs. For example, many people depict themselves holding their loved ones, caressing them or lifting their spirits to heaven in a way that restores some measure of empowerment to them that was denied at the time of the death. In such interventions, therapists actively join clients in engaging rather than merely trying to suppress the imagery and seek to overwrite the visualization of the trauma with imagery that embodies the client's love for the deceased, rather than only his or her horror.

Finally, working with healing imagery directly can be helpful in therapy, especially after the hard but supported retelling described earlier. For example, Jack Jordan writes about the use of guided visualization of peaceful scenes and settings as an aid to emotion regulation, and I have found it helpful to encourage clients to display pictures of their loved ones at a time of health and happiness in the home to provide prominent portrayals that offer alternatives to troubling images of the deceased at the end of life or after death. Although these more benign interventions alone are often insufficient to overwrite traumatic imagery when it is present, they can contribute to a positive reconstruction of memory when such imagery has been processed and defused through exposure. For specific procedural descriptions of several of the methods noted earlier, you might wish to consult the *Techniques of Grief Therapy* series [listed in the following chapter on *Resources for Therapists*].

—Dr. Neimeyer

## Group Therapy for Traumatic Loss

*Dear Dr. Neimeyer,*

My colleagues and I are currently recruiting clients for a traumatic loss group in our clinic, one that draws on your approach to grief therapy as meaning reconstruction, which has strong relevance when losses are sudden and often violent. The group is designed to run 12 weeks, and is closed, meaning that the same 8 to 10 members should be in the group from the beginning to the end. In terms of referrals received, I have already been in touch, through a bereavement support organization in our area, with a mother who lost her daughter to suicide, and she is still thinking about whether she wants to attend or not. Another bereavement service also mentioned two people, one of them also bereaved by suicide, whom they might want to refer, and I have been contacted by someone who lost her father recently to cancer and had support for this from another organization, but this recent bereavement has triggered unresolved issues around her mother's suicide 30 years ago, which she believed was connected to her father leaving her mother, and she is wondering if she could attend the group. I do not know anything else yet. The question would be whether this would be too complex for the group to address or, if we ask her to focus on the suicide mainly, whether this would be possible or, indeed, desirable, as it seems her feelings in connection with the one are so closely connected with her feelings in connection with the other.

What do you think? Our eligibility criteria do not stipulate a maximum period since the bereavement, and it would be fine to include her from a criteria perspective, but before arranging to meet her, I was wondering if you have any other thoughts on this and whether I have missed anything.

**Edith S., PhD**

*Dear Edith,*

I appreciate your recognition that those who have lost loved ones to traumatic death, such as suicide, homicide and fatal accident, have special needs that are often poorly accommodated in a group whose members have often had more normative losses to anticipated natural causes.

But I do have questions about the long-term maternal suicide/recent paternal death case in the context of the group. Understandably, these two losses will be conjoined for the client and can't truly be separated. I would be concerned that one dynamic of most group members would be to find a villain responsible for the suicide—and that they could join with the client in blaming the father in this respect, potentially complicating her fresh grief for her father's death by arousing anger at his possible role in motivating her mother's tragic action. On the other hand, her long-term perspective on a traumatic loss could make a valuable contribution to the group, just as their fresh perspective could help her revisit her mother's loss in a helpful way—especially with the meaning-making tools offered throughout the treatment, which could help her revisit an old loss in a new way.

Perhaps the ideal response to questions of this sort would be to ask the true expert—the client herself—about her readiness for the group in an initial interview to consider its appropriateness for her. So, I would screen her for the group, and discuss the issue of her tandem loss directly, but slowly, one small piece at a time—not in a big clinical conjunction like I've provided earlier: *How do you imagine the group might help you with your old grief for Mum? Your fresh grief for Dad? How do you think the other group members might handle your own mixed/troubling feelings about why your mother ended her life? If they responded with anger at your father, how might this be helpful to you? Harmful to you in your grieving?* You get the idea: these kinds of questions would be salted through a half-hour of conversation. Then you could make a more informed decision together: *Would this be better handled in the group, which could provide some specifically helpful advice and member perspectives, even from other suicide loss* survivors, or in an individual therapy, which could focus more time on what is uniquely important to you? I'd tend to trust her thoughtful conclusion.

—Bob Neimeyer

## Doctor Depressed by Patient Suicide

*Dear Dr. Neimeyer,*

I have a professional colleague who is a retired obstetrician/gynecologist from a world-renowned medical group. He ruminates and is depressed about a patient he had many years ago. She suffered from postpartum depression after giving birth and then died by suicide.

He tells the story that she came to him, and he believed at the time she would be okay. Then her husband called him to relay that she had taken her life with a gun, leaving behind several young children.

Dr. Neimeyer, is this Disenfranchised Grief or Complicated Grief, being that he has carried this with him for so many years? Any advice for him to forgive himself?

**Lisa T., MD**

*Dear Lisa,*

Thanks for your compassionate outreach on the part of your colleague and friend grieving the tragic death of a patient so many years ago. When suicide strikes, it leaves many questions unanswered and a great well of potential guilt for all those who knew and cared for the victim, including those who cared for him or her in a professional capacity. And guilt certainly complicates grief, reinforcing our rumination about the death as we seek to make sense of it or "undo" it in some fashion, or repeatedly engage in inner dialogues of self-blame for what we did or did not do that could have contributed to the tragedy. Physicians, who are often the first-line professionals having contact with the potentially suicidal person, may be especially prone to this, and the trauma of the death can be all the more shocking and horrific for specialties beyond psychiatry, whose members are likely to have less experience and training in evaluating and treating suicide risk, as well as in dealing with patient loss as an all-too-common occurrence across a long career.

You also ask if the grief of your colleague could be considered disenfranchised, in the sense that it receives little social recognition, validation and support. The answer, of course, is almost certainly "yes," as few consider professional caregivers legitimate "mourners" and indeed may blame them for presumed negligence in insufficiently evaluating or treating the condition leading to the suicide. These responses on the part of much of the social world are understandable, even if they do not take into account the realities of time pressures in clinical practice, the difficulty in assessing suicide risk, the expectation that prescribed medication would reduce the symptoms of depression and attendant risk, etc. Alas, suicide prevention is an inexact science, and even with the best of efforts, tragedies will continue to occur.

So what might your friend do? Rational considerations of this kind typically have little effect, unfortunately, as the moral and emotional part of us that cultivates ongoing self-accusation and grief resides at deeper levels than our conscious consideration of these factual or logical responses. What might be more helpful is attempting to learn something of value from the experience and translate it into action. This might take the form of visible action in the world, as in using one's professional skills in retirement in a compassionate, healing way, perhaps speaking to relevant groups about depression as a form of community or professional education or joining in suicide awareness walks or other attempts to make a difference through mitigating the risk of future tragedy or offering support to survivors. But this might also take a more inner form, as in meditating seriously on our own fallibility as human beings; our own imperfect efforts to understand, predict and control events in life; and to practice humility and compassion in response to ourselves and others in our professional and personal lives. This is deep work, commonly reserved for our later years, when we can review life's lessons and cultivate the wisdom they might yet confer.

—Bob Neimeyer

## Alzheimer's Loss: Fixating on the Present

*Dear Dr. Neimeyer,*

I am providing emotional support to the family of an advanced Alzheimer's patient who has been institutionalized for five years. The patient was a brilliant scientist, greatly loved and admired by his sister and three daughters.

As the scientist approaches death, his sister and daughters are troubled by the fact that their thoughts of him are fixated on his current condition. They cannot think or talk about their lives and experiences with him in the past. They suppress any thoughts or conversations about him and wonder if they will ever be able to create a more balanced memory of him.

Do you have any suggestions for them, especially any reading material on this type of reaction to losing a loved one?

**Linda D., LCSW**

## QUESTIONS FROM PROFESSIONALS

*Dear Linda,*

Sadly, the reaction you describe, in which positive memories of a loved one are overshadowed by the darker cloud of the circumstances of the death, is not uncommon. It occurs with great frequency when the death is itself traumatic, as by violent means, but as this family's experience testifies, it occurs as well even when the death is a natural one, anticipated by many months or years. Indeed, the slow demise that characterizes an Alzheimer trajectory like this one may be even more insidious, installing vivid memories of a loved one's gradual reduction of ability and personality over half a decade. In such a case, the "dominant narrative" of the illness can eclipse for survivors the "preferred narrative" of the loved one's special qualities and accomplishments, rendering them scarcely visible through the veil of anguishing memories.

Beyond the sheer vividness and primacy of the more traumatic memories are motivational factors, even if these are only half-conscious. That is, the attempt to recall the loved one brings with it painful contact with the dominant memories of this same person in advanced illness—leading to avoidance of memories of the loved one altogether. Although this unintended reliance on avoidance coping is negatively reinforced by a reduction of grief in the present moment, the cost of this form of protection is high, effectively stealing from mourners the psychological as well as physical presence of the deceased.

Fortunately, there are several ways forward through this dilemma, though none of them is easy. And just as you imply in your apt phrasing, this involves active attempts to "create a more balanced memory." One of these is commonplace—bravely stand up to the pain and revisit cherished stories, photos, videos and mementos, in full recognition that initial instances of doing so are likely to bring tears that will only gradually be leavened by smiles and, eventually, perhaps, laughter and pride. To be most effective—as in approaching any other fearful situation—these chosen exposures to the memories should be long enough to engage the emotions associated with the remembered experiences or artifacts and to promote some initial level of mastery of them, which usually requires 20 to 30 minutes. Because this will initially be quite stressful, early "exposure trials" of this sort might be done in your office, where you can invite the clients to walk you slowly through a photo album, for example, as you inquire compassionately and with interest about the person and relationships behind the pictures, while also helping the clients "breathe through" the experience and modulate the strong emotions they evoke.

Another more ambitious approach would be to pursue a "legacy project" that honors the deceased—perhaps constructing a virtual memorial on the internet, preparing a family dinner that includes his favorite food or taking a pilgrimage to a place that was special to him, any of which could naturally lead to sharing stories and memories and reflecting on the indelible impact the loved one's life had on friends and family, and in the case of this prominent scientist, the larger world. Anything that honors that legacy helps sustain us in our grief, whereas anything that silences it wounds us further.

And finally, there are specialized therapeutic procedures that work specifically with our ongoing connection to the deceased and seek to restore it in a healthy form. These include various practices of visualization and imaginal dialogue that can directly work with our inner (and avoided) relation to the loved one, differentiating the person from the pain of his or her passing. For a detailed case study that illustrates such work in an actual session of therapy, both you and your clients might like to read my chapter (among others) in the book by Dennis Klass and Edith Steffen entitled *Continuing Bonds in Bereavement*, published by Routledge. Repeated experiences with clients like the family you describe have convinced me that a tense avoidance of memories is not the only option in dealing with the grief-saturated recollections of a loved one's dying and that with some guidance and courage, survivors can distinguish positive emotions regarding the loved one's life from more painful memories associated with the death, ultimately embracing the former and grieving the latter.

—Bob Neimeyer

## Therapy for a Deep and Isolating Grief

*Dear Dr. Neimeyer,*

I am currently working with a woman who lost her adult son to sudden death when he was residing in a foreign country five years ago. Since then she has been absorbed in a deep and isolating grief, though she has two other adult children and a husband who remain quite concerned about her. I have seen her with her husband in therapy for 12 sessions, but her grief remains intense and unremitting, to a point that she seems to have cut off from all other relationships with friends and family, and although not actively suicidal, clearly wants to die. Her psychiatrist has been unable to alleviate her anguish with several adjustments in antidepressants, and my best efforts to empathize with her suffering only seem to reinforce it. She presents with a deep feeling of being all alone, and she even looks this way, leaning away from her husband on opposite ends of the sofa in my office and sending few signals of feeling connected to me as well. I feel very stuck in this therapy, but am reluctant to "abandon" her by suggesting that she consult another therapist, as this client describes vividly the pain caused by a childhood experience of being "unwanted" and even felt abandoned by her son when he left to live in another country. What could I do to help restore momentum to the therapy and help this woman find the hope and meaning that seem to have died with her son?

**Beverly F., LPC**

*Dear Beverly,*

As central as empathy and compassion are in attending to those in deep grief, there are times when they are not enough, and this appears to be one of them. We ourselves can ultimately be drawn into their hopelessness, as the therapeutic options seem to narrow to the point of trying "more of the same," only harder! In the service of opening some options, let me therefore brainstorm a few alternatives, each with a brief explanation. I'll start with a few easy-to-implement suggestions and then work up to more complex interventions.

1. *Shift the proxemics*: If part of your client's problem is a sense of isolation from others, move your chairs closer together by one foot when partway through a session. Then continue as before, and after a few minutes, process with the client whether she noticed a difference, and if so, which felt more comfortable and why. Likewise, invite her to sit closer to her husband, or him to her, in a separate experiment with physical closeness. If the closeness is welcome, ask in what other ways she would like to invite more of it in her life. If it is uncomfortable, ask to talk with that part of her that prefers distance about what makes that necessary, despite her loneliness.
2. *Take a walk:* If the problem is "no movement," literally mobilize her by conducting your session as you stroll together through the neighborhood of a nearby park, speaking therapeutically about how it feels to be in motion, as you literally walk alongside her going forward. In addition to helping promote psychological movement, the exercise can itself be a form of behavioral activation, promoting self-esteem and self-care. It can also set the stage for walking with friends or family as homework.
3. *Investigate motherhood:* Interview her about the best part of being a mother during those special years she had with all three of her kids. Ask: *What did your son represent to you?* Consider how she can still be a good mother to her living (and grieving) children and what her son—and his death—means to each of them.
4. *Open the photo album:* Stimulate the stories of her family and their interrelationships over time, considering what endures in each even following this hard, mutual loss.

5. *Talk **to** her son, not just **about** him:* Use chair work to encourage her to express to her son, placed symbolically in an empty chair, just where she is in her grief, what she feels and what she needs. Then change chairs, have her loan her son her voice and invite him to "respond" to Mom, offering advice, counsel and—almost surely—love and appreciation.
6. *Go to the source:* In this variation, consider chair work with her mom about the abandonment your client felt as a child and what she needs and is seeking as a result.
7. *Family meeting:* Invite the other adult children into therapy with their mom and dad to talk with them about their perception of who is hurting most, next most and least and what each needs from the others to feel or adapt better. Help them plan a shared ritual that honors their brother to reduce their individual isolation.
8. *Ground the client:* When her heart is overwhelmed by emotion, move her back into her head by discussing problem-solving strategies or coaching in diaphragmatic breathing to modulate and tolerate the effect.

Note that most of these approaches can be used in tandem rather than as stand-alone interventions, but beware of overloading her by implementing too many at one time.

—Bob Neimeyer

## Since Her Son's Death . . . Cut Off From the World

*Dear Dr. Neimeyer,*

As a director of a bereavement center myself, I am very concerned about a friend. Her mother died about four years ago. Her father died about eight months ago. Then, her son, as far as we know, died of an accidental overdose about one month after her father. The truth is it seems she never quite was able to adjust after the death of her mother. She was a devoted daughter to her parents. The following information comes to me by a mutual friend.

Since her son's death she has become completely cut off from the world. She does not drive or leave the house. She is completely terrified of doing anything. I'm told she does not turn on the TV, listen to music, answer the phone. She does not pick up a pencil.

I believe there is a housekeeper in the home making sure she eats. Her husband and surviving children are fed up with her state of mind. Apparently, they were told that anything they do for her would be enabling her situation. So they do nothing to help her. I'm told she has a psychiatrist who has her on medication. Our mutual friend, who is also a therapist, believes that she has become numb to her situation, her family and the world.

My experience with her over the years is that she was always a somewhat fearful and cautious person. Any suggestions made to her are met with resistance. We are at a loss for how to help.

**Karen R., LCSW**

*Dear Karen,*

First, I applaud and appreciate your engagement with your friend's sad retreat from life, which seems to have exhausted her family's patience and resources, and perhaps that of her professional caregivers as well. So, let me join you here in offering a few ideas that you might bring to her, and perhaps her family, as you jointly seek a way to begin reengaging your friend in life after far too many deaths in quick succession.

To begin, it is important to acknowledge the profound challenge to your friend's sense of attachment occasioned by the death of her mother, followed by that of her father a few years later. As you describe, she was a loving and devoted daughter, likely receiving and then giving care in her relation to her parents across a lifetime. Especially when our bonds are close in this way, their severance through death often thrusts us into a very vulnerable place, which in her case was almost unspeakably compounded by the intentional or unintentional death of her son just a month following that of her father. Cut off nearly simultaneously from the last of two parents who had long nurtured her and a child who she had long nurtured, it is not surprising that she collapsed into a wounded self-isolation over these four years.

What, then, might be done about this? The profundity of your friend's apparent grief and its intractability over time certainly suggests that it could qualify as prolonged grief disorder (PGD), a serious complication in bereavement that persists in an incapacitating, seemingly unchanging form for at least six months that has been given global recognition in the World Health Organization's International Classification of Diseases (ICD-11). Although this or any other diagnosis would require confirmation by a qualified mental health professional, PGD typically requires specialized intervention beyond that provided by caring family, bereavement support groups or even generalists in professions such as psychology, social work or psychiatry. Antidepressant medication could make a contribution to your friend's treatment by mitigating symptoms of sleep disruption, anhedonia, impaired concentration and so on, but evidence clearly indicates that this alone is insufficient to address the profound separation distress that PGD represents. Instead, a specialized form of treatment, like that developed by Katherine Shear and her colleagues at Columbia University, represents the state-of-the-art approach to intervention, one that is being disseminated to a large and growing cohort of therapists around the country, and indeed around the world. Investigating whether there are trained practitioners of this or related models of cognitive-behavioral therapy (CBT) or meaning-focused therapy in your friend's region of the country could therefore be a helpful step.

In addition to this attachment-informed approach to treatment, a trauma-informed approach could also be relevant, as the loss of your friend's son in particular could present unique challenges associated with the circumstances under which he died. Here again, Shear's PGD treatment, Rynearson's restorative retelling and other forms of exposure therapy offer specific "revisiting" procedures for helping clients integrate the hard reality of the story of dying without experiential avoidance, which can be extended by attention to the many questions that ambiguous losses and suicide deaths typically pose. When orchestrated by a trained practitioner, such interventions can encourage and prompt relevant forms of social support by family, friends and perhaps mutual support groups, optimally helping your friend adapt to three cardinal losses without compounding them with further relational estrangement in her ongoing life.

—Bob Neimeyer

## Telling the Story of a Tragic Death to Find Meaning

*Dear Dr. Neimeyer,*

I have read and heard you speak about the need to revisit and retell the story of the tragic death of a loved one in order to find meaning in the event. What stands out in your comments is obvious but should be underlined, in my view: the profound truth about the need to address the traumatic event of a loved one's dying, that is, the "ugly and difficult" narrative itself, before the full back story of the lost one, in context, can be freed. I just had to comment on this. It seems so apparent.

When I was initially searching for an adequate therapist three years ago after losing my loved one, several therapists, including one who supposedly was a specialist in treating complicated grief, began their assessment with the question, "How did you meet your friend?" I was speechless. Are you kidding? I did prolonged exposure therapy three years ago, which at least allowed me to tell the story!

What has helped me the most, finally, after three years, has been to write a creative nonfiction piece over this summer. I will submit it to a literary review, but even if every journal rejects it, I have finally gotten a sense of mastery. I included the details, restrained but factual, about the reality in an overall framing device of assumptive world dissolution and reclamation, which I believe roughly jibes with your position of meaning reconstruction. I continue to be so aware of the mental health field's zeal to just move this pain off stage at whatever cost to the client, so as to reach the goal of shutting the whole thing down.

Am I off base about this, or do you also see the need to retell the hard story of the loss before accessing the real narrative of the relationship that the bereaved is trying to reconnect with? Your ideas about making sense of the loss are so helpful to me in thinking about this, for myself and for my clients.

**Nancy D., LCSW**

*Dear Nancy,*

I appreciate your wise words, which are thoughtful in both senses—reflective and intelligent, on the one hand, and generous and kind to share with me, on the other. In return, I'm happy to think through with you a bit more these issues of timing in grief therapy in terms of whether to tackle the event story of the death first or the back story of the life shared with the loved one.

A cardinal precept for me in therapy is to allow clients to direct us to what they (1) deeply need and (2) are ready for in this moment of meeting. Sometimes I encounter clients who are desperate to share something of their loved one—especially when death seemed to place a cone of silence over their even mentioning the deceased person's name. But at other times, as you discovered for yourself, finding a listener who is willing to stand into the retelling of the hardest and darkest parts of the story of the death is a compelling existential necessity—to find an audience for it, a responsive witness, someone not eager to pretty it up or push it aside. Here, finding a partner in the work who will help the retelling become restorative and not retraumatizing is what is deeply needed and is precisely what the mourner is ready for. This was clearly the case for you, and your artful and authentic narrative in which you found words for your loved one's death eloquently met this need. Even if the creative nonfiction that resulted focused more on her or his death than life, I can imagine that your friend would feel pride and hope at the courage this huge step required.

A second thought stimulated by your inquiry bears on the form of the narrative that you wrote to frame your story, which began with all of the profound changes or ruptures introduced into your assumptive world—perhaps a shattering of your sense of predictability or control or an erosion of your trust in a world that is just or benign. Starting by exploring the brokenness of the previous meanings you had held and then in a second step tracing your discoveries or your attempts to reclaim or reconstruct them seems like a powerful prescription for how to pivot from grief to growth and one that is very much in keeping with our current research. In one recent study, for example, we found that challenges to our worldview of taken-for-granted beliefs was precisely the process that bridged between the anguish of complicated grief on the one hand and the unsought benefit of posttraumatic growth on the other. Other recent studies conducted with colleagues have also documented the power of creative writing to promote meaning and reduce grief-related suffering among the bereaved. Thus, in the form of your story as well as its specific content (which I would welcome a chance to read!), I can't imagine a more significant form of meaning reconstruction.

—Bob Neimeyer

## Lost Her Son in a Drowning Accident

*Dear Dr. Neimeyer,*

I'm a family therapist who has been working with a couple who lost a young adult son in a drowning accident in a distant country and in which the mother has remained in a deep, unshakeable grief for over three years, for two of which I have been working with her and her husband in therapy. At this point I feel like I've tried everything with her, grounding our work in deep compassion, making a safe place for the expression and exploration of her feelings, nudging her to take small steps toward something that could bring her pleasure, pointing out the irrationality of her self-blame and trying to foster greater closeness to her husband. Nothing has made a dent in her grief or her guilt, though her relationship to her son was a good one and she had no hand in his trip or his death. Nor will she accept my referral to a physician who could evaluate her for antidepressant medication, which she probably needs, or do anything more with her husband than ruminate about the loss, as she pushes away his efforts to reach out to her in a consoling way. We've reviewed the story of the death, though it doesn't feel like she is dealing with trauma, per se, and we've also tried to explore her relationship to her son, with little effect. In short, I feel quite stuck, even though she seems committed to seeing me weekly and says she feels more desperate on weeks that we are not able to meet. My client says that she will never be happy again, even though her other children and grandchildren try to involve her in their lives. At this point, I am beginning to believe her, though I have tried to remain supportive.

Is there something more I could be doing to help her?

**Harriet B., MFT**

*Dear Harriet,*

I can hear your clear frustration with the impasse in this case, as your earnest efforts to make a difference seem continually to be rebuffed or seem to be drawn down into the quicksand of your client's grief. Compassionate attunement is surely the place to begin, and validation and exploration of her feelings and great pain surely are a big part of what most bereaved people need. But it sounds like in this case this often-necessary foundation for intervention is clearly insufficient. So, here are a few quick suggestions that occur to me, with no omnipotent conviction that any of them will be a magic key that opens a door out of the prison of her grief. These are simply some things I might try.

1. *When what you are doing isn't working, do something different.* Rational disputation and emotional expression and exploration haven't made much difference so far, so I would tend to let them go. Releasing these approaches could make way for something else.
2. *Shift the context.* Your office seems to have become a safe haven for this mother, as suggested by her missing it when you skip a session, but also seems to have become a confessional for her unwavering grief. So, consider a change up: greet her at the door and take a walk. Stroll to a nearby park or green space as you talk, with only occasional eye contact as you both necessarily focus on the changing landscape. In my experience this has sometimes injected movement and outward attention for clients stuck in ruminative constriction, allowing a conversation that varies naturally from observations about the world around you ("What a beautiful flower!" "Do you recognize the call of that bird?") to reflective probes that are lightly metaphoric ("Where would you like to see your path heading as we move into summer? What do you imagine the next step might be?"). If nothing else, the walk may be more enjoyable and stimulating for you personally and could contribute to her wellness at a physical level. More optimistically, making a practice of this could begin to build a sense of mastery, self-care or more regular exercise for her in a way that has been demonstrated to be useful in the treatment of depression, and it might even prompt movement in her foreclosed psychological world as well.
3. *Interview the resistance.* There is ample evidence in this case for what my colleague Bruce Ecker would call "pro-symptom positions" (PSPs), deeply entrenched and largely unconscious meanings of suffering and thriving that make this particular form of grief more important to have than not to have, despite the genuinely life-vitiating pain associated with it. For example, preserving a conviction of her own responsibility for her son's death might prove less anguishing despite her terrible guilt than reckoning with her own maternal powerlessness to protect her child, or her intense grief might stand as an accusation to God or the universe that the death was cruelly unjust and leaves a permanent wound that will not heal. Alternatively, a part of her might believe that allowing the grief to

recede, even a bit, would be tantamount to loving him less, or the grief itself might have become the way she is now attached to him. Pursuing such hidden meanings is not an intellectual guessing game, however, as it requires special methods for indirectly inviting and encountering these entrenched beliefs that make her suffering in just this way necessary. If getting to the roots of these PSPs is a direction you'd like to pursue, you might like to check out "coherence therapy" and Ecker's work on the internet, as well as the module Holding onto Grief in the rich menu of recorded training offered by the *Portland Institute for Loss and Transition*. This thoroughly experiential, non-psychoeducational or interpretive approach to therapy offers a clear alternative to pushing harder for change. Instead, it provides a methodology for encountering and dialoguing with the resistance, with no overt effort to change (and for this very reason it often provokes profound and rapid transformation). Coherence work greatly informs my own practice and is a mainstay in my work with complicated grief cases, as displayed in several clinical videos in the Portland Institute curriculum.

4. *Go social*. Therapy can become its own little world, especially when a client has cut off from (or been cut off by) many others. As a counterbalance to this, secure your client's commitment to engage in some form of regular social activity, whether it is a weekly "meet up" group announced on the internet, a knitting circle, a tennis class, a book club or a gourmet club. In keeping with the Dual Process Model of grief, which emphasizes both the need to process the loss but also to restore life, the goal would be to venture weekly into restoration, just as she ventures regularly into loss-oriented work with you. Make time for both, and push her gently to reconnect with a world in which grief is not the singular focus.

5. *Use the grief instead of trying to lose it*. Suffering can be borne nobly, rather than merely wasted in rumination and self-indulgent anguish. Seek ways to draw on her pain in order to engage a deeply broken world, filled with loss and suffering. Meeting others in compassion, whether in a self-help group, by volunteering for an organization promoting social justice, tending to rescued animals or doing good work with suffering communities, could be a way of reaching out from her own broken heart to embrace others who know their own form of pain and loneliness. Performing such acts of kindness in her son's name also honors him and extends his impact beyond the grave.

Best of success with this. But also, humbly recognize that we do not save all lost souls; sometimes we just make their purgatory a little less hellish.

—Bob Neimeyer

QUESTIONS FROM PROFESSIONALS

## The Widow Is Ready for a New Relationship, But Nobody Else Is

*Dear Dr. Neimeyer,*

I am a bereavement counselor at a hospice. I have a client who has done amazing work after the death of her husband. She is in her mid-60s and very healthy. She and her husband had counseling before his death, and she continued after his death. She has written and read everything she can get her hands on. She has recently met a man in whom she is romantically interested who is concerned she has not grieved enough. It has been ten months since her husband died. She feels she is ready to explore a new relationship. Her family is not.

Can you help me with some helpful advice for her?

**Diana R., LPC**

*Dear Diana,*

As you know, one sign of resilience following the loss of a spouse is genuine readiness to open one's heart to another partnership, though this is by no means an inevitable outcome of positive adaptation to loss. Across much of human history and most cultures, committing to a new partner in marriage would be considered the normative and approved course, though cultures vary in whether this expectation applies equally to men and women. Thus, there is nothing unusual about your client's interest in exploring a new relationship, even as she approaches the first anniversary of her husband's death, and certainly the therapeutic work she has done with you and on her own seems to have contributed to her readiness for this step.

But of course, such decisions are not simply individual matters, as they implicate other stakeholders in the family and social system. Adult children in particular can feel an invisible loyalty to a deceased parent and be reluctant to imagine the surviving parent in the arms of another. Some also may be concerned about their parent committing to someone who will ultimately require exhausting caregiving in later life or who will deplete or inherit their parent's financial resources. Most, but not all, eventually come to terms with this natural desire for new love and companionship on the part of their surviving parent, though acceptance and perhaps even celebration of this development commonly take time.

More crucially, it takes two to say "yes" to a relationship, so the concern of the potential partner that your client "has not grieved enough" has to be taken seriously. Is this a general cultural norm that he subscribes to, or if he himself is widowed, is his concern grounded in his own intimate experience of being reluctant to embrace someone new? Or does it reflect subtle signals that he seems to be receiving from your client, perhaps in the form of a careful avoidance of triggers for sadness or grief, or an overly needy reaching out for security in a new bond? Faced with these questions, and the need for the prospective partners to be "on the same page" in their readiness to step toward one another, I would likely invite a session with both of them to consider what each is ready for now and what they might be open to some months down the road. A wonderful new resource for older adults considering new intimacy after loss is the very readable and practical book, *Open to Love*, by Gloria Horsley and Frank Powers, two seasoned psychologists who themselves have come together as a couple in later life. The book is packed with engaging and wise counsel on everything from online dating sites to physical intimacy and family resistance of just the kind you describe.

Of course, a conversation about hopes and fears regarding a blossoming relationship might be relevant for many couples who are negotiating possible intimacy, whether or not either of them had recently lost a partner. But in the case of widowhood, I might introduce the invisible third party to the conversation—namely, the deceased husband—to explore how comfortable each is in speaking about him and what would be considered a normal and healthy loving place your client might still hold for him in her life. At the point that both members of the potential couple are comfortable with that as well as with one another, I trust that the relationship might move forward in a way that could be embraced by both, as well as the larger circle of their families.

—Bob Neimeyer

## Resilience and Posttraumatic Growth

*Dear Dr. Neimeyer,*

As a counselor myself, I was interested to read recently that the majority of people who experience a significant loss react with a surprising degree of resilience, to the extent that the grief process can, in the longer term, be a positive experience for them. This tends to counter a prevailing, if rather archaic, view that counseling is routinely a valuable process to help people deal with bereavement. In your opinion, what should grief therapists expect about how people will cope following a recent bereavement?

**John S., MA**

*Dear John,*

Well, to say that the death of one's child, partner, sibling, parent or friend could in the long run be considered a "positive experience" may be a bit of an overstatement; I've met very few grieving people who wouldn't give back in a heartbeat any degree of personal growth they've achieved to have their loved one back physically in their lives. But at the same time, as the research of my colleague George Bonanno clearly demonstrates, resilience is a reality for close to half of the bereaved. The fact is that many people weather the storm of mourning surprisingly quickly, finding that they retain their footing in the world or recover it once again within a short period, even if they continue to miss their loved ones keenly. For many others, the loss more profoundly disrupts their mood and functioning for several months, but they too ultimately grieve adaptively, integrate the loss into their lives and return to their emotional baseline while revising their life routines and goals accordingly.

As Bonanno reports, however, another 25% tend to fare worse, experiencing exacerbations of previously problematic patterns (e.g., of chronic depression or substance abuse), family and work-related conflicts or prolonged and anguishing grief, experienced by about 10% of the bereaved. The point I'd like to make is that grieving can lead to surprisingly different outcomes, only a minority of which are likely to benefit from psychotherapy. Most people will adjust to their loss quite well over time, drawing on their own strengths and those of others who care about them, without the aid of a grief therapist.

But allow me to conclude with a few more remarks about your implication about the upside of grief. Beyond *resilience* per se, which refers essentially to a rapid return to baseline following a significant stressful event, a surprising number of people also report what my colleagues Tedeschi and Calhoun call *posttraumatic growth* (PTG) in the long-term wake of loss. PTG refers to a cluster of developments in the wake of a "seismic" life transition, which include a greater sense of strength and maturity, deepening of relationships and compassion for the suffering of others, keener appreciation for life, greater readiness to embrace possibilities and often a renewal of spiritual and philosophic frameworks for living. Nothing about this is inevitable, of course, and our own research and that of others suggests that PTG is typically a hard-won outcome of a good deal of painful reflection and meaning-making, which is probably most accessible when the distress of bereavement is sufficiently intense to challenge life as usual but not so overwhelming as to make constructive change impossible. Sometimes on their own, and sometimes with the aid of an understanding counselor, many bereaved people experience this form of loss-related growth as well as grief.

—Bob Neimeyer

# 16
# TRAINING RESOURCES FOR PROFESSIONALS

### Grief Therapy Masterclass
### *Featuring Robert A. Neimeyer, PhD*

This 8.5-hour online course features an in-depth training in advanced skills for working with a variety of challenges in bereavement, seen through the lens of a meaning-focused approach to grief therapy. The four-part program provides case-based instruction, drawing on extensive demonstrations of work with seven clients, punctuated by probing clinical dialogue between Neimeyer and program host, Victor Yalom, PhD. Among the losses encountered are the death of a spouse after nearly 60 years of marriage, prolonged grief following the cancer death of a mother over 20 years before, the shocking suicide of a young husband, the COVID-19 death of a father, the drowning of an adult daughter, the murder of a son and the perinatal death of two children accompanied by the profound brain damage of a third. Viewers will complete the program with a substantial toolbox of techniques for responding to both normative and traumatic loss and a nuanced understanding of the therapeutic relationship that makes profound transformation possible. For more information and a special discount on the program, navigate to https://academy.psychotherapy.net/grief-therapy-masterclass-Neimeyer?mc_cid=0e4e0c386b&mc_eid=34df19236d.

### Certification in Grief Therapy

The *Portland Institute for Loss and Transition* (PI), the leading institute for global online and onsite training in bereavement support, grief counseling and grief therapy, offers a comprehensive and affordable training and optional certification in *Grief Therapy as Meaning Reconstruction, Family-Focused Grief Therapy, Grief Therapy for Non-Death Loss, Arts-Assisted Grief Therapy* and *Grief Therapy for Suicide Bereavement*, offered by over 20 world-class faculty presenters and mentors. For information about training for individual therapists, conferences or organizations, navigate to www.portlandinstitute.org/.

TRAINING RESOURCES FOR PROFESSIONALS

## Association for Death Education and Counseling (ADEC)

The leading North American organization for professionals specializing in grief counseling, therapy, death education and research, ADEC hosts annual conferences as well as monthly webinars on a variety of topics of professional interest, as well as certification in thanatology, the study of death, dying and bereavement. For more information, navigate to www.portlandinstitute.org/.

## The Routledge Series on Death, Dying and Bereavement

As the leading publisher of professional books in the field of grief counseling, the Routledge series features such recent titles as *New Techniques of Grief Therapy: Bereavement and Beyond*, *Attachment-Informed Grief Therapy*, and *Compassion-Based Approaches in Loss and Grief*. For details of relevant titles, navigate to www.routledge.com/Series-in-Death-Dying-and-Bereavement/book-series/SE0620.

## The Handbook of Grief Therapies

*(Edith Steffen, Evgenia Milman and Robert A. Neimeyer, Eds.)*

This comprehensive sourcebook features a pluralistic range of contemporary approaches to grief therapy, including meaning-focused, cognitive-behavioral, family-centered, existential, expressive arts, narrative, Two-Track, attachment-informed, psychodynamic and mindfulness-oriented perspectives, as well as chapters focused on diverse losses, populations and issues. For a detailed table of contents, navigate to https://uk.sagepub.com/en-gb/eur/the-handbook-of-grief-therapies/book272994.

# INDEX

AAS *see* American Association of Suicidology
abandonment 136, 149; chronic anxiety regarding 194; fears of (Rita) 97; feelings of (Beverly) 220; feelings of (Ken) 58–59; professional (Beverly) 220; sense of (Eileen) 64; sense of (Wanda) 107
absenteeism 199
absent grief 74
absent other 210
abuse: alcohol 46, 97; childhood sexual 107, 120; memories of 106; reporting 107; satanic ritual abuse panic 105; sexual 30; substance 137, 166, 190–191; *see also* drug use and abuse
abuser, father as 211
acceptance 113, 229; of human condition 72; of limits of human knowing 138; moving to place of 166; self-acceptance 146, 180
ADEC *see* Association for Death Education and Counseling
ADHD *see* attention deficit hyperactivity disorder
adult children, loss of 198, 220, 222, 226; daughter 87–88, 232; son 67–68, 96, 220, 226; suicide of adult son (Anna) 148–149; suicide of adult son (Joanne) 155–157; suicide of adult son following his loss of two infant (Loretta) 149–152; teenage daughter 84–85; teenage son 158–160; unfinished business between parents and 208–211; *see also* children, loss of
adversity: coping with 58, 201; facing 157, 179; finding one's way through 129; suffering 86; surmounting 185

a-fib *see* atrial fibrillation
AfterTalk column and website 4, 16, 111, 125, 132, 211; integrating AfterTalk Letters to the Deceased into Grief Therapy 203–206; letter of appreciation to a daughter who has passed (Doreen) 80; letter to daughter who was murdered (Anabel) 170; letter to a daughter who has passed (Anna) 85; letter to a father who has passed (Eileen) 64; letter to a first husband who has passed (Nicole) 24; letter to husband who has passed (Johanna) 29; letter to husband who has passed (Dina) 31; letter to husband who has passed (Moira) 21; letter to a husband who has suddenly passed (Rachel) 22–23; letter to a husband who has suddenly passed (Sabrina) 20; letter to a mother who has passed (Amy) 104–105; letter to a mother who has passed (Fran) 74; letter to a mother who has passed (Laurie) 101; letter to a mother who has passed under complex circumstances (Charlene) 164; letter to partner who has passed (Miles) 52; letter to a sister and other family members who have passed (Paulina) 94; letter to a son who has passed (Kaitlyn) 83; letter to a son who has passed (Katia) 82; letter to wife who has passed (Bob) 33; letter to wife who has passed (Enrico) 40; letter to wife who has passed (Rodney) 36; letter to wife who has passed (Theodore) 43; Private Conversations function 55, 101
alcohol abuse 46, 96–97

# INDEX

alcohol and drinking 117; advice to avoid 45; advice to exercise to mitigate negative effects of 178; advice to limit 161; advice to refrain from offering to grieving individuals 181; combining medication with 117; coping via 138
alcoholism 211
Alliance of Hope (suicide survivors support group) 154
ALS *see* amyotrophic lateral sclerosis
Alzheimer's disease, loss from 69, 93, 218–220; *see also* dementia
ambiguous cause of death 143, 180
ambiguous loss 114–115, 224
American Association of Suicidology (AAS) 145, 146
American Foundation for Suicide Prevention support groups 154, 158
American Psychiatric Association 195; see also DSM 5-TR
amyotrophic lateral sclerosis (ALS) 58
anger 3, 63–64, 72; avoidance and 38; bargaining shifting into 113; constructive outlets for releasing 166; cultivating 108; depression and 82, 85, 113; feeling misunderstood and prolonged anger over loss of son (Bette) 85–86; forum for venting 107; at God 168; guilt and 76, 130; isolation in bereavement and 132; processing 74; releasing 165; son's anger over sister's death (Stella) 91–92; sorting through 141; suppressed 129; survivor guilt and 136; understandable 74
anorexia 211
antianxiety medication 128, 153
anticipatory grief 118–119, 197–198; complex 208
antidepressants 53, 62, 89, 116–117, 120, 127–128, 153; advice regarding exercise as form of 177; getting through grief without 175–176
anxiety 113; advice to accept 123; advice to expect 23; antianxiety drugs 128, 153; antidepressants and 176; antidotes for 23; chronic 194; depression and 97–98; exposure treatments for 38; medication for 37; moral injury and 135; panic attacks and 122; Prolonged Grief Disorder and 190–191; self-blame and 177; spiking 119; strong 22

"Ask Dr. Neimeyer" column 5; *see also* AfterTalk
Association for Death Education and Counseling (ADEC) 233
atrial fibrillation (a-fib) 117; *see also* heart
attention deficit hyperactivity disorder (ADHD) 142
atypical depression 153–154
autopsy: of a child 142–144; psychological 138
autopsy report 144, 212
avoidance 59, 70; anger and 38; awkward avoidance of others 83; experiential 224; of memories of the deceased 220; of pain 93; of reminders of loss 125, 148; task 26; social 56; of triggers for sadness or grief 230; vigilant mutual 12
avoidance-based coping in bereavement 178, 219; *see also* bereavement; coping

bargaining 113
Bereaved Parents of the USA group 114
bereaved, the: allowing to speak 6; background of 193; everyday experiences of 15; listening to 3–5; professionals who support 6–7; parents 82–83, 85, 124; regrets acknowledged by 54; risk factors for prolonged grief relative to 193; self-reflections by 27; separation distress felt by 53; spouses 13; trauma-informed therapy for 116
bereavement: aftermath of 190; alcohol abuse during 46; antidepressants and 127, 175–176; avoidance-based coping in 178; bereavement camps 86; bereavement care 53, 194, 197, 199; bereavement center 192; bereavement complication 193; bereavement counseling 122; bereavement outcome 194, 198; bereavement overload 94; bereavement research 196; bereavement studies 3; bereavement services and support 215; bereavement support groups 65; compassionate understanding in 182; configurations of 9; complicated 97, 119; continuation of bonds in 36; *Continuing Bonds in Bereavement* (Klass and Steffen) 220; as depressive disorder 175; early months of 50; exercise (physical) and 177–178; "living losses" and 128; pain of loss in

# INDEX

relationship to 72; problems ushered in by 96; prolonged 16; seasonal affective disorder (SAD) and 88; self-care in 178; sense of isolation in 132; sleepless 45; significant, due to loss of father 69; suicide bereavement 147–149, 154; support for 4; traumatic 137; unfinished business in 208–209; violent death bereavement 214; *see also* Dual Process Model of Coping with Bereavement (DPM); Unfinished Business in Bereavement Scale (UBBS); Violent Death Bereavement Society

bipolar disorder 88–89

Bogatin, Lisa 4–5

brain tumor, death from 30–31, 115

Buddhist concepts of suffering 138

Buddhist "Middle Way" 47–48

bullying 146; cyber bullying 146

burnout 188; caregiver 42, 199, 201

caffeine 45, 178

cancer: ambiguous situation caused by diagnosis of (Sandy) 114–115; boyfriend's death from (Charlene) 54–55; brain tumor 115; colon 61; death of a boyfriend 54–55; death of a child from 4; grief and depression over loss of father to (Caitlin) 61; grief over loss of husband from (Lee) 31–32; guilt and grief over husband's decline from (Dolores) 117; holding over good memories following death of son from (Leah) 115–116; inability to speak about loss of father to (Rachel) 69; loss of ex-husband to (Carla) 100; loss of both parents to (Julie) 72–73; loss of father to (Edith contacted by a person with story of) 215; loss of mother to (Amy) 104; loss of sister to (Stella's son) 91; loss of sister after long battle with (Nita) 92–93; loss of son to (Eva) 89; loss of teenage sibling to (Sandy) 114–115; lung 119; no justice in (i.e. randomness of) 157; prostate 117; recent loss to (Johanna) 28; recent loss to (Renata) 13–15; suicidal thinking of wife following loss of husband from (Andrea) 119–121; suicide following diagnosis of (Carla's story of her brother) 139–140; suicide following loss of children to (Loretta's story of her son) 149–152; *see also* oncology unit

cancer therapist 30

CBT *see* cognitive-behavioral therapy

child, loss of 4; anniversary of daughter's passing (Doreen) 80–81; coping with autopsy of (Jeanmarie) 142–144; coping with multiple losses including sister and son (Paulina) 94–95; cycling from mania to depression following death of daughter (Sandy) 87–89; daughter murdered by father of daughter's children (Miriam) 166–168; daughter's murder by gunshot (Anabel) 169–171; feeling misunderstood and prolonged anger over loss of son (Bette) 85–86; loss of son in drowning accident (Harriet) 226–228; loss of teenage daughter (Anna) 84–85; loss of two girls in car accident (Margie) 126–128; mother who cut herself off from the world following death of son (Karen) 222–244; online sharing and memorialization of grief following 85; second year following death of son (Eva) 89–90; senseless loss of son (Kaitlin) 83–84; spouses differently grieving death of daughter (Lorinda) 86–87; suicide of nephew and son (Hannah) 158–160; symbiotic relationship with daughter who has died (Lisa) 211–212; time as "healing all wounds" and time to heal following (Katia) 81–82; violent death of son (Briana) 161–162; violent death of son (Miriam) 165–166; *see also* adult children

Chodron, Pema 130

chronic anxiety 194; *see also* anxiety

chronic depression 231; *see also* depression

chronic fatigue 45

chronic inflammatory demyelinating polyneuropathy 75

chronic mental illness 76

chronic sorrow 128–129, 133

*Chronic Sorrow* (Roos) 119

cigarettes 178

civil union: no partner rights without marriage or 55; *see also* partner or close relationship, loss of

cognitive-behavioral therapy (CBT) 224

# INDEX

coherence therapy 228
coma-like state 30
Compassionate Friends, The 85, 114
compassion fatigue 199
complicated relationships: choosing isolation from children following death of husband (Bethany) 102–104; daughter accusing father of molesting her and widow (stepmother)'s response (Wanda) 105–108; disenfranchised grief following death of ex-husband (Carla) 100–101; guilt at mother's passing (Amy) 104–105; loss of mother with "good" and "bad" personalities (Laurie) 101–102; widow cut off by oldest son following death of her husband/his father (Selena) 108–109
*Continuing Bonds in Bereavement* (Klass and Steffen) 220
Cooper, James Fenimore 95
coping in bereavement 86, 175, 179; alcohol to self-numb as form of 138; avoidance-based 178, 219; contextualizing 87; coping capacities 94; coping with child's autopsy (Jeanmarie) 142–144; coping with loss of multiple members at one time (Paulina) 94–95; positive 203; *see also* Dual Process Model of Coping with Bereavement (DPM)
coping style (styles of coping) 59, 96, 114, 193, 194
Correa, Fanny 214
COVID-19 pandemic 183–185, 183, 208, 211

dementia, loss from 42–43, 73, 93, 119, 210; encroaching 117; vascular 117
depression: chronic 231; cycling from mania to 87–89; disconsolate 4; grief and 60–62; incapacitating 85; managing 61–62; postpartum 217–218; rumination and 17; self-management of 98; walking to improve 75; *see also* antidepressants; bipolar disorder
depressive disorder, bereavement as 175
depressive symptoms 176
*Diagnostic and Statistical Manual of Mental Disorders, Fifth Edition* (DSM 5-TR) 189–191, 195, 209
disenfranchised grief 100–101

disrupted sleep 45, 98, 176
Doka, Ken 56
DPM *see* Dual Process Model of Coping with Bereavement (DPM)
drowning accident 226–228
Drug Induced Cardiomyopathy 142
drug overdose 87
drug problem 155
drugs: antianxiety 42; lethal 159; as means of dealing with emotional pain 181; pain-regulating 55; sleep 169; trading sex for 148
drug use and abuse 96, 142–143, 149–150, 155–156; children with history of 211
DSM 5-TR *see Diagnostic and Statistical Manual of Mental Disorders, Fifth Edition*
Dual Process Model of Coping with Bereavement (DPM) 14–15

Eker, Bruce 227–228; *see also* coherence therapy; PSP
electrocution 129–130
EMDR *see* eye movement desensitization and reprocessing
EMDR Institute 160
emotion regulation 39, 204, 214, 215
empathy 32, 71, 92, 108, 182, 209; professional liability of 188–189; radical 138; therapeutic 188–189
end-of-life care 57, 197, 199
euthanasia 130
exercise: advice on alcohol and 178; advice on exercise as form of antidepressant 177; advice to build into one's day 46; breathing 116; as form of self-healing 142; on grieving and (Brittany) 176–179; mindfulness and 68; staying busy with 26; *see also* yoga
exposure therapy 244
eye movement desensitization and reprocessing (EMDR) 116, 128, 151, 170

family death 6; family get-togethers in wake of (Mary) 11–13; loss of both parents and all siblings (Devorah) 95–96; loss of multiple members at one time 4; loss of multiple members at one time (Paulina) 94–95; loss of multiple members to suicide (Hannah) 158–160; therapist's own feelings of grief following multiple deaths in the family (Briana) 201–203; *see also* child, loss of; husband, loss of; partner or close relationship, loss of; sibling, loss of; wife, loss of

fatal accident: daughter who accidentally killed another in motorcycle accident (Lynn) 134–135; death of mother in car accident caused by seizure in son (Phil) 130–131; electrocution of teen son (Fred) 129–130; loss of soldier husband to car accident (Donna) 131–133; loss of teen son in car accident (Ellen) 122–124; loss of two girls in car accident (Margie) 126–128; unanswered questions in wake of husband's death (Connie) 133–134

fatal illness: anticipatory grief for daughter diagnosed with fatal disorder (Victoria) 118–119; autoimmune disorder, loss of a child to (Felicia) 113–113; cancer, loss of adult son to (Leah) 115–117; cancer and other co-morbidities, loss of husband to (Dolores) 117–118; cancer, loss of teenage sibling to (Sandy) 114–115; suicidal thinking following loss of husband (Andrea) 119–121

firearms *see* gun violence

forgiveness 17; asking for 43, 170; choice of 166; extending 17; giving "moral gift" of 165; lack of 209; offenses beyond 211; postmortem negotiation or 204; seeking 135; self-forgiveness 152; virtue of 166

Frankl, Viktor 121

gender minorities 146
Gestalt Therapy Institute 160
God: accusation of 227; anger at 168; being with, after death 34; caring 167; complicated spiritual grief and conflicting views of 130; "letter to" 151, 152; seeking forgiveness from 135; punishment from 150, 151; strength from 22, 124; suffering and 69, 182; understanding from 30
God's eye view 107, 138
grief and grieving: absent 74; complicated 119; complicated spiritual 130; deep and abiding, therapy for (Beverly) 220–222; daily, over loss of brother (Meika) 98–99; depression and 60–62; grief class, attending 89–90; grief and guilt over husband's long decline (Dolores) 117–118; guilt as complicating factor in 217; Holding onto Grief module 228; normalcy of 190; prolonged, risk factors for (Elaine) 192–194; stages (or not) of 179; requiring clinical intervention, questions regarding (Maria Teresa) 194–196; ruminative 30; stages of 179; steps of 113; therapist's own feelings of grief following multiple deaths in the family (Briana) 201–203; unpredictability of, questions regarding (Sofia) 179–182; *see also* anticipatory grief; Prolonged Grief Disorder (PGD)

Grief After Suicide blog 154
grief therapy: certification in (Portland Institute) 232; *Handbook of Grief Therapies* (Steffen, Milman, and Neimeyer) 233; integrating AfterTalk into (Bryan) 203–206; Routledge Series on Death, Dying and Bereavement 233

Grief Therapy Masterclass (online course) 232

grieving period 180
guilt 3–4, 96, 104, 189; caregiver's regret and (Theodore) 42–43; corrosive 71, 159; death of daughter and feelings of (Felicia) 113; feeling consumed by 190; grief and guilt over husband's long decline (Dolores) 117–118; grief complicated by 217; guilt busting 23; irrational 24, 84; long-term 212; mother's passing and (Amy) 104–105; remorse and 131; trauma and guilt over loss due to violent death 134; survivor guilt following suicide of wife (Gill) 136–137

gun violence: daughter's murder via 169–171; postpartum depression and suicide by 217–218; suicide and 159; traumatic suicide from 153–157

hanging of oneself 149
heart attack 186
heart problems 45; cardiac stress 71; Drug Induced Cardiomyopathy 142
heroin 142

# INDEX

heroism, everyday 185
Holland, Jason 208
homicide and mass tragedies: accidental arson death of mother by her roommate (Charlene) 162–165; daughter murdered by father of daughter's children (Miriam) 166–168; grieving war and terrorism (Lisa) 171–172; murder of daughter preceded by relationship rupture with mother 169–171; violent death of son (Briana) 161–162; violent death of son (Miriam) 165–166
Horsley, Gloria 49, 230
hospice 108, 195, 196–198, 229
hospice social worker 192
husband, loss of: choosing isolation from children following death of (Bethany) 102–104; creation of bedroom shrine following (Dara) 77–78; being cut off by eldest son following death of his father (Selena) 108–109; daughter's wedding in wake of 18–19; disenfranchised grief following death of ex-husband (Carla) 100–101; gift of grief from (Lee) 31–32; guilt and grief as a result of (Dolores) 117; in holiday season (Mary) 11–13; how to live in wake of (Netta) 15–16; husband accused of molestation after his death (Wanda) 105–108; losing final piece of him (Moira) 20–21; loss of husband and father (Dolores) 67–69; moving forward after (Dina) 30–31; moving on after husband's suicide (Katie) 137–139; opening oneself to new love after (Rachel) 21–23; quilting a new life after (Johanna) 28–29; recent (Renata) 13–15; remarriage following (Nicole) 24; starting over after (Vanessa) 27–28; sudden death of (Cynthia) 16–18; suicide of 158–160; turning over a new leaf after (Phyllis) 25–26; a widow's complicated grief ritual following (Marie) 206–208

ICD-11 see International Classification of Diseases
"indwell" another's feelings, capacity for 189; see also empathy
inner mother 74

insensitive consolation 182–183
International Classification of Diseases (ICD-11) 189–192, 195, 223

kidney failure 211
Klass, Dennis 220
Kübler-Ross model 179
Kushner, Harold 130

Lamictal 89
*Last of the Mohicans* (Cooper) 95
Lewis, C.S. 130
LGBTQ+ youth 146
lithium 89
Loss conference, The 146
Lynn, Larry 4–5

MADD *see* Mothers Against Drunk Driving
making meaning out of loss: on telling the story of death to find meaning in it (Nancy) 224–225; *see also* meaning-making; narrating loss
"Map of Mourning" 14
mass tragedy *see* homicide and mass tragedies
meaning-focused therapy 224
meaning-making 194, 203, 214, 231; tools for 216
mental illness 75, 137; chronic 76
Milman, Evgenia 233
mood disorders 88
Mothers Against Drunk Driving (MADD) 166
murder *see* homicide and mass tragedies
*Music and Medicine* journal 199
mystical experiences following loss 33, 36

narrating loss: on telling the story of death to find meaning in it (Nancy) 224–225; using creative writing for 226; *see also* restorative retelling
National Center for Health Statistics 159
Nazi concentration camps 121

oncology unit: dealing with loss on 198–201
online dating 49
online or onsite training in grief therapy 7n1
online resources *see* AfterTalk
online sharing of grief 85

239

online support forums 68, 152, 154
Open to Hope website 85
*Open to Love* (Horsley and Powers) 49, 230
overdose 186; coping with death of son from (Jeanmarie) 142–144; *see also* drug overdose

palliative care 194, 197–199
pancreatitis 142
parent(s), loss of: accidental arson death of mother by her roommate (Charlene) 162–165; blaming oneself for death of mother (Carrie) 70–72; creation of bedroom shrine by wife following death of husband (daughter Dana's concerns regarding) 77–78; death of mother in car accident caused by seizure in son (Phil) 130–131; delayed grief following death of parents and grandmother (Robin) 66–67; finding father dead on Father's Day (Mimi) 64–65; grief and depression in wake of (Caitlin) 60–62; grieving not permitted by father's second wife in wake of father's death (Eileen) 63–64; guilt at mother's passing (Amy) 104–105; loss of both parents and all siblings (Devorah) 95–96; loss to cancer of both parents (Julie) 72–73; loss of father to Alzheimer's and inability to speak of it (Rachel) 69–70; loss of husband and father faced by (Dolores) 67–69; slipping back into grief following death of father (Mara) 78–79; struggling with "What If's" in wake of father's schizophrenia and (Carol) 75–77; waiting to grieve death of mother (Fran) 73–75
Parents of Murdered Children advocacy group 166
partner or close relation (uncles, friends, etc.), loss of: cancer death of boyfriend (Charlene) 54–55; death of uncle and grieving niece (Meghan) 57–58; feeling abandoned and confused by friend following loss of his wife (Ken) 58–59; feeling lost in limbo following (Miles) 50–52; finding meaning in life following (Yvonne) 52–54; veterans' suicide and fear of loss following (Brad) 55–57

path: to adaptation 141; of avoidance 59; of compassion 71; of humility 71; of logic 71
PGD *see* Prolonged Grief Disorder
PI *see* Portland Institute for Loss and Transition
Popkin 200–201
Portland Institute for Loss and Transition (PI) 7n1, 228, 232, 233
posttraumatic growth (PTG) 231
post-traumatic stress disorder (PTSD) 124–127
powerlessness, feelings of 33, 166, 186; maternal 227
Powers, Frank 49, 230
practical and philosophical questions: COVID-19 and future pandemics, dealing with (Shirley) 183–185; getting through grief without antidepressants (Demi) 175–176; on grieving and exercise (Brittany) 176–179; insensitive consolation, dealing with (Helen) 182–183; on the meaning of life (Nicolae) 185–187; on the unpredictability of grief (Sofia) 179–182
professionals, questions from: on Alzheimer's patient, counseling for (Linda) 218–220; on dealing with patient loss in the oncology unit (Joyce) 198–201; on deep and abiding grief in a patient (Beverly) 220–222; on doctor colleague who is depressed by patient's suicide (Lisa) 217–218; on friend who cut herself off from the world following death of son (Karen) 222–244; on grief that requires clinical intervention (Maria Teresa) 194–196; on group therapy for traumatic loss (Edith) 215–217; on integrating AfterTalk into grief therapy (Bryan) 203–206; on loss of son in drowning accident (Harriet) 226–228; on prolonged grief disorder in DSM 5-TR (Luis) 189–192; on reaching out to hospice families (Holly) 196–198; on resilience and posttraumatic growth (John) 230–231; on risk factors for prolonged grief (Elaine) 192–194; symbiotic relationship with daughter who has died (Lisa) 211–212; on telling the story of death to find meaning in it (Nancy) 224–225;

# INDEX

on therapist's own feelings of grief following multiple deaths in the family (Briana) 201–203; on traumatic images of loved one's death (Kerry) 213–215; on unfinished business between adult children and their parents (Sonya) 208–211; on whether empathy is a liability for grief therapists (Megan) 188–189; a widow's complicated grief ritual, therapist's questions regarding (Marie) 206–208; on widow who is ready for a new relationship (Diana) 229–230
professionals, training resources for 232–233
prolonged grief, risk factors for 192–194
Prolonged Grief Disorder (PGD) 190–191, 223–224
pro-symptom positions (PSP) 227–228
PSP *see* pro-symptom positions
psychotherapy 105, 176, 231
PTG *see* posttraumatic growth

questions from professionals *see* professionals, questions from

radical empathy 138
radical honesty 121
radical questions 121
random act of kindness 184, 205
random behavior 26
random loss 71; automobile accident 157
random medical condition 114
random sexual encounters 149
random violence 171
Rando, Therese 133
regret 101, 104; Amy's feelings of 208; bereaved peoples' acknowledgement of 54; caregiver's guilt and (Theodore) 42–43; COVID-19 and 208; living in such a way so as to minimize 119
resilience 23; posttraumatic growth and 230–231
restorative retelling 116, 128, 151, 160, 170, 214, 224–225
restorative sleep 45–46, 133
Roos, Susan 119
Routledge Series on Death, Dying and Bereavement 233

rumination 17, 44, 71, 170; anxious 80; corrosive 138; getting up and going to counteract 177; intrusive thoughts and 142; occasional 133; self-blame and 134
ruminative grief 30
Rynearson, Edward (Ted) 214, 224

SAD *see* seasonal affective disorder
safety 37–38, 68, 164; conditions of 135, 204; finding safety in isolation following death of husband (Bethany) 102–104; loss of 92, 120
safety net 192
safety plan 158
safety protocols 193
safety program, launching in wake of deaths of 186
"safety zone," school as 114
Sands, Diana 147
Schut, Henk 14
schizophrenia 75
Schwartz Rounds 199–201
seasonal affective disorder (SAD) 88
secondary emotion *see* anger
secondary losses 46, 115, 133–134
self-acceptance 146, 180
self-blame 134
self-capacities for emotion regulation 204
self-care 71, 88, 98, 113, 118, 152, 161, 170, 173, 178, 199, 204, 221, 227
self-compassion 6, 69, 80, 129, 138, 161, 178, 180, 202, 213
self-healing 142
self-management of depression 98
self-medicating 96–97, 131
self-soothing 116
shame 54, 61, 136, 148, 208
sibling, loss of: anxiety and depression following death of brother (Rita) 97–98; coping with multiple losses including sister and son (Paulina) 94–95; daily grieving following loss of brother (Meika) 98–99; loss of both parents and all siblings (Devorah) 95–96; self-medicating after loss of brother (Cyma) 96–97; sister's mourning of sister's death from cancer (Nita) 92–94; son's anger over sister's death (Stella S.) 91–92
Shear, Katherine 223–224

# INDEX

sin: self-harm or suicide as 34
sleep *see* disrupted sleep; restorative sleep
Steffen, Edith 220, 233
Stroebe, Maggie 14
stroke 34, 111
suicidal thinking: following loss of husband (Andrea) 119–121; following loss of son (Jacqueline) 157–158
suicide awareness and prevention 160
suicide and overdose: attempted by daughter (Lisa) 211; attempted/successful suicide by husband and successful suicide by nephew and son (Hannah) 158–160; coping with death of son from overdose (Jeanmarie) 142–144; death of adult son from (Anna) 148–149; death of adult from (Joanne) 155–157; death of adult son following loss of children (Loretta) 149–152; death of ex-boyfriend from (Ros) 141–142; death of friend's teen daughter from (Jack) 146–148; death of life partner and military veteran from (Brad) 55–57; death of son from (Jacqueline) 157–158; death of teen daughter from (Melissa) 144–145; death of teen son by shotgun (Nancy) 153–155; on doctor colleague who is depressed by patient's suicide (Lisa) 217–218; following diagnosis of cancer (Carla's story of her brother) 139–141; following loss of children to cancer (Loretta's story of her son) 149–152; from gun violence (Nancy) 153–155; moving on after husband's suicide (Katie) 137–139; survivor's guilt following wife's suicide (Gill) 136–137; *see also* American Association of Suicidology; American Foundation for Suicide Prevention support groups
*S Word, The* (film) 146

TAPS *see* Tragedy Assistance Program for Survivors
terrorism *see* war and terrorism
TIAs *see* transient ischemic attacks
Tragedy Assistance Program for Survivors (TAPS) 132
transient ischemic attacks (TIA) 117

trauma-based learning 38
trauma-informed therapy and care 116, 124, 128, 135, 140, 151, 152, 156, 158, 168, 214

UBBS *see* Unfinished Business in Bereavement Scale
unanswered questions 133–134
unfinished business 43; between adult children and their parents 208–211
Unfinished Business in Bereavement Scale (UBBS) 208
Unfulfilled Wishes 209
unpredictability of grief 179–182
Unresolved Conflict 209

violent death *see* fatal accidents; homicide and mass tragedies; war and terrorism
Violent Death Bereavement Society 160

war and terrorism 4, 171–172
White, Michael 4
WHO *see* World Health Organization
widow: complicated grief ritual of 206–208; ready for a new relationship 229–230; *see also* husband, loss of
widower 23, 35, 48; *see also* wife, loss of
wife, loss of: deep grief in wake of (Bob) 33–34; fear of loss and moving on in wake of (Harvey) 37–38; grieving and inability to sleep in wake of (Dave) 44–47; husband's caregiver's guilt in wake of (Theodore) 42–43; inability to get over sudden death of (Gordon) 43–44; inconsolable grief in wake of (Samuel) 38–40; parting with belongings of wife following (Jerry) 47–48; ready to love again following (Kent) 48–49; seeking a reason to live in wake of (Gary) 34–35; writing to deceased wife following (Enrico) 40–41; yearning for deceased wife in wake of (Rodney) 35–37
World Health Organization (WHO) 195; *see also* International Classification of Diseases (ICD-11)
writing to a deceased person 77, 82, 85, 181, 204–205; to daughter 81; to mother 74, 101; to son 83, 152; to wife 36, 40–41, 43; *see also* AfterTalk

yoga 178

For Product Safety Concerns and Information please contact our EU
representative GPSR@taylorandfrancis.com
Taylor & Francis Verlag GmbH, Kaufingerstraße 24, 80331 München, Germany

www.ingramcontent.com/pod-product-compliance
Lightning Source LLC
Chambersburg PA
CBHW050521170426
43201CB00013B/2039